KU-205-924

046713⊄-C

THE SCHOOL IN THE MULTICULTURAL SOCIETY

THE SCHOOL IN THE MULTICULTURAL SOCIETY

A Reader

edited by
Alan James and Robert Jeffcoate

Harper & Row, Publishers
in association with
The Open University Press

Selection and editorial material
copyright © The Open University 1981

Reprinted 1982

Harper & Row Ltd
28 Tavistock Street
London WC2E 7PN

All rights reserved. No part of this publication may be reproduced, stored
in a retrieval system, or transmitted in any form or by any means,
electronic, mechanical, photocopying, recording, or otherwise, without
the written permission of the Publisher.

British Library Cataloguing in Publication Data

The School in the multicultural society.
   1. Minorities – Education
   I. Jeffcoate, Robert
   II. James, Alan
370   LC3705

ISBN 0-06-318195-9
ISBN 0-06-318196-7 Pbk

Phototypesetting by Parkway Group, London and Abingdon
Printed and bound by The Pitman Press, Bath

CONTENTS

PREFACE

Three companion volumes of readings have been prepared for the Open University course *Ethnic Minorities and Community Relations* (E354). The other two are *Discrimination and Disadvantage in employment: the experience of black workers;* and *Social and Community Work in a Multi-Racial Society.*

The readers form one component of the course which also includes correspondence texts, radio and television programmes and personal tuition.

The editors wish to acknowledge the help of the course team and its consultants in the compilation of these readers. Opinions expressed in the readers are, of course, not necessarily those of the course team or of the University.

INTRODUCTION

This collection of readings, assembled as part of the education component of Open University course E354, 'Ethnic Minorities and Community Relations', raises issues of importance to everyone concerned with the role of the school in the multicultural society. We have selected readings both theoretical and practical, descriptive and prescriptive, discursive and polemical, systematic and anecdotal, seeking among the more interesting contributions to the argument since 1971 a representative selection of answers to the question 'what can schools do to educate children for life in the multicultural society?'

A consensus developed during the 1970s that schools should do something, and a kind of orthodoxy began to emerge as to what 'multicultural education' might look like in practice. However, as teachers have found, well-intentioned initiatives can go awry if their aims and rationale are not thoroughly thought out. Our selection of 'Critical Perspectives', with which this reader begins, should encourage such fundamental consideration. A theoretical framework for a multicultural curriculum must begin with a definition of its aim – essentially, a concept of 'the good life' in a society which is both 'plural' and 'just'. This entails explicit affective and ethical objectives, such as respect for self and others, and implies specific curricular content. The first paper (Jeffcoate) was an early attempt to provide such a framework.

But such a framework can be challenged on several grounds. In the first place, the preoccupation with affective objectives derives from ideas about the nature of a child's self-concept, and the significance of the self-concept in the child's intellectual and social development. While psychological and philosophical studies emphasize the complexity of this aspect of personality, the practice of ' multicultural education' sometimes reduces it to a simple matter of bolstering self-esteem, encouraging teachers to intrude into sensitive, private areas of the child's psyche, dabbling in social work and psychotherapy. Educational practices motivated by a concern for the individual child and for social justice may prove ineffective or even harmful;

the fourth paper (Stone) suggests that this kind of 'multicultural' education may be a factor in black children's underachievement. Like Dhondy (in the later section, 'Pupils and Teachers'), this writer is hostile to 'multicultural' education because, in effect, it fails to attack underlying injustices and so is irrelevant to the real needs of black children. What may seem to be a reactionary demand for emphasis on instruction in 'basic skills' is motivated by the recognition that such skills may be needed (along with the discipline and self-organization that goes with learning them) if black children are to grow up to change society, to achieve justice and respect for themselves.

Even more fundamentally, the very idea of 'cultural pluralism' is beset by fuzziness. To present aspects of different cultures in a 'positive' way may mean distorting the evidence just as much as in the justly condemned 'ethnocentric' curriculum. To 'respect' and 'value' other ways of life can sometimes be interpreted as an abdication of ethical judgement. Extreme forms of relativism seem to deny the possibility of cross-cultural under-standing, so that objectivity shades into nihilism, suspending judgement and the exercise of empathy into a withdrawal from any attempt at comparative analysis, and cultural pluralism into apartheid. The third paper (Zec) calls for clear thinking: children should learn how to ascertain the truth and how to make rational judgements, in the context of their own cultures and in understanding others. A 'weak relativism' is valid as a methodological approach to the unfamiliar, but 'strong relativism' contradicts the very purpose it claims to further.

Similarly, while the 'multicultural' curriculum claims to foster the kind of openness and flexibility of thought that only a 'dialogue' can achieve, in practice it often seems to take the form of 'banking' (to use Paolo Freire's terms). Concern with curriculum content – with 'positive images' – may lead us to lose sight of educative processes, with their implications for children's progress towards rational autonomy and learning to cope in a plural society. The second paper (James) draws attention to the need for a context of discourse in the classroom where children are listened to, and listen to each other, learning the skills of democratic participation.

All the papers in the first section ask one way or another what social ideology underlies the 'multicultural' curriculum? The fifth paper (Hall) makes this question explicit, challenging those who favour such educa-tional practices to make clear their understanding of the relationship between what goes on in the classroom and the economic and political realities of society at large. While subsequent sections are more closely directed to classroom practice, we feel that none of the writers we have selected loses sight of these issues, and in the final section, 'Pupils and Teachers', they emerge again quite explicitly.

When, in the 1960s, discussion focussed on the educational needs of children of recently-arrived immigrants, 'language', in the sense of teaching English as a second language, was the centre of attention. As interest shifted to curriculum content and the development of attitudes to self and others, language became a somewhat peripheral concern, restricted to specialist teachers in language centres and classes. However, the papers we have selected for our second section assert the importance, indeed the centrality, of language in multicultural education. A child's use of language shapes his world, establishes his concepts of himself and others in that world, and determines the quality of his interaction with others. The first paper (from the Bullock Report), in calling for 'sensitivity to language in all its forms', defines a quality in the process of educating without which changes in curricular content are ineffectual or counter-productive. The other two papers (Richmond, Miller) give practical examples of such sensitivity in action, emphasizing the importance of the children's own languages, stressing that bilingualism or bidialectalism are assets, and showing how the multi-lingual classroom can be an arena for self-fulfilment and curriculum enrichment.

We then draw attention to another major question in multicultural education: do ethnic minority pupils enjoy equality of opportunity in the school system? Unfortunately the data do not at present exist to answer this question with any confidence. The first paper in the section (Tomlinson) warns against 'blanket statements', but the review of relevant research between 1960 and 1980 confirms the widespread subjective impression that there is serious cause for concern, especially about the attainment of many children of Caribbean ancestry. On the other hand, certain groups of ethnic minority children enjoy striking success (at least when measured against pupils of other backgrounds attending the same schools). The second paper (Driver and Ballard) examines the achievements of some children of South Asian ancestry, suggesting that their high level of persistence reflects cultural strengths: are such Asian children less 'socialized to failure' than their Caribbean or working-class white peers?

In the section headed 'Curriculum', we begin to draw together themes from the first three sections. For all the discussion of the multicultural curriculum in principle, it has not been easy to find well-argued sets of proposals for specific areas of curricular practice, and carefully evaluated records of the implementation of such proposals are even rarer. The bias in the section towards the humanities, and towards curricula for the middle and secondary years, reflects the dearth of serious examinations of the implications for other areas of the curriculum and for younger children.

The pieces we have chosen attempt to answer, one way or another, the questions 'what to teach?' and 'how to teach it?'. Several are concerned with extirpating racist and ethnocentric elements from curricular materials (Hicks and Worrall especially), but others emphasize the positive, the celebration of cultural diversity (e.g. Cole, Nandy, Goody). Such examples may be seen as implementations of the kinds of objectives outlined in the first paper in 'Critical Perspectives' (Jeffcoate), but the paper by the same writer in this section draws attention to the possible pitfalls of such well-intentioned multiculturalism, and emphasizes once again sensitivity to the children's own part in negotiating and shaping the knowledge presented to them.

So this section also stresses the importance of curricular process: notably of the 'creative collaboration' of pupils working together, and of 'the part that talk and classroom interaction can play in helping all pupils to make sense of the world' (Goody). The ideal of the open classroom, in which pupils air and exchange views freely while observing the ground rules of democratic debate, faces its sternest test when 'race' is the issue under consideration. The style of teaching pioneered by Lawrence Stenhouse and his colleagues, with teachers committed to 'procedural neutrality', represents one of the most controversial and fraught ways of maintaining such openness. It is possible, though difficult, to achieve this, as another paper in this section shows (Parkinson and Macdonald).

In returning our focus to the processes of educating we are underlining once again the central importance, for any attempt to educate for life in a multicultural society, of the relationship between teachers and pupils, the theme of our final section. The papers in this section all examine, in different ways, interaction between teachers and black pupils, so they take further the questions raised by Stone in 'Critical Perspectives'. Are teachers too much concerned with affective and emotional aspects of their work (Stone), or are they guilty of the daily denial of black identity (Coard)? In a multicultural classroom 'the chances for misunderstanding are very much higher' (Driver) so the demands on a teacher's 'cultural repertoire' are very much greater. On the other hand, are the negative stereotypes and expectations held by white teachers the explanation for black underachievement? This proposition was raised in the section on 'Attainment', and two papers in 'Pupils and Teachers' suggest that it may be too simple: not only are some ethnic minority pupils relatively successful, but there are differences among the 'underachieving' black pupils, notably between boys and girls (Driver and Fuller). Black girls, perceiving themselves accurately as victims of double discrimination, seem to respond with greater determination to succeed in school and in the job market, and their relative success is 'not related to whether teachers [see] them as good or bad pupils' (Fuller). Moreover, what looks to white teachers like apathy and failure among boys of Caribbean ancestry (perhaps, Driver suggests, specifically Jamaican ancestry) may even be a conscious, deliberate rejection of a schooling that seems to lead only to dead-end jobs or the dole queue: so argues the final paper (Dhondy), bringing us back to the theme of the location of multicultural education in its economic and political context in 'Critical Perspectives' (Hall).

This collection presents, then, a diversity of contributions to the debate about multicultural education, which go beyond simple answers and blanket prescriptions. It emphasizes the need for more research – for more comprehensive and reliable data on relative levels of achievement, more detailed curricular evaluations, more analysis of the processes of education and of interaction among pupils and between teachers and pupils. It underscores the need to pay careful attention to such evidence as there is, warning that educating for life in a multicultural society entails much more than a decision – on the part of teachers and those who would influence teachers – to adopt some new curricular content. Content cannot be separated from process any more than teachers' teaching can be separated from pupils' interpreting and negotiating. Equally the learning that goes on in school is inextricably bound in with the economic and political reality of the society in which the school 'educates'.

SECTION 1

CRITICAL PERSPECTIVES

CHAPTER 1.1

CURRICULUM PLANNING IN MULTIRACIAL EDUCATION*
ROBERT JEFFCOATE

The primacy of objectives

The objectives I am concerned with in this paper are objectives for pupils. By this I mean a statement of what pupils should know, be able to do, feel, think and so forth, at a given point in their formal educational career. The intentions of the paper are to establish the primacy of objectives in curriculum planning in multiracial education, to explore the factors governing their selection and to suggest, in a general way and in the form of a Bloomian classification (Figure 1) what they might be, and the kind of criteria for choosing learning experiences that could be derived from them (Figure 2).

There is nothing particularly original or revolutionary about the idea that schools should be prepared to make explicit their objectives for the children they teach. It is commonplace to curriculum developers and teacher educators, and accepted by most of them. However, the tenets underlying the objectives model of curriculum planning have been questioned in a number of theoretical critiques, and it continues to lack credibility with many classroom teachers.[1]

Most of the reservations refer to the behaviourist version of the model associated with the American school of rational curriculum planning. According to this version the curriculum process is a simple temporal sequence which starts with the selection of objectives, moves on to the identification of learning experiences to achieve those objectives and terminates with an evaluation of how successful the learning experiences have been. For evaluation to be possible the objectives must be behavioural, that is, so precisely stated as to be observable and assessable. The model on this interpretation ascribes learning experiences a purely

* *Educational Research*, vol 18/3, 1976, pp. 192–200. This article arose out of the Schools Council Project 'Education for a Multiracial Society' (1973–76).

Figure 1 A classification of objectives in multiracial education

(A) Respect for Others
   Cognitive (Knowledge)
All pupils should *know*
A 1.1   the basic facts of race and racial difference;
A 1.21   the customs, values and beliefs of the main cultures represented in Britain and, more particularly, of those forming the local community;
A 1.22   why different groups have immigrated into Britain in the past and, more particularly, how the local community has come to acquire its present ethnic composition.

   Cognitive (Skills)
All pupils should *be able to*
A 2.1   detect stereotyping and scapegoating in what they see, hear and read;
A 2.2   evaluate their own cultures objectively.

   Affective (Attitudes, Values and Emotional Sets)
All pupils should *accept*
A 3.1   the uniqueness of each individual human being;
A 3.2   the underlying humanity we all share;
A 3.3   the principles of equal rights and justice;
A 3.4   and value the achievements of other cultures and nations;
A 3.5   strangeness without feeling threatened;
A 3.61   that Britain is, always has been and always will be a multi-ethnic society;
A 3.62   that no culture is ever static and that constant mutual accommodation will be required of all cultures making up an evolving multicultural society like Britain;
A 3.71   that prejudice and discrimination are widespread in Britain and the historical and socioeconomic causes which have given rise to them;
A 3.72   the damaging effect of prejudice and discrimination on the rejected groups;
A 3.8   the possibility of developing multiple loyalties.

(B) Respect for self
   Cognitive (Knowledge)
All pupils should *know*
B 1.1   the history and achievements of their own culture and what is distinctive about it.

   Cognitive (Skills)
All pupils should *be able to*
B 2.1   communicate efficiently in English and, if it is not their mother tongue, in their own mother tongue;
B 2.2   master the other basic skills necessary for success at school.

   Affective (Attitudes, Values and Emotional Sets)
All pupils should have developed
B 3.1   a positive self-image;
B 3.2   confidence in their sense of their own identities.

Figure 2: Criteria for the selection of learning experiences

(a) An insular curriculum, preoccupied with Britain and British values, is unjustifiable in the final quarter of the twentieth century. The curriculum needs to be both international in its choice of content and global in its perspective.

(b) Contemporary British society contains a variety of social and ethnic groups; this variety should be made evident in the visuals, stories and information offered to children.

(c) Pupils should have access to accurate information about racial and cultural differences and similarities.

(d) People from British minority groups and from other cultures overseas should be presented as individuals with every variety of human quality and attribute. Stereotypes of minority groups in Britain and of cultures overseas, whether expressed in terms of human characteristics, life-styles, social roles or occupational status, are unacceptable and likely to be damaging.

(e) Other cultures and nations have their own validity and should be described in their own terms. Wherever possible they should be allowed to speak for themselves and not be judged exclusively against British or European norms.

instrumental function, and believes that ideally it should be feasible to ascertain which learning experiences will lead to the achieving of which objectives. The objection to this is that it does not begin to approximate to the complexity of school life. It is as unrealistic to imagine that objectives and learning experiences can enjoy the same kind of casual relationship as physical phenomena as it is to expect the selection of learning experiences to attend upon the stating of objectives. If the latter are to be so precisely stated as to be observable and measurable, then, in the view of one critic,[2], six years of schooling will need something in the order of 25,000 of them. In any case there is a wide scepticism as to the usefulness of such an exercise. Available examples of behavioural objectives suggest that only lower order cognitive objectives, dealing with elementary knowledge and skills, can be expressed in this way. Higher order cognitive and affective objectives may very well not be conducive to what the behaviourists call 'operationalization', nor is it desirable that they should be. The mismatch between the 'rationality' of the behaviourist version and the multifoliate complexity of school realities has been nicely pointed up by Marten Shipman:

> Curriculum development does not proceed through a clear cycle from a statement of objectives to an evaluation of the learning strategies used. It consists of interaction, accommodation and compromise. Horse trading and horse sense are the concrete curriculum scene, not the clinical alignment of means with ends that is the official version.[3]

Even an interactionist version of the objectives model, however, has to meet a number of objections, which seem to me to emanate from the child-centred progressivist ideology that dominates the theory, if not always the practice, of primary and lower secondary school education. Behind the idea of having objectives is the assumption that the business of teaching is to bring about desired changes in children. The child-centred ideology queries this assumption: not that children will change as a result of experience at school, but that the school can, or should, prespecify what these changes are to be. To prespecify the outcomes of learning situations, the ideology argues, is to make education synonymous with instruction, to ignore the objectives children may have and to discount the value of unintended outcomes – what has been called, following Horace Walpole, 'serendipity' in the classroom. The progressivists advance a rather different view of the educational process. Their overall concern is with children becoming autonomous. The teacher's task is not to prespecify outcomes, rather to place children in learning situations which stimulate them in a host of ways but whose outcomes will emerge gradually from the constant interaction and negotiation between teacher and pupil.

It would be a caricature of the progressivist position to suggest that it admits no kind of objectives at all. What it does do, if my understanding is correct, is, in its preoccupation with autonomy, to confine them to the development of overall skills. These skills include literacy, numeracy, information gathering, deduction and the formulation of hypotheses, and creativity in the arts. Notably excluded are knowledge objectives, on the grounds that there is no longer a consensus in our society on the facts children need to know, and that therefore it is important that they should be equipped with the skills to determine for themselves which knowledge is of the most worth. My impression is that the importance attached to skills, procedural knowledge, and the depreciation in the value of facts, propositional knowledge, are part of a marked trend in the education of children in the five to thirteen age range. A further impression is that there is ambivalence over objectives in the affective domain. By and large primary schools will be found to agree that they have responsibility for children's spiritual, moral and emotional development, but are distinctly reluctant to translate this recognition into affective objectives for the formal curriculum. What the school can do in this domain, they are likely to insist, is best done indirectly through the tacit lessons of its ethos. Secondary schools, on the other hand, are increasingly prepared to incorporate aspects of the domain into the curriculum in the form of subjects such as moral education and education for personal relationships.

Eisner, in his constructive critique of behaviourist curriculum planning, draws a useful distinction between 'instructional' and 'expressive' objectives.[4] Broadly speaking this distinction corresponds to the Bloomian distinction between cognitive and affective domains. In the cognitive domain of knowledge and skills there will generally be identifiable objectives that can be prespecified, and the teacher, in view of his more complete mastery of that knowledge and those skills, will rightly expect to have overriding authority for deciding what the objectives are to be. Contrary to the beliefs of some of their advocates this situation is not significantly affected by the use of progressive methods – discovery, individualized and resource based learning and so on – in maths and the sciences. In the affective or 'expressive' domain of the arts and the humanities, on the other hand, or, to put it in another way, where there are no simple or correct outcomes and where the ultimate targets are to do with creativity or forming one's own opinions and conclusions, only the learning situation can be prespecified; the outcomes will be various and arise out of negotiation between teacher and learner.

Multiracial education is primarily affective, about attitudes and dispositions, and only instrumentally cognitive. But it is a different sort of affectivity from the affectivity of creative work or aesthetic judgement. Even though the overriding objectives, respect for self and others, stipulated in the classification could hardly be called 'correct', they are ones we believe to be necessary for children and for society, and we could go some way to justifying their selection; equally they are not objectives that could be said to be open to negotiation. Many of the objectives in the classification are knowledge objectives, and I have called these 'instrumental'. In order to come to respect themselves and others, I am suggesting, children must be in possession of certain facts. The first three specific knowledge objectives (A.1.1, 1.21, 1.22) are, then, a necessary (but not, of course, a sufficient) condition of the overriding objective of respect for others. It is at this point that we find ourselves at odds with the dominant progressivist ideology. We do not dissent from the importance they attach to skills but we also attach importance, in a way they would not, to specific items of knowledge which we feel to be predicated by our overall affective targets.

Prespecified objectives are necessary in multiracial education because we share the basic assumption of the objectives school that the function of formal education is to bring about desired changes in children. We want them to have acquired certain identifiable knowledge and skills and developed certain identifiable attitudes and behaviours by the time they leave school. We must be prepared to make these knowledges, skills, attitudes and behaviours the starting point and focus for our curriculum planning. At the same time we have to think rather more flexibly about the way we define our objectives, recognizing the force in Eisner's caveat that, whilst providing windows, objectives may also 'create walls',[5] and adopt a more fluid interactional model for the curriculum process which bears a closer resemblance to quotidian classroom realities. This means, among other things, that prespecified objectives should not acquire the status of sacrosanct unalterable absolutes. Instead they should be open to constant review, adaptation and revision, both to allow for the objectives of pupils and their parents and to accommodate Eisner's principle of 'serendipity' in the classroom. Hilda Taba best conveys this notion of flexibility in the definition and use of objectives when she suggests they should be seen as 'developmental', representing 'roads to travel rather than terminal points'.[6]

Factors governing the selection of objectives

Apart from certain obvious practical constraints, a school's selection of objectives in multiracial education will be signficantly affected by two factors which are themselves interrelated – its value system or educational philosophy and its definition and analysis of the situation (problems, needs and so on) which it finds itself confronted with.

The simple relationship between a school's stated objectives and its overall educational philosophy has long been recognized. 'The objectives to be finally included', write the authors of the Bloomian taxonomy, 'should be related to the school's view of the "good life for the individual in the good society"';[7] or, as Hilda Taba puts it, 'an organized statement of objectives expresses the philosophy of education of a particular school system or of a particular school'.[8]

Within the framework of its educational philosophy the school's answers to two questions will bear upon its choice of multiracial objectives. The first is general and well-worn: What is school for? The second is specific and of recent origin: What kind of future for multiracial Britain are we envisaging and what part can the school properly perform in bringing it about? The answers to these questions are also obviously interconnected.

I have already suggested that there is a discernible trend increasingly affecting primary schools and the first two years of secondary school whereby the school's function is confined to the development of a range of skills. The notion that children should leave school in possession of an agreed body of facts, once taken for granted, now lacks credibility, and ambivalence surrounds the development of feelings and attitudes. Teachers' ambivalence towards the affective domain is understandable; it reflects a number of very real anxieties – of indoctrinating, of producing counterproductive effects, and of trespassing on parental terrain. One simple fact goes some way to resolving these anxieties and precludes the need for a lengthy philosophical wrangle. The affective domain falls within the area of the school's discretion whatever its collective wishes or the wishes of individual members of staff. The period of statutory education is a crucial one for the development of racial attitudes. It would be unreasonable to maintain that the time spent at school during those eleven years had no influence on children's values and feelings, which is not, of course, to say that the school's influence can match the home's or the peer group's or even the mass media's. But it is to say that schools are in the attitudes business anyway, and that therefore they have an obligation to ensure that their influence is benign.

Concern for the evolution of a just multiracial society leads us to apportion overriding importance to the affective objectives of respect for self and respect for others. The achievement of these goals, it seems to me, predicates not only certain skills but also certain knowledge; hence the form and substance of the classification. Ann Dummett shares this somewhat unfashionable position:

> We need to return to the idea that there is some limited, distinct body of knowledge worth transmitting to the entire younger generation.[9]

It scarcely needs adding that this 'distinct body of knowledge', represented by objectives A 1.1, 1.21 and 1.22 for example, will bear little resemblance to that which schools used to think it was their business to transmit.

The verb 'transmit' and the idea of a 'distinct body of knowledge' can serve to introduce a further dimension to the debate. There is a longstanding discussion as to whether the school's function is to transmit or transform culture. Traditionally all societies have sought to transmit their cultures to the next generation, whether through formal or informal educational processes, and there are those who, albeit defining 'culture' more narrowly, would continue to regard this as the school's main purpose today. But there is clearly a difference between a 'simple' society which can still boast of a discrete common culture – an agreed set of rituals, beliefs and values – to pass on to its young, and contemporary Britain fragmented and diversified culturally by industrialization and urbanization and which, even when discounting for the moment the cultures of recently arrived racial and ethnic minorities, incorporates a great variety of rituals, beliefs and values.

In the sphere of formal education awareness of the plural nature of our society – of the multiplicity of knowledge and the diversity of beliefs available – has produced a number of responses. One sort of response, associated historically with Victorian writers like Matthew Arnold and Herbert Spencer, argues for the necessity of sifting out from what is available the knowledge that is of most worth. What Arnold called 'the best that has been known and thought in the world' would then become the substance of a common curriculum for all children and the foundation on which a new common culture could be constructed. Two modern exponents of part of this view (they have not, so far as I know, addressed themselves to the concept of a common culture) are the educational philosophers Paul Hirst and R. S. Peters. Their case, in brief, is that there exist clearly identifiable 'forms of knowledge', corresponding more or less to the established academic disciplines, into which, because they are basic to the development of rationality (to, in effect, being 'educated'), all children should be initiated.[10] Schools, then, are conceived of by this view as passing on to the next generation a cultural heritage defined by criteria of intellectual excellence.

The other sort of response derives some rather different inferences from its recognition of the plural character of our society. Partly it distinguishes itself through a sharp critique of the Arnoldian view. In practice, the critique contests, the 'best that has been known and thought in the world' and the revered 'forms of knowledge' represent, at least as enshrined in the school curriculum, merely fossilized formulations of the values and interests of the middle class;[11] a genuinely common curriculum and a genuinely common culture (and these ideals are shared by some advocates of both sorts of response) would need to draw equally on the various social and regional subcultures making up our plural society and which up to now have been discounted and devalued. It is a simple extension to this argument to acknowledge that the cultures of recently established minority ethnic groups also have an entitlement to contribute to this process of forging new cultural syntheses. 'In our present multiracial society,' writes Ann Dummett, 'we need to develop a new unifying culture that means something to everyone'.[12] A recently published adumbration of what might be called the 'transformationist' view of the relationship between school and culture, and, unlike Ann Dummett, not specifically concerned with the multiracial complexion of our society, extends its argument to include the same acknowledgement:

> We might . . . speak of the need for immigrants to accommodate to the way of life which is now in the process of creation – a process in which their influence is as valid as ours, and our efforts at reaccommodation as necessary as theirs.[13]

It would not be too fanciful to claim that new cultural syntheses, drawing on wider sources than the narrowly British or European, have already begun to take shape in the twentieth century, if as yet only at a superficial level or in relatively specialist spheres, and one thinks, for example, of the influence of African art on contemporary painters and sculptors, of Asian influences on cuisine and design, and of experiments in fusing African, Caribbean, Indian and European traditions in classical and popular music.

However, the argument for a broader, less elitist and less ethnocentric definition of both a common culture and a common curriculum is only part of the transformationist position. What distinguishes it, above all, is its conception of the relationship between the school and the culture it serves. The traditional view, I have suggested, has been that the school should transmit what it takes to be 'culture' to each new generation. The transformationists contend that if a new viable common culture is to emerge, adequate to the needs of the final quarter of the twentieth century, what has previously passed for the 'cultural heritage' requires to be opened up to critical revaluation, and indeed that future cultural health will demand that critical revaluation becomes an established feature of British society. The school's function will be to involve its pupils in just this process, and it is here that it becomes possible to relate the increasing sway enjoyed by various versions of transformationism with the increasing sway enjoyed by skills objectives. If schools are to participate significantly in the process of cultural revaluation, and if pupils are to be able to formulate their own beliefs, values and life-styles (become, that is, autonomous rational beings), then it seems logical to set greatest store by the skills without which neither of these two aims could be achieved.

That the school should aspire to the function of social critic and cultural synthesizer is both justifiable and realistic in contexts which are culturally uniform, for instance in remote and rural areas, and indeed in the far greater number of contexts where some measure of cultural variation is encompassed by overall common ground. The multicultural school, however, presents a rather different proposition. It does not serve one society or culture or even a congeries of related sub-groups and sub-cultures. It serves several quite discrete and sometimes markedly diverse cultures whose beliefs and values may well not only differ but actually conflict. It is hard to imagine how the school could aspire to serve such diverse cultures in quite the same way. The school, after all, is not a value free institution; nor could it hope to be, no matter how 'open' its relationship with the surrounding community. Not only does it serve a society and a culture or cultures; it *is* itself a society and a culture with identifiable values and rituals to which its members are expected to conform.

It has been argued in the past that there is a discontinuity between the culture of the school and the culture of the working class child, and that, because the culture of the school is to all intents and purposes synonymous with the culture of the dominant middle class, implicit in this discontinuity will be the disparagement of everything – language, expectations, behaviour – the working class child brings to school with him. It is now being argued that the minority ethnic group child is in a similar, only more acute, position. His culture too is likely to be ignored, underestimated or disparaged by the school. The outcome of this analysis is that the multi-cultural school incorporating a number of ethnic groups in its pupil population and serving a socially heterogeneous catchment area will find itself in different kinds of relationships with the different ethnic and social sub-cultures, and obliged, therefore, to consider the possibility of developing different objectives or, at any rate, different emphases for children from the different groups. A white middle class child, for example, with confidence in his cultural inheritance will clearly not have the same sort of needs as a black working class child with unsure or ambiguous feelings about his identity and ancestry. If we look at the classification, it would be reasonable of the school, on the strength of this analysis, to underscore, as far as the white child is concerned, respect for others and a very specific objective such as A 2.2 (being able to evaluate one's own culture objectively), whilst interpreting its obligations towards its black pupils first and foremost in terms of enhancing self-respect.

The ability to evaluate one's own culture objectively (that is to say, viewing it from the point of view of an outsider) remains, of course, an ultimate objective for all children. To recognize this is to recognize, notwithstanding the research evidence indicating a causal link,[14] the very real tension between creating respect for others and creating respect for self. But what I am saying is that it only becomes a realistic objective *after* objectives to do with self-respect, such as B 1.1, 3.1 and 3.2, have been achieved. One can only begin to evaluate one's own culture objectively when one knows what it is and what its accomplishments have been. With the white middle class child this prior knowledge is unlikely to be at risk; the risk in his case is that confidence in his cultural identity will be coupled with contempt or condescension towards cultures that are different and especially towards those which are not European.

The trouble is that some minority ethnic groups, insofar as it is proper to speak of them as totalities, will find it difficult to accept even as ultimate targets the objectives, such as the ability to evaluate one's own culture objectively, which are associated with the view of the school as social critic and cultural synthesizer, or with the view of the child as possessed of an inalienable right to determine his own career and life style. Let us take a concrete example. Most Moslem children in Britain attend Koran schools in the evening. Here they will be taught the tenets of Islam, the life of Mohamed, Moslem ethics as matters of faith; they will not be encouraged to view what they have been told critically. During the day at school, on the other hand, they may well find themselves in quite different learning atmospheres where the emphasis is not on their learning facts or items of faith but on being creative and critical, on reaching their own conclusions, forming their own opinions and making their own judgements and decisions. In other words, and referring back to an earlier part of the discussion, the Moslem child in Britain will be put in the perplexing position of attending a school in the day time which interprets the school's function as 'transformationist' and one in the evening which interprets its function as 'transmissionist'.

It would be mistaken, however, to imagine that all minority group individuals, or indeed all British Moslems, looked at their own cultures quite so uncritically as this most extreme case, the often open conflict between British school and Moslem community, would lead us to believe. At least one Asian commentator, for example, does not accept the full 'ethnic reinforcement' philosophy. In the *Times Educational Supplement* in September of last year A. S. Abrahams wrote:

> Learning about one's culture to establish identity and self-pride is one thing, learning about it so that it impedes acculturation in a modern, egalitarian, technological society is another.

The preservation of minority cultures in a fossilized form is not what multicultural schools should be doing, he went on; instead their objective for minority group pupils should be just the one we have been discussing –to make them 'critically aware of their culture and equipped to decide themselves how much to retain'.[15] It is instructive to compare this statement with a more famous one by the American authors, Stephen and Joan Baratz, who concluded an article on early childhood intervention with a demand for programmes 'that utilize the child's differences as a means of furthering his acculturation to the mainstream while maintaining his individual and cultural heritage'.[16] Inherent in Abrahams' statement, but missing from the Baratz's bland prose, is the recognition of the very real tension imposed on both the child and the school by biculturalism, by the need to be competent in two sometimes mutually contradictory cultures, and that the right, rather than the obligation, for resolving this tension must rest finally with the child. The school's role is, of course, to be as 'open' and supportive as is possible; but, as I have already argued, there is a limit to its openness. Its very existence predicates certain values and it is just these values which find expression in its stated objectives and which are at issue.

For a new, and more broadly based, common culture to evolve, the tensions implicit in biculturalism will have to be resolved and we shall perhaps need to reach beyond the idea of cultural identity altogether. Another American commentator, P. S. Adler, has written eloquently of the emergence of 'multicultural man', 'a new kind of person, a person who is socially and psychologically a product of the interweaving of culture in the twentieth century'. Not only will multicultural man be 'able . . . to look at his own original culture from an outsider's perspective', and to 'negotiate the conflicts and tensions inherent in cross cultural contacts', but also he can 'serve as a facilitator and catalyst for contacts between cultures'.[17] All this might seem rather futuristic for the pressing concerns of contemporary British multiracial schools, but it is a line of thinking they will need to get to grips with and it is to some extent echoed in the objectives in the classification.

At this juncture it might be useful to turn for a moment to the questions I isolated from within the framework of the school's educational philosophy: what kind of future for multiracial Britain are we envisaging and what part can the school properly perform in bringing it about? It has become customary to present the range of possible models for a future multiracial Britain as a continuum whose poles are occupied by the pure types of pluralism and assimilation. Assimilation is the older hypothesis and it continues to appeal, tacitly rather than overtly, to many teachers and schools, despite its diminished credibility following the failure of the American 'melting pot' to materialize. The expectation that minority cultures will adapt to the mainstream culture to such an extent as to forsake all distinguishability apart from the dark skins of their adherents seems now, however, not only unrealistic but also cramping in depriving the mainstream of sources of potential enrichment and, above all, inegalitarian in its failure to recognize minority group rights and damaging in its threat to the identity and self-image of minority group children.

All in all, it could be said that as a 'final solution' the pluralist model, according to which minority cultures come to retain their essential identities and to stand in a relationship of equality and mutual respect to the cultural mainstream, is preferable if only because whereas assimilation seems effectively to exclude the possibility of individuals making pluralist choices for their own lives the converse does not hold.

It is really more useful, however, to speak of individual life decisions than of models for the future of society as a whole, simply because the school has more influence over the former than over the latter. What one can say of the school is that its philosophy, policies, curricula and so on should be such as to enable and accommodate as many choices as feasible for minority group children. There will be some who will choose to adapt fairly closely to British norms; others who will choose to retain the customs and beliefs in almost identical shape to those they or their parents or their grandparents knew in their countries of origin; and there will be all sorts of other possibilities in between. The bounds of feasibility and accommodation will be marked out by the values the school believes it cannot leave to chance and those will be embodied in its objectives.

The other broad factor governing the selection of objectives is the way the school defines and analyses the situation it thinks it is confronted with – what, in effect, it believes it is up against. I do not propose to say very much about this, because it has been fully covered elsewhere, merely to point to the outlines of the argument. There is a wealth of sociological and psychological evidence which the school in defining its multiracial objectives needs to take into account. There is, to take the most important examples, the evidence on the various manifestations of prejudice and discrimination in the country provided by PEP reports and government white papers;[18] there is the conclusive international evidence on the early onset of racial awareness and attitudes; and there is the evidence on the way young children are socialized into prevailing norms.[19] In addition, and coming nearer home, the school will need to establish what the climate of race relations in the immediate vicinity is, and how the children it is responsible for see themselves and others as members of distinctive racial and ethnic groups. Crucially, perhaps, it will have to try to conclude whether it is up against prejudice or racism. For it will make all the difference to the definition of objectives, and the development of curriculum strategies, whether, to simplify the debate for the sake of brevity, the school identifies its target group as a handful of disturbed prejudiced personalities, the product of loveless or authoritarian child-rearing or whatever, or whether it defines racial prejudice as a social norm with a describable history and causation which will have left its imprint to varying degrees, and in different ways, on all children.

The behaviourist version of rational curriculum planning has been faulted for proposing a model of curriculum development which does not appear to take account of the realities of school life. It would be equally remiss, and sort ill with the explicit recognition of the plural character of our society, if this paper were to imply that a comprehensive school, say with a hundred staff, should reach a consensus on the various issues that have been raised. Nevertheless the conviction behind the paper is that these issues must figure in formal staffroom discussion, and, beyond that and most importantly, that a written statement of objectives of the order of generality represented by the classification presented here is incumbent on all schools and on faculties and subject departments in secondary schools. The undertaking will, of course, be onerous and even hazardous, not only because the affective domain is an area in which it is hard to be precise about one's intentions but, above all, because, as the authors of the Bloomian Taxonomy concede, the domain is, in their memorable phrase, 'a Pandora's Box'.

> We are not entirely sure that opening our box is necessarily a good thing; we are certain that it is not likely to be a source of peace and harmony among the members of a school staff.[20]

Acknowledging the task's difficulties, however, is maybe only another way of indicating its urgency.

Notes and references

1. Recent critiques have been: Eisner, E. W. 'Instructional and Expressive Educational Objectives', *Instructional Objectives*, AERA Monograph 3 (Rand McNally, 1969).
   Stenhouse, L. 'Some Limitations on the Use of Objectives in Curriculum Research and Planning', *Paedagogica Europaea* (1970/71).
   Chanan, G. 'Objectives in the Humanities', *Educational Research* (NFER, June 1974).
2. Eisner, E. W. *op. cit.*, p. 14.
3. Shipman, M. 'Contrasting views of a curriculum project', *Journal of Curriculum Studies* (Collins, November 1972), p. 147.
4. Eisner, E. W. *op. cit.*, pp. 15/16/17. 'An expressive objective describes an educational encounter. It identifies a situation in which children are to work, a problem with which they are to cope, a task in which they are to engage; but it does not specify what from that encounter, situation, problem, or task they are to learn . . . instructional objectives emphasize the acquisition of the known; while expressive objectives its elaboration, modification, and, at times, the production of the utterly new.'
5. Eisner, E. W. *op. cit.*, p. 14.
6. Taba, H. *Curriculum Development Theory and Practice* (Harcourt, Brace and World, 1962), p. 203.
7. Bloom, B. *et al. Taxonomy of Educational Objectives – Handbook I Cognitive Domain* (Longman, 1956), p. 27.
8. Taba, H. *op. cit.*, p. 211.
9. Dummett, A. 'Education for a Unifying Culture', *The Times*, 9 July 1974.
10. Hirst, P. H. and Peters, R. S. *The Logic of Education* (RKP, 1970).
11. It is convenient to label the view 'Arnoldian'. To do justice to Arnold he saw culture as 'not a having and a resting, but a growing and becoming' and as essentially classless making 'the best that has been thought and known in the world current everywhere'. Arnold, M. *Culture and Anarchy* (CUP, 1963), pp. 48/70.
12. Dummett, A. *op. cit.*
13. Chanan, G. and Gilchrist, L. *What School is For* (Methuen, 1974), p. 129.
14. Thomas, J. B. *Self-concept in Psychology and Education: A Review of Research* (NFER, 1973).
15. Abrahams, A. S. 'Time to Help the Underdog'. *Times Educational Supplement*, 27 September 1974.
16. Baratz, S. C. and Baratz, J. C. 'Early Childhood Intervention: the social science base of institutional racism', *Harvard Educational Review*, February 1970.
17. Adler, P. S. 'Beyond Cultural Identity: reflections on cultural and multicultural man', *Topics in Culture Learning*, vol 2 (East-West Center, Honolulu, 1974).

18. See, for example, Daniel W. W. *Racial Discrimination in England* (Penguin, 1969). Home Office *Racial Discrimination* (HMSO, September 1975).
19. See, for example, Allport, G. *The Nature of Prejudice* (Doubleday Anchor, 1958) Chapter 18.
    Goodman, M. *Race Awareness in Young Children* (Macmillan, 1964).
    Milner, D. 'Prejudice and the Immigrant Child', *New Society,* 23 September 1971.
    Hartmann, P. and Husband, C. *Racism and the Mass Media* (Davis-Poynter, 1974).
20. Krathwohl, D. R. *et al., Taxonomy of Educational Objectives* – Handbook II *Affective Domain* (Longman, 1964), p. 91.

CHAPTER 1.2

THE 'MULTICULTURAL' CURRICULUM*
ALAN JAMES

Over ten years, since the Labour Government's about-turn on immigration and Powell's 'rivers of blood' speech, there has developed in British educational thinking an increasingly influential and coherent philosophy and range of practices which is most often labelled 'multicultural'. Its advocates seek to reflect and to value in the curriculum that diversity of lifestyles, beliefs and cultural traditions which post-war immigration has brought to our country. They justify these curricular changes by reference to the need to prepare all children for life in a society where such diversity is functional, a source of social energy and a richer life, and they support their arguments with psychological evidence as to the importance of a positive awareness of these differences both for ethnic minority children in developing a concept of their own identity, and for all children in developing favourable attitudes towards others different from themselves. The optimistic tenor of this philosophy, the very real fear of worsening racial conflict and of a brutal authoritarian response from the white majority, as well as the solid evidence of progress in increasing numbers of attractively 'multicultural' books, teaching materials and curricular practices, have all given strength to this growing 'multiculturalism'.

But the attractiveness of this ideology does not protect it from serious critical analysis. Teachers are bound to operate within the framework of economic, political, social and cultural realities of which the education system is only a part. We are not compelled to fit children for predestined places in society as it is, we *can* raise the possibilities of society as it might be, but if we ignore the difference between things as they are and things as we would wish them to be – if we obscure that difference in the images of reality we present to the children – we shall neither equip them for competence in society as they shall find it, nor give them the skills and knowledge they will

* *New Approaches in Multiracial Education*, vol 8/1, 1979, pp. 1–5.

need to change it. We need to ask: how far can 'multi-culturalism' be a valid educational ideology in a society whose institutions are not geared to tolerant pluralism?

The channels leading to employment, promotion and the trappings of success in our society still prescribe – to a large extent – mastery of a standard language (in its written form, and within a rather wider range of tolerance, in its spoken form), and a high degree of acquiescence in a 'common culture'. By this, I mean not the critical 'high culture' which followers of Arnold, Leavis and Hoggart would wish us to share in common, but rather the twin demands of the work ethic and the consumer ethic which between them constitute the real 'common culture' of advanced industrial society. The work ethic imposes conformity in the disciplines of work, in obedience and reliability, in foresight and deferred gratification. The consumer ethic is in many ways contradictory – indeed, the contradiction between our identities as workers and consumers seems to me to be a major factor in those conflicts within society which are reflected in the recent arguments about curriculum and teaching practices – but that, too, demands conformity by the creation of wants, the lure of instant gratification, the presentation of ideal, or at least fashionable, life-styles. The kinds of life we shall lead are predicted and prescribed to a substantial extent by the very physical structure of our cities, our houses, the goods in our shops, by our laws and by the expectations of those who enforce them. The jigsaw puzzle envisaged by Roy Jenkins, with diverse cultural groups co-existing in a harmonious atmosphere of mutual tolerance cannot be a reality when the chances in life of members of cultural minorities – and of many of their neighbours in the inner-city areas – are limited by inequality in wealth and access to power. Does the 'multicultural' ideology presuppose that a harmonious society of equals, where such differences in status as remain are achieved, not ascribed by the accident of birth, does exist, or can exist in the foreseeable future? Can 'multicultural' education be an instrument for social justice?

Multicultural education, I have said, sets out to influence children's attitudes towards themselves and others. The hope is that ethnic minority children, if they acquire a more positive evaluation of those factors (skin colour, home life, communal history and traditions) which give them their own identity, will have higher aspirations for themselves reflected by greater achievements in school, and also that such self-confidence in all children will enable them to respond more positively to the different appearances, beliefs and behaviours of others. A major assumption seems to be that both sets of attitudes, to self and to others, are largely determined by the input of information, the 'images' which growing children encounter, of people like or different from themselves. Hence the emphasis on the visual and textual content of children's books; the presentation of non-white people, their ways of life and cultural achievements, in text-books for history and geography, in stories and novels for children, in posters and audio-visual materials.

Recognition that schools are concerned with the formation of attitudes, and cannot escape responsibility for the incidence of hostility towards ethnic minorities, is an important achievement of the last decade. Equally valid is the view that one's behaviour towards others is powerfully determined by one's estimation of oneself. But the self is a much more complex entity than this philosophy suggests; the subject, the 'first person' is continually being re-created, re-integrated, as we live and communicate in human society. As soon as we think about ourselves, we form detached, fictional concepts of our 'selves'. Of these self-concepts we may have many, created for us in our interaction with 'significant others', and projecting our (often conflicting) ideas of what we would wish to be and what we most fear we are. So to talk of a child having a 'positive' or 'negative' self-image is unhelpful: we all have both, many times over. A model of conflicting 'high' and 'low' self-concepts may be more appropriate to the understanding of the personalities of ethnic minority children than the conventional assumption of consistently 'low' estimation. Nor is such conflict necessarily destructive: in the individual, and in society, a degree of conflict may be a valuable source of creative energy: members of ethnic minorities who have grown up with the conflicting demands of their own communities and wider society, and with the conflicting images of their selves projected by others, have often acquired an advantage in their understanding of themselves and of the human environment in which they are living.

However, the individual's response to conflict is a crucial variable, and this needs more careful examination in relation both to the self-concept and to attitudes to others. Where authority is imposed – by brute strength or by inconsistent and frequently withdrawn affection – a child learns only that safety depends on unquestioning obedience to rules which have no explicit logic, which must not be exposed to criticism. Individuals who lack a personal reference system for planning their own actions or for judging those of others, are dependent on externally-imposed systems. Diversity, ambiguity, complexity and open-mindedness are, for such personalities, sources of fear and threat. Changes that affect them personally send them seeking some scapegoat to blame, and looking for some charismatic leader to rescue them. The theory of the 'authoritarian personality' as an explanation for racism has been criticised for treating the phenomenon as a pathological symptom rather than a product of historical and socio-economic factors, but it is quite possible to locate it in the conflicting context which I have already described – in the authoritarian work-ethic with its implications of self-control, suppression of desires, and the massive burden of guilt which this generates, brought into conflict with the legitimation of desire by the consumer-ethic. Such a theory helps us to relate the development of prejudice to the development of the individual self, and to see racism in a context of economic change and social conflict to which the socially incompetent can only respond with the rigidity of racism, closely allied to sexism (dependence on male dominance, in males and females), the search for 'leadership', and the recrudescence of religious superstitions and censorious puritanism.

So how can teachers help children to cope with these conflicts and complexities – in their own personalities and in society? I am arguing that the ability to understand and to master complexity is not dependent only on the input of 'positive' information. That is not to say that the elimination of factually inaccurate and racially (and sexually) insulting materials and their replacement by truthful, exciting and attractive sources of 'images' is a misguided enterprise: it is very necessary, but it must not be considered sufficient in itself. Equally important is the context of discourse in which the information is acquired. We should not be concerned with replacing one form of 'bucket-filling' indoctrination with another. If the uncomprehending racist response is to be prevented, schools must be places where all children's identities are valued, and this must be more than pious intention: close study of the use of language in classrooms can show us to what extent children's own utterances are encouraged and listened to seriously, to what extent co-operation and listening to each other are fostered. Anti-racist teaching cannot take the form of the imposition of the teacher's construction of reality – however enlightened – on children who are deprived of negotiating rights by the rules of the language-game in which they're involved: this can only spread a thin veneer of multiculturalism, a polite surface of acquiesence. It is never easy to give children the confidence to articulate their own interpretations of reality while at the same time fostering the skills of co-operation, the ability to empathize, to take the role of another. Ultimately this approach to 'multi-cultural' education, embracing all the teaching that goes on at all stages in the child's career, must press teachers to the limits of what is possible within the structure of the school system and the social and political context within which it operates.

Moreover, if we take a more complex definition of the self of the ethnic minority child, so we must consider more critically what we mean by such a child's 'own' culture and language. Culture is not transmitted from one generation to another in fixed and permanent forms: rather it is broken down, reinterpreted and made the source of new growth, like the organic matter of physical life. The quasi-permanent *forms* of culture – works of literature, art or music, traditional and symbolic clothing, customary food, ritual practices and, most of all, language – can be transmitted, passed on, but the ideological meanings they incorporate are not transmitted with them wholly or unchanged. Thus children as they grow, in each generation, create for themselves a living culture out of elements of the various existing cultures to which they have access. To illustrate this point: when we ask what is the 'mother tongue' of, say, a Pakistani child from Mirpur or an Italian child from Sicily, the answer 'Urdu' or 'Italian' is thoroughly misleading – his/her 'own' language is almost sufficiently different from the standard language of the parents' country of origin to be regarded as a separate language; the same is more obvious to us in the case of Creoles as against the Caribbean forms of standard English. The parents, and the community to which they belong, may have ambivalent attitudes towards their own dialect, regarding it – perhaps – as an inferior, deficient form of the standard language. But the situation is even more complicated by the way in which children growing up in this country may be changing their mother-tongues (if they are not abandoning them altogether) in use among themselves, intruding loan-words and simplifying grammatical forms until the language becomes a kind of Creole hybridized on English. Again, this is most apparent to us when we examine the range of language to which many Caribbean children have access – not merely bidialectal, as between standard English and Creole, but evolving a whole 'Black English' repertoire.

The same point can be made about 'cultures', in the sense of lifestyles, religious beliefs, social customs and the visible symbolic forms of food, dress, hairstyle, music and so on. For the first generation, there is the gulf between the metropolitan 'high culture' of the country of origin and their own regional and class subcultures: for the second generation, there is the compound contrast between their parents' cultures and the values and ways of life offered by school, work and the mass media – and within all these, there are the ways which they themselves develop in response, asserting their own identities and individuality against those imposed both by white society and by their parents.

So there are several problems for the teacher who seeks to identify, in order to validate and celebrate, the children's 'own' cultures and languages. In the first place, there is the problem of relevance – of presenting elements from the history, traditions and present-day achievements of people with whom they can identify, in ways which are not fossilized, but which can be taken by the children and recreated as living elements in their own 'action-knowledge'. Examination of the curriculum has made us increasingly aware of the difficulty of steering between the shallows of a superficial raree-show which emphasizes the quaint and colourful aspects of exotic cultures while insulating them against the possibility of their challenging predominant Western assumptions, and the rocks of an interpretation of all human endeavour as being directed towards the implicit aims of Western industrial society – so that all non-Western cultural forms are judged as more or less successful attempts at doing what white men have (by implication) done best, while avoiding at the same time the storms that blow up when we attempt to present the truth about inequality and injustice (within Britain and in the whole world) without implying that the victims are to blame or that their exploitation is inevitable.

Then there is the problem of accessibility for the teacher, given – as I say – the ambivalence of many of the first generation towards their 'own' cultures and languages, and the painfully acute tension for the children – a teenage Asian girl, for example, faced with the prospect of an arranged marriage, yet painfully aware of her emotional dependence on her parents and of the insecurity and threatening racism and sexism of society outside her parents' community. And then if distinctive life-styles, language, dress, music, hairstyles, etc. are being adopted by youngsters as forms of defensive solidarity, as a protection against the challenges to their self-esteem from school and society, what happens if the school tries to co–opt these? Does 'multi-culturalism' become a form of control?

All these points seem to call for a more thorough examination of our aims, and of our motives for seeking to give value to the identities of ethnic minority children – for their own benefit and for the education of all children. In terms of conventional success, the getting of jobs and the avoidance of trouble, acknowledgement of 'non-standard' ways of life and language can only be justified as a limited means to motivating the children, capturing their interest and, perhaps, enhancing their self-confidence. But presumably we hope to do more, interpreting 'success' more demandingly: giving to the children in inner-city schools the skills for analyzing and criticizing the assumptions of the social worlds they are growing up in, of articulating their own interpretations, of questioning and controlling.

This entails access to the spoken and written standard language. Standard English evolved from the dialect of fifteenth-century Westminster as a result of historical accident – it has no particular intrinsic virtues, it just happens to be the form which became standard. It evolved as the dialect of a dominant class, but it is no longer a class dialect – it is a necessary common code for communication within a complex society.

I distinguish dialect from accent; the standard form may be pronounced in many ways, and these do have social class associations. I also recognize that the standard is by no means fixed and unchallengeable – the language, being alive, is constantly changing and evolving in use. And I certainly take the view that the standard language need not, and should not, be taught in a way which implies inferiority or inadequacy for any child's 'mother' dialect of English or non-English mother-tongue; rather we should be encouraging the use of these in appropriate contexts and celebrating the diversity of linguistic skills and means of expression to which these give access. Much rather, we should be fostering critical awareness of language, of the ways in which any forms of language may be used for clear expression, explicit elaboration and incisive criticism of ideas, or for the obfuscation of ideas, for concealing presuppositions and denying critical examination. Consciousness of the differences among forms of English, and of the arbitrary character of the social values attached to these differences, is a necessary prerequisite for such critical awareness. While it is obviously much more difficult to extend this active acknowledgement to languages other than English, it would seem a reasonable indication of a teacher's professional attitude that she/he should take an interest in the identity of the languages known to the children, perhaps attempt to acquire a rudimentary knowledge of some of them, and encourage the children to use their languages as she/he celebrates the diversity of their skills.

So a mastery of standard English as well as confidence in the mother-tongue or dialect must be among our objectives, and I would link these with the development of logical thinking, regarding mathematics as a particular form of logical language and regretting the separation between the different ways of studying language – and of enabling children to use language – that is characteristic of English education. Such mastery cannot be achieved by passive learning of prescriptive rules, but implies a learning situation in which children receive constant encouragement to use language – both spoken and written – with increasing versatility, precision and expressiveness.

Secondly, all children must acquire sufficient knowledge and understanding to locate themselves in the physical and social world – in relation to neighbourhood, nation, continent, planet in physical space, in relation to family, community, social class in 'social space', and in relation to the historical and evolutionary time-scales. Of course this entails much more than 'knowing one's place': if one really knows one's place, one knows and understands how it comes to be, and how it might be otherwise. It entails a concept of the curriculum which is fundamentally integrated, but this raises familiar problems and dangers. It may well be that distinctive areas of knowledge require separate handling for much of the time to ensure coherence, but the ultimate inter-relation among these areas must be made explicit by teachers to themselves and to the children.

In history, for example, the most valuable developments in recent years have been in approaches centred on local social history, giving children access to the sources for understanding the ways of life of earlier inhabitants of the area which they know best and for interpreting these; such history teaching, well done, may foster the ability to understand unfamiliar lifestyles and to empathize with those whose social location and way of life are different, in spite of its apparently parochial focus. If the area in question is a city, it is likely that the subject matter will include evidences for the lives of many earlier communities of immigrants, from overseas or from elsewhere in Britain, and also for the struggles of working people of all ethnic groups to protect themselves from exploitation and to make a better living for themselves and their families. Such approaches must, of course, be linked as time goes on with a broader perspective on English, European and world history, and this perspective must certainly highlight the histories of the countries of origin of the immigrant communities. But there is danger in a disjointed approach to 'world history' which fails to develop an understanding of historical cause and effect, of the time-scales entailed, of the tests of historical 'truth', replacing one set of 'kings and battles' myths with another.

Similarly, the study of literature should lead – as well as to a sensitivity to the uses of language, already mentioned – to an understanding of the ways in which different people at different times have interpreted the world, creating 'models' of human nature and behaviour which can be judged as being more or less close to the infinitely complex truth. To achieve this understanding and to pass such judgements we should go beyond the kind of crude censorship and the lists of 'good' and 'bad' books that have characterized multiculturalism to a reading of texts which recognizes their historic location and enables us to separate the distortions which the author's social context and ideology impose from the essential truth or falsehood to human experience in the text she/he wrote. Of course, such reading depends on a sophisticated knowledge and understanding of the historical contexts, and the development of such skill in children or even adults must be a long process, but I am arguing that it is not sufficient simply to 'protect' children from books containing racist images or themes: somewhere in the process of learning they need to come to terms with these and to begin to judge them in relation to the contexts in which they occur.

My argument, once again, suggests the division between 'imaginative' and 'factual' components of an understanding of one's location in the world is artificial: literature is concerned with 'facts' of human experience subject to the test of truth just as much as history, geography, or science. Science in particular needs to be established as an integrated and essential element in the multicultural curriculum. Without entering into a detailed critique of 'Man, a Course of Study', we can recognize the strength of Bruner's justification for locating the study of ourselves in an evolutionary context – giving children skills and concepts for interpreting characteristics of human societies, their similarities and differences, their internal logics and conflicts, for thinking about their own experience of learning, for reflecting (yet again!) on the nature and uses of language. The issue of skin-colour and other physical differences, like the issue of sex difference, needs to be examined in the context of a scientific understanding of the evolution of the species and of the physical environment. Moreover, children need to be made aware of the possibilities and dangers of scientific research – the history of scientific freedom and its subversion is a necessary element in the study of science, and a pre-requisite for understanding present-day struggles, whether they be about race, sex or about nuclear technology or microprocessors. Our aim should not be mere emotional commitment to the ideal of a harmonious multi-cultural society, but objective scientific understanding of the processes by which mankind has gained mastery of the physical environment, by which human behaviour in society has evolved, and a fundamentally logical and scientific approach to the diversity and complexity of modern life – an approach characterized in all spheres by the absence of prejudice, the ability to suspend judgement, to argue rationally and to change one's mind in response to evidence or argument.

To the examples I have given I would of course add the study of geography, of legal and political institutions (to be understood by the children playing an increasingly active and responsible part in processes of collective decision-making on matters which affect their lives and work at school) and would include active participation in, as well as study of, the visual arts, music and the design of the man-made environment. All these would be centred on the life of working people in the environment where the child is growing up, but this would, of course, be only a starting point: a starting-point in the sense of the prime focus of interest in the early stages of education, and a constant reference point, a starting-point for each new stage, as education progresses. The focus would extend, in space and time, to allow particular attention to the nature and development of the social, economic and political system of Britain and Europe, and to the historical background and cultural achievements of the people and nations with which the ethnic minority children can identify and in which all children should be encouraged to take a legitimate interest. Thus all children should identify themselves primarily with working people, like their parents and neighbours, and secondarily with people whose language, skin colour and way of life is similar to theirs and their parents. But as time goes on, this local and personal emphasis must be replaced by wider reference to other ways of life, other cultures and languages. Ultimately our aim should be to enable all children to achieve autonomy, and this includes independence from their own 'roots': they should be able to look at the ideas and work of any human being and judge them on their own merits, irrespective of the skin colour, cultural background or socio-historical location of their maker – to identify themselves with other human beings as fellow-workers with a common interest in ending exploitation and injustice based on race, sex or way of life.

Such an education can only be provided, as I have argued, in a context where children are encouraged to articulate their own ideas, to question, to listen to each other, to co-operate rather than compete – and, as they grow, to take an increasing part in the practice of democracy – in debate and negotiation, and the election of representatives within school, and in informed and critical use of sources of information and opinion in society – the press, television, newspapers, libraries. This is not an afterthought, civics or social studies grafted onto the traditional curriculum: democratic education and education for democracy are inseparable, and must stand at the core of the curriculum for life in a multicultural society.

CHAPTER 1.3

MULTICULTURAL EDUCATION : WHAT KIND OF RELATIVISM IS POSSIBLE?*
PAUL ZEC

No discussion of multi-cultural education at a philosophical level should seek to mask the wretched experience, for many of our newer settlers and their children, of social and economic inequality rendered more damaging by racial prejudice and discrimination. But Karl Marx may only have been partly right when he denied that philosophy could change the world. A philosopher is, let us suppose, confronted with a prescriptive attitude concerning some social practice. The attitude may be in principle unexceptionable, but at the same time may be based on intellectual foundations which logically support policies and specific practices inconsistent with the general prescriptive attitude. A philosopher is at least in a position to expose this kind of inconsistency, and has a role to play in rebuilding the foundations and showing how these can support the sorts of policies and practices which *are* consistent with the attitude. A particularly apt example of this is multicultural education. Most people who think about it are in favour of it; I shall assume that their motives are as often as not unimpeachable; nevertheless the rationale for much prescriptive talk in this area is obscure or – as I shall try to show – mistaken.

On the evidence provided by the prescriptive literature in this field a generally favourable attitude towards multicultural education usually entails a rejection of cultural elitism and an explicit or implicit acceptance of some notion of relativism. In this paper I want to show that cultural relativism as often understood cannot yield a general framework for the education of all in a culturally diverse society, and in fact provides logical support for the sorts of policies and practices which are inimical to what many concerned with and for multicultural education would want. I also

* *Journal of Philosophy of Education*, vol 14/1, 1980, pp. 77–86.

want to sketch some elements in a positive rationale for multi-cultural education which eschews what I shall prematurely but unapologetically call crude relativism, but at the same time rests upon a kind of relativism that I believe to be sensible and acceptable. Furthermore, I hope that what I have to say will to some small extent speak to those urgent and difficult questions about the educational needs of minority groups and about prejudice and discrimination in society at large (although I should say immediately that that cannot be the main burden of this paper, and is in any case a task which has been very effectively undertaken by others).[1]

1

Consider these three brief extracts: (a) '. . . positive attempts should be made to build upon the considerable strengths and riches that children of diverse cultures bring to the school environment';[2] (b) 'A system of public education sympathetic to a legitimate cultural diversity demands standards drawn from more than one culture . . . the curriculum requires that due recognition be given to all who contributed to our national heritage';[3] (c) '(There is a need for) the inclusion of themes and topics which relate to multicultural Britain . . . (students should be brought) to value cultural differences and to accept the others' right to be different and British at the same time'.[4]

The spirit, at any rate, of all these extracts is clear enough. It amounts to the view that, in some sense, differences between cultures are to be celebrated rather than denied, distorted or used as a justification for invidious comparisons between cultures. What we have here are fairly typical examples of a generally relativistic attitude. Now, suppose we call a generally relativistic attitude 'weak' relativism (fortunately there are plenty of philosophical precedents for this all-too-convenient stratagem). A 'weak' relativist would, for example, take into account another person's cultural background, with its prescribed norms, shared beliefs, etc., before passing judgement on the other's conduct. To look at the matter in another way: a 'weak' relativist would be disposed to put himself in another's shoes, to try to see what it was that was exercising the other, when confronted with an enthusiasm or distaste or indignation that was rooted in that other's culture. 'Weak' relativism, then, seems to unpack cognitively into objectivity, and emotionally into empathy or compassion. A 'weak' relativist is someone who takes seriously the truism 'circumstances alter cases' and has the appropriate emotional make-up to go with this.

'Weak' relativism as I have just characterized it would no doubt be seen by many – probably including the authors of at least two of the passages quoted above – as providing quite the wrong sort of basis for multi-cultural education, if only because it fails to repudiate ethnocentrism unequivocally enough. I shall leave that point aside for the moment. The immediate task is to see what a 'strong' relativist might say about 'weak' relativism: he would surely see it as begging all the important questions. In the first place a 'strong' relativist would argue that the 'objectivity' claimed for the 'weak' relativist is a will-o'-the-wisp; he would deny that beliefs, social practices and conduct rooted in cultures other than one's own are understandable and analyzable except by means of the concepts employed within those other cultures. There is, on this view, no extra-cultural metalanguage in terms of which cultures can be described. One can only understand another culture by coming to see how its concepts etc. function within that culture – in short, by making them one's own. Dispositions like empathy or compassion – the other plank of 'weak' relativism referred to above – might be necessary, but certainly could not be sufficient, conditions for this. So, for the 'strong' relativist, intercultural understanding is a highly circumscribed possibility. Furth-ermore, *evaluation* of beliefs, values and conduct across cultures is only possible under the same conditions applying to intercultural understand-ing. Standards of rationality and right conduct (to use two umbrella terms for brevity's sake) are neither independent of particular cultural contexts nor commensurable as between cultures; they are culture-bound.

This 'strong' version of cultural relativism has its pedigree in the writings of, among others, Malinowski, Westermarck, Radcliffe-Brown and Melville Herskovits.[5] Peter Winch's book *The Idea of a Social Science* was one of the generators of recent controversies in philosophy of the social sciences on matters like intercultural understanding and explana-tion, rationality and so on.[6] But 'strong' relativism is, of course, available – and, in these uncertain times, rather fashionable – as a general orientation wherever questions arise about social analysis and description and moral appraisal within, as well as between, cultures and societies. I do not propose to criticize it directly and in isolation now, since to do so would take us too far for too long from the specific subject-matter of this paper. But there are two important points to be made now about this 'strong' version of relativism.

First, whilst few people now would unreservedly espouse relativism in quite such an extreme form as that summarized above, because of the obvious logical difficulties that arise, its proponents have tended to have more in mind than just setting the theoretical record straight. Relativism of the kind which says that standards of rationality and right conduct are culture-bound is widely deployed both explicitly and implicitly as an antidote to ethnocentrism, cultural imperialism and so on. An example of this would be the view that there can be no 'culture-free' or 'culture-fair' test of intelligence. The proponents of this view see intelligence tests in a multi-cultural context as a vehicle for the unjust treatment of pupils with a different background from that of the dominant culture; and they reject the ethnocentrism they see as embedded in such tests. This example alone shows how relativism, curiously enough, may be used to generate positive value positions on such matters as intercultural relations and multi-cultural education, with the emphasis on favourable treatment of minority groups and the cultures they exemplify. It only needs to be said at this point that it is, of course, at least doubtful whether one can consistently be a relativist in the present sense and at the same time hold positive values.

The second point that I wish to make, arising out of the brief account of 'strong' relativism, concerns the policies for educational practice which tend to be advocated by relativists. It is not difficult to detect the flavour of 'strong' relativism in the following recommendations: (a) Because standards of rationality are culture-bound, aspects of the curriculum which are vehicles for the development of rationality in pupils should be contextually rooted in the various cultures from which different pupils in a multi-cultural society come; (b) Because moral, aesthetic and religious beliefs are relative to cultures, and not understandable except in terms of the concepts employed within particular cultures, one should, in a multi-cultural school, either refrain from transmitting these in a positive way or, perhaps, leave them to be dealt with in supplementary schools for separate cultural groups, manned by teachers who are rooted in the particular cultures; (c) If stereotyping of groups of pupils by teachers is partly a reflection of the barriers which cultural relativity necessarily erects against intercultural understanding, either teachers must be appropriately equipped to overcome such barriers – which will in practice only be possible for some teachers – or, again, different cultural groups should as far as possible encounter teachers who share the same cultural background. Now, all I want to say at this point about the recommendations just mentioned is that they are in my experience frequently uttered, and that both they (together with other recommendations of a similar type) and their provenance are in need of close scrutiny.

So, to summarize so far: throughout the educational system concern is being expressed that education should be responsive to the fact that Britain is a multicultural society, and that cultural diversity should both be reflected in school curricula and be valued by those who work in education – especially teachers. Underpinning the prescriptive force of this general position is cultural relativism; the widely advocated implications of this general position for educational practice are also, *prima facie*, strongly relativistic in character and basis.

2

Now, if relativism is right, there would seem to be a problem inherent intalking about *an* education for all in a multi-cultural society – and this would be a particular case of the more general problem posed by relativism about whether, in other than a purely formal sense, there can be a concept of education that is not culture-bound. It seems that to accept relativism is to accept the view that in a multicultural society the only choice is between on the one hand the maintenance through education of a dominant culture (which is undesirable because elitist, anti-democratic, etc.) and on the other hand the institution of separate but equal educational programmes for the transmission of their cultures to co-existing cultural groups (which is also undesirable because it smacks of apartheid). Ruled out, it appears, by relativism is a non-ethnocentric, non-imperialist education for *all* in a multicultural society. But it is precisely this latter ideal to which many educators and others whose thinking is relativistic, aspire. It is here, then, that the philosophical difficulty arises, and the opportunity occurs to attempt its resolution.

In what immediately follows I shall expose in more detail what I consider to be the incongruity between cultural relativism of the 'strong' kind and a sensible approach to the education of all pupils in a multicultural society – an approach which is unitary and at the same time takes diversity fully into account. This will be preliminary to an attempt to erect some signposts for a multicultural education for all.

Let us then consider the proposition – extracted from one of the passages I quoted earlier in the paper – that education should build upon the strengths and riches that children of diverse cultures bring to the school environment. Now people usually support such a proposal because they believe it reflects a desire to treat other cultures with respect. Two major points need to be made about the proposal and the outlook upon which it is based.[7]

The first point concerns what it is to respect anything at all: it is surely impossible for someone to respect another's way of life, or another culture, unless he is in a position to a certain extent to understand it – to see what is there. Furthermore, if the only thing that is to count as understanding of another culture is possession of the concepts of that culture (the position taken by cultural relativism) then one can hardly talk about respect *for* that culture. This is because respecting something implies not only that one to a certain extent understands what one is respecting, but also that one is looking at it from a *standpoint* – a standpoint located outside the object of respect. Finally, since respect for another culture presupposes seeing what is there, and picking out aspects of it which, from a certain standpoint, seem worthy of respect, cultural relativism cannot be the basis for intercultural respect.

Three objections might be made to this argument. First, it could be said that the perfectly comprehensible notion of *self*-respect puts paid to the assertion that the subject of respect necessarily stands in an external relation to its object (this conceptual point is needed by the cultural relativist in order for him to be able to maintain consistently the proposition that we ought to treat other cultures with respect and the proposition that evaluation of a way of life from a culturally different standpoint is impossible). Secondly – and this is connected with the first objection – it obviously makes sense to say that one respects one's own culture, and since one can, on a relativistic account, only understand another culture by in some sense making it one's own, respect for other cultures is no different in principle from respect for one's own. That puts paid to the notion that the external standpoint has to be a culturally different one. Thirdly, the cultural relativist might rule out *a priori* the assumption that respect for another culture entails seeing what is there and picking out aspects of it relevant to what, from a particular standpoint, is held to be valuable. Respect for other cultures would, for a relativist, itself presumably be an *a priori* matter; we should automatically respect other cultures because they have their own concepts, beliefs and norms which we, imprisoned as we are in the universe of our own discourse, cannot appraise or evaluate.

None of these objections holds water; first, the notion of self-respect, common enough as it is, either has more to do with overall mental health than with self-analysis, in which case it involves a quite different application of the concept of respect from that which we are concerned with; or it refers to the favourable result of self-appraisal, in which case it implies just those conditions, of understanding and, as it were, an external standpoint, that I took to be necessary for respecting another culture.

The second objection, it will be recalled, was that (on a relativistic account) respecting other cultures could not be the result of appraising them from a culturally external standpoint, and in any case did not have to be; it could and had to be the same in principle as respecting one's own culture. Well, the relativist is right, but for quite the wrong reasons: in any but an *a priori* sense, respecting one's own culture implies appraisal according to criteria, and the criteria must be other than the object of appraisal itself. If, for example, I respect Britain's parliamentary institutions (this is not meant to be a far-fetched example) it is because they presumably fulfil certain criteria other than the *defining* characteristics of parliamentary institutions. If I respect – or, let us say, value – the British concept of fair play, it is because it connects up with a larger, more general concept of justice, and/or with some other value. So the possibility of respecting one's own culture entails the further possibility of appraisal from a standpoint external to what is appraised; it is for that reason that *intra*cultural respect is no different in principle from *inter*cultural respect.

The third objection – that respect for other cultures is an *a priori* matter, precisely because we cannot appraise or judge them from an external standpoint – is all too easily rebutted. It just makes no sense to say that we are obliged to adopt a respectful and tolerant attitude towards something of which we can understand nothing, *because* we can understand nothing of it. It does, of course make sense to say that we should not judge harshly that which we do not understand (after all, that is what we are saying when we repudiate prejudice). But the point is that no evaluation of anything at all is possible independently of understanding. If this is what the relativist is saying (with his rider that understanding is in the intercultural context very unlikely) then he cannot logically enjoin respect upon us. If he is saying that we should adopt an attitude of respect towards other cultures *a priori*, then he not only fatally undermines his own relativism, but offers us no good reason why our *a priori* attitude should not be one of hostility or contempt (if he does offer a good reason why not, he again ceases to be a relativist, because of what is entailed by the notion of a good reason).

So respect for other cultures is only possible for a non-relativist; for someone who from where he stands sees something in another culture and values it. That is just what is entailed by the proposition that education should build upon the strengths and riches of diverse cultures: respect for other cultures is justified by their strengths and richness.

The second major point about the proposition under consideration arises out of the first: how are we to get from the essentially negative point about the impossibility of relativism as a basis for intercultural respect, to a positive interpretation of the principle that education should build upon the strengths and riches of diverse cultures? There *is* clearly a problem here: reference to the strengths and riches of other cultures than one's own, if it is not either to be patronizing or vacuous, must be based on a judgement about what is valuable in other cultures. Now, such a judgement, if serious, will of course be rooted biographically in one's own reflections on one's own culture. But how can we arrive after reflection at some assertion that we take to be morally or aesthetically or scientifically true about our own culture, if we turn our back on the possibility of applying the same processes of thought to other cultures? We could not be said to be taking our own or other cultures seriously if we were only prepared to think critically – that is to evaluate after reflection – either only about another culture (ethnocentrism) or only about our own (cultural relativism). It is, of course, usually more difficult to see what a given belief or practice is a case of, in another culture, than in one's own; but there is only a difference of degree here, no difference in principle.

On these grounds, reference to the strengths and riches of other cultures is an inevitable prelude to a specification of those strengths and riches, based on evaluative criteria. Whatever they are, these criteria, however culture-bound in origin, will have the logical character of universalizable maxims: to welcome some aspect of another culture because of its richness or whatever, is not just to say that it is good for that culture or even one's own, but that it is the sort of thing that is in general worthy of value.

The relativist might reply that we are just not entitled to say of any aspect of any culture that it is in general worthy of value. But this leaves him in a very difficult position as far as multicultural education is concerned. For, granted that there is to be multicultural education in a society, on what basis could it then be constituted? Either no criteria for the selection of material are available, or the criteria for selection must be internal to the various cultures themselves – in which case, in the absence of some justifiable form of adjudication we are left with a model of multi-cultural education that can best be described as well-intentioned apartheid. So, however difficult the task may at first appear, those who profess a concern for multi-cultural education are likely to base their educational programme upon sounder foundations than that which relativism provides, if they can accept the challenge and opportunity for appraisal and evaluation which diverse cultures offer.

3

I come now to the final section of this paper, in which I try to identify some of the principles upon which a multicultural education for all might be based. I shall discuss this under three main headings: first, the educator's perception of cultural diversity itself; secondly, the problem for the educator of doing practical educational justice to the possibility which I have affirmed above of reconciling objectivity and universality with cultural diversity and relativity; thirdly, an ethical issue which I take to be crucial to multi-cultural education.

First, then, the educator's perception of cultural diversity. It is nowadays perhaps natural, but misleading and dangerous, to see Britain as a society of different and separate cultures. Cultural relativism, unfortunately, encourages that view, because of the theoretical barriers it erects against interpenetration between cultures. That it is a misleading view has been very effectively demonstrated by Mary Midgley:

> Our society . . . is a fertile jungle of different influences – Greek, Jewish, Roman, Norse, Celtic . . . into which further influences are still pouring – American, Indian, Japanese, Jamaican, you name it. If we think about this history for a moment, we can see that the . . . picture of separate, unmixable cultures is quite unreal. The world has never been like that; it couldn't be like it . . . Except for the very smallest and most remote, all cultures are formed out of many streams. All have the problem of digesting and assimilating things which, at the start, they don't understand. All have the choice of learning something from this challenge, or, alternatively, of refusing to learn, and fighting it mindlessly instead.[8]

That the view of multi-cultural Britain as a unique locus of separate unmixable cultures is dangerous needs no further evidence than that the 1977 Government Green Paper on Nationality Law suggests such possible new criteria for British citizenship as willingness to identify with British society, and general behaviour acceptable to one's fellow-citizens. The implication here is that, *prima facie*, a British-born black, for example, is less likely to fulfil these criteria than his 'indigenous' counterpart.

It is surely vital that educators should understand that cultural plurality is neither unique to Britain nor just the result of recent immigration nor manifested in the form of a homogeneous 'host' culture, surrounded by a motley bunch of 'satellite' cultures; nor a matter of separate unmixable cultures. It hardly needs saying that a correct perception by educators of cultural diversity, in theory and actuality, is a necessary condition for their being able to seize opportunities for illuminating and enlarging pupils' understanding of what binds humanity together and what differentiates people.

I turn now to the difficult question of the basis – if any – upon which the educator is to do practical justice both to the possibility of an objectivist framework for multicultural education, and to a legitimate recognition and celebration of cultural diversity. This sort of problem has been raised more generally in the context of the debate about whether there can be universal (i.e. transcultural) criteria of rationality in human thought and action. The problem I am concerned with can be seen as a particular case of the more general debate if we characterize it in the following way: it is, of course, widely held that education is largely a matter of developing the rational mind (i.e. *inter alia*, a mind that abhors contradictions and inconsistencies, superstitions and compulsive fantasies, and that is capable of formulating appropriate ends and appropriate means to those ends). The question immediately arises: is a unitary conception of education for rationality possible in the context of a classroom containing pupils of different cultural backgrounds – some of them, perhaps, fairly exotic to Western eyes?[9] To answer that question one inevitably has to consider the wider debate concerning whether or not what I shall for brevity's sake call criteria of rationality are totally culture-bound. (Much is implied by this, of course, for consideration of people from different cultures as knowers, believers, language-users, agents and so on. Much is also implied for consideration of the processes and products which are the concrete evidence of the thought processes, etc., of different cultural groups. Furthermore, much is implied for consideration of the modes of enquiry, analysis and criticism employed in the West for appraisal of 'other' cultures.)

Detailed rehearsal of the relativistic and anti-relativistic arguments employed on this subject by such writers as Winch, Jarvie, Horton, Lukes, Gellner and others[10] would be out of place in this paper (although consideration of them would be a necessary part of a fully detailed treatment of these issues). In any case, I have already nailed my colours firmly to the mast of objectivism. I tend to share the view of those who hold that we question the rationality of some of the beliefs and practices of exotically alien or primitive cultures, precisely because the beliefs or practices are recognizably rational at some level – and this, in turn, is because rationality is not confined to some human groups as opposed to others. It is not that Azande witchcraft, or arranged marriages, have nothing whatever to do with rational belief or conduct; it is rather the case that they are describable from one point of view as instances of a flawed – perhaps badly flawed – rationality.

An alternative way of seeing the matter would be to suggest that '. . . some criteria of rationality are universal, i.e. relevantly applicable to all beliefs, in any context, while others are context-dependent, i.e. are to be discovered by investigating the context and are only relevantly applicable to beliefs in that context'.[11]

Now it seems to me that, whichever of the above two positions is adopted, there are certain immediate implications for multi-cultural education. First, all children should be treated as potentially rational in at least some respects which are cross-culturally identical. There would be no warrant for treating some children as opposed to others – even to any extent – as being *locked into* a 'prelogical' state, by virtue of their cultural or ethnic heritage as distinct from their developmental stage.

Secondly, the multicultural educator, *qua* educator for rationality, is able on the basis I have outlined to select curricular material according to criteria which are educational and rational, rather than on the purely intuitionist grounds that the fact that an item 'belongs' to a minority culture self-evidently qualifies it for inclusion in a multicultural curriculum. He has every reason to search for, and use, examples from various cultures which manifest in different ways the same facet of rational human thought or activity. He is further entitled to examine – first on his own, perhaps, and then with pupils – beliefs and practices from 'other' cultures both in terms of universal criteria of rationality and in terms of, as it were, local criteria. As an educator, he is also entitled – indeed obliged – to evaluate (as well as explain) the 'local' in terms of the universal. Lastly, such processes would have to be applied by the multicultural educator to 'this' as well as to 'other' cultures.

Music education provides a good example of what has just been generally suggested. In all music there are the same fundamental elements of rhythm, pitch and intervals. I am not just saying that there is rhythm and melody in all music, but that the fundamental elements *are* fundamental in an identical way across all cultures. Thus, for example, near the end of the Scherzo of the Eroica Symphony, there is a simultaneous occurrence of simple and compound metre (2- and 3-time) which is no different from one of the commonest cross-rhythms to be heard in African music. It is easy not to notice the similarity, because the idioms and superstructures are so different between the two. But the fact that the rhythmic feature in question is identically explicable in both musical settings is not the result of some random coincidence, of the sort exemplified by the case of the chimpanzee typing all of Shakespeare's plays – given enough time. It is rather a reflection of the fact that there is very much in common between human cultures in their ability to erect internally coherent structures and appreciate their internal coherence. The example does suggest at least a part of the rationale for the multicultural music educator: find examples for appreciation and performance from as broad a range of cultural experience as possible – which reflect as well as possible the interplay between what is common to all music and how each musical idiom handles the commonly fundamental structures.

A large part of the basis, then, for a general multicultural education must be a readiness to find in a diversity of cultures just those things which one values or recognizes as rational in the culture that one is most used to – even if one finds them in strange forms. It really is not that difficult an operation. To put it briefly: an objectivist approach does not entail a monocultural (or ethnocentric) education; nor, conversely, are multi-cultural learning and teaching activities which deserve to be called educational, guaranteed by relativism. One good reason for drawing educational experiences from a diversity of cultures rather than from one, is that the development in pupils of awareness of the variety of forms which common human experiences may take, is one means of rendering cultural diversity less of a 'problem'. If inter-cultural understanding is to be an aim of multi-cultural education, it cannot develop solely on the basis of the notion – however well-meaning – that culturally different beliefs, practices, values and so on are in principle incommensurable.

I come finally to deal with an ethical issue which seems central to multicultural education – that of respect for persons. Once again, I shall try to show that relativism provides no support for a reasonable working-out of that principle in the context under discussion.

The concept of respect for persons has received much attention from philosophers of education. Paul Hirst and Richard Peters, for example, have approached it on the basis of what seems to be a rather special concept of a person: 'This use of "person" is connected conceptually with having what might be called an assertive point of view, with evaluation, decision and choice, and with being, to a certain extent, an individual who determines his own destiny by his choices'.[12]

Now many teachers have to deal with pupils who are apparently lacking in a point of view; who (even in adolescence) are precisely not sources of evaluation, decision and choice, and who through various sorts of circumstances are relatively incapable of determining their own destiny by their choices. It is precisely because many people of Caribbean origin are so widely treated in accordance with the stereotyped image with which White society saddles them, that many children and youths of Caribbean parentage seem to lack the defining characteristics of personhood in the sense under consideration. But whilst it is perfectly proper that teachers should seek to engender in such pupils the prerequisites of a capacity to be the source of evaluation, decision, choice, etc., such a project is surely doomed to fail if its starting-point is the assumption that the intended recipients are not yet 'persons'.

But what content is the multicultural educator to give to the principle of respect for persons – especially in his work with pupils from so-called ethnic minority groups? The importance of the concept is surely that one of the things it entails is looking behind the structures of racial and cultural differences to the person as a centre of consciousness. What it rules out, of course, is the pigeon-holing, stereotyping and problematizing of pupils belonging to such groups.

What underlies what I have just said is the issue of teacher expectation: the teacher who meets a new class of children containing some West Indians, who expects these latter to be relatively poor at academic subjects and good at dance and physical education, and who behaves towards them accordingly, differentiates them in advance of good reasons being produced; stereotypes them; shows a lack of respect for them as persons, and possibly helps to create those situations which he anticipates. But a teacher who refuses to treat any pupils as being locked into a particular culture; who does not regard cultural differences as irreducible and impenetrable in every respect, denies in his everyday practice the false perspective of relativism. His pragmatic recognition that cultural differences *can* generate special educational needs is indeed a reflection of what I earlier called a relativistic attitude (or 'weak' relativism). But relativism of the other kind: (a) fails to support any general moral principle such as that of respect for persons; (b) approaches cultural difference as something 'given' and not to be, as it were, tampered with, and thus provides logical support for just that which people most concerned with multi-cultural education abhor – stereotyping of pupils by teachers. So respect for persons – incompatible with relativism because it is itself a universal principle – in a multicultural context demands teacher behaviour and attitude of a sort which are a *practical* repudiation of relativism.

I have in this paper suggested that there can be a unitary approach to multicultural education which sets its face against the relativism of knowledge, understanding and values, and against educational separatism. I also hope to have shown that a unitary approach does not entail any sort of indifference to, or belittling of, cultural diversity – on the contrary. Finally, I have begun – and no more than begun – to sketch what this approach might entail in terms of certain cognitive and ethical aspects of multicultural education. Some might say that grim social realities stack the cards so heavily against educational justice for all in this society that my quest is as futile as trying to square the circle. But I really do not see any alternative strategy to the one to which I am committed, for anyone who wants the educational experiences of all pupils in a multicultural society to live up to the name of education. And saturation of classrooms with images from a diversity of cultures, necessary though this may be, cannot be sufficient; while the crudely relativistic concentration on different cultural diets for different cultural groups comes nowhere near to meeting the case, based as it is on false intellectual assumptions and generating as it does educational consequences which potentially celebrate division rather than diversity.

Almost everything remains to be done in the task of building a full rationale for a general multicultural education, and of translating the rationale into direct curricular prescriptions. In particular, a full working-out of the objectivist proposition that items from 'minority' cultures should be selected according to their educational value, remains to be accomplished (I am uncomfortably aware that in this paper I have done little more than open up that particular topic for discussion). Furthermore, a great deal of work needs to be done on the question of how far school curricula might approach cultural diversity and connected phenomena directly, and how far, as it were, adverbially to other, more established, activities. No less important than either of these issues is that of the sort of society which the approach I have taken to multicultural education might be aiming to promote. All of the above problems have a philosophical dimension, and I hope to say more about these and other related questions at another time.

Notes and references

1. The literature in this area is, of course, immense. But see, for example: Milner, D. (1975) *Children and Race* (Harmondsworth, Penguin); Giles, R. (1977) *The West Indian Experience in British Schools* (London, Heinemann); Smith, D. (1977) *Racial Disadvantage in Britain* (Harmondsworth, Penguin); Rex, J. (1973) *Race, Colonialism and the City* (London, Routledge & Kegan Paul); Commission for Racial Equality (1978) *Five Views of Multiracial Britain* (London); Jeffcoate, R. (1979) *Positive Image: Towards a Multi-racial Curriculum* (London, Chameleon Books).
2. White, J. and Houlton, D. (1977) 'Biculturalism in the Primary School', *Forum*, 20, Autumn.
3. Pratte, R. (1978) 'Cultural Diversity and Education', in: Strike, K. & Egan, K. (Eds) *Ethics and Educational Policy*, p. 162 (London, Routledge & Kegan Paul).
4. Giles, R. (1977) *Op. cit.*, pp. 163–164.
5. See, for example: Malinowski, B. (1944) *A Scientific Theory of Culture and Other Essays* (Chapel Hill, N. C.); Radcliffe-Brown, A. R. (1952) *Structure and Function in Primitive Society* (London); Herskovits, M. J. (1948) *Man and his Works* (New York).
6. See, for example: Winch, P. (1958) *The Idea of a Social Science* (London, Routledge & Kegan Paul); Wilson, B. (Ed.) (1974) *Rationality* (Oxford, Basil Blackwell) – articles by P. Winch, E. Gellner, A. MacIntyre, R. Horton, and S. Lukes; Borger, R. & Cioffi, F. (Eds) (1970) *Explanation in the Behavioural Sciences* (Cambridge University Press) – articles by I. C. Jarvie, P. Winch, and A. MacIntyre.
7. And/or because they are disposed to regard the contents of other cultures positively. In fact, this section would have profited from a distinction I failed to make explicit between a formal respect for other cultures – a variation, perhaps, on the relevant Kantian Imperative; and a substantive regard (or distaste) for the *contents* of other cultures. No doubt the reader will be able to decipher which of these I am referring to at particular points in the text. But the most important educational implication I should wish to draw from this part of the discussion is that enthusiasm for incorporating material from 'other' cultures into an educational programme should not be accompanied by a refusal, on relativistic grounds, to make assessments of the contents of 'other' cultures. I am therefore mostly talking in this section about substantive regard (or distaste) rather than formal respect.
8. Midgley, M. (1977) 'Trying Out One's New Sword,' *The Listener*, 15th December.
9. Several commentators on this paper have asked me whether in this discussion of education for rationality in a multicultural context I meant to imply: (a) that there is a 'pure' (Platonic?) version of rationality which is entirely *independent* of all cultures and which could constitute a common core of learning experiences for all pupils in the world; (b) that the development of rationality is necessarily the paramount aim for education qua *multi-cultural* education. The answer to both questions is no.

10. See references given for note 6 above.
11. Lukes, S. 'Some Problems About Rationality', in: Wilson, B. (Ed.) *Rationality, op. cit.*, p. 208.
12. Hirst, P. H. & Peters, R. S. (1970) *The Logic of Education*, p. 53 (London, Routledge & Kegan Paul).

CHAPTER 1.4

THE EDUCATION OF THE BLACK CHILD*
MAUREEN STONE

In reality a mediocre teacher may manage to see to it that his pupils become *informed*, although he will not succeed in making them better educated; he can devote a scrupulous and bureaucratic conscientiousness to the mechanical part of teaching – and the pupil, if he has an active intelligence, will give an order of his own . . . to the 'baggage' he accumulates. With the new curricula . . . there will no longer be any 'baggage' to put in order . . . A date is always a date, whoever the examiner is, and a definition is always a definition. But an aesthetic judgement or a philosophical analysis? (Antonio Gramsci, On Education in *Selections from the Prison Notebooks* (1971) Lawrence & Wishart.)

Gramsci's argument against the romantic idealism of the Gentile Reform of 1923, which sought to change Italian education from mere 'instruction' to an 'active, creative' process, is very relevant to any discussion on urban schooling in Britain today, and particularly to the schooling of West Indian children within that system. There is almost unanimous agreement amongst researchers and teachers that the development of positive self-concept and high self-esteem are important to attainment in schools. The practical results of these assumptions is that teachers act more and more like social workers and consequently neglect their primary role of 'instruction'. We have seen from the research undertaken as part of this work that there is no basis in fact for the belief that black children have poor self-esteem and negative self-concept. Further, we questioned the belief that high or low self-concept in itself can make a difference to the structural forces in society which largely determine distribution of income which in turn determines class and status positions.

* *The Education of the Black Child: the Myth of Multiracial Education*, 1981, Fontana, pp. 240–54. This extract is from the concluding chapter. Maureen Stone's argument is based on her research into black children's self-concept and self-esteem and on her observations of black supplementary schools and multiracial education 'in action' in London. Findings are reported in earlier chapters.

Here we examine the implications of the critique and the research for the schooling of West Indian children. We are not here concerned with developing relevant curricula; the details of what Gramsci called 'the baggage' may not be as important as has been recently stressed. What is of overriding importance is that children should acquire the means to put 'the baggage' in order; something they cannot possibly do if they have not mastered the fundamentals and are virtually semi-literate.

The proposals which follow may appear controversial or conservative. The intention is that the debate over the schooling of working-class and black children should be opened up to rigorous academic scrutiny so that discussion of issues such as the place of emotions in the classroom, self-concept and self-esteem should be linked to discussions of the structural factors which regulate social and economic life and so teachers are not further encouraged into teaching methods based on romantic ideas of 'self-realization' and 'self-fulfilment', to the detriment of their pupils' interests.

Neville Bennett, in trying to explain the poorer academic performance of the 'informal' pupils in his sample observed that one explanation may be:

> that the poorer academic progress of informal pupils is an accurate reflection of the aim of informal teachers . . .
> Formal teachers stress academic aims while informal teachers prefer to stress the importance of self-expression, enjoyment of school and the development of creativity.

This seems to lend support to my thesis that teachers who emphasize self-concept, self-esteem and enjoyment, do so at the expense of more concrete objectives. Although it is possible to test whether or not a child can read, write, spell or do sums to most people's satisfaction, there is no agreed method of telling whether a child is 'self-actualized' or not – even if it were important to know. It is for these reasons that the central recommendation of this study is for the use of more formal methods of teaching West Indian children throughout primary and secondary schools. These methods are understood and approved of by West Indian (and other working-class) parents and in the light of the dismal failure of the present approach, formal teaching methods can only offer an improvement on the present situation. The present methods have resulted in low attainment by West Indian pupils and concentration of black children in lower streams of the comprehensive school, remedial classes and special schools for the educationally subnormal.

300 in mind 1991

We turn now to a general discussion of the work as a whole and its implications for (a) policy, (b) theory and research, (c) schools and teachers and (d) parents, children and the West Indian community.

The aims of education

With Brian Simon (1965) I would argue that sociological theory must be able to explain and demonstrate plausibly, at a number of levels (of which the empirical is only one), the ways in which anomalies and inconsistencies within schools reflect wider contradictions within the social structure. In looking critically at the ideas underlying self-concept theory and research and in examining the process involved in projects which attempt to apply these theories within schools, one major contradiction has emerged: given the level of dislike of teachers it is virtually impossible for teachers to be 'significant others' in the lives of West Indian children. This factor is compounded by evidence which suggests that teachers are not all that keen on black children either ; Brittan showed that teachers in general had negative, stereotyped views of West Indian pupils (Brittan, 1976). Willis (1977) suggested that the one tension-free area between 'the lads' (who belonged to the school counter-culture) and the teachers was their mutual resentment of the immigrants in their midst. Willis wrote:

> Certainly it is quite explicit that many senior staff associate the major immigration of the 1960s with the break-up of the 'order and quietness' of the 1950s and of what is now seen more and more retrospectively as their peaceful, successful schools.

My own research suggests that West Indian pupils, at least, have equally negative feelings towards teachers. Individuals or small groups of children develop 'relationships' with a particular teacher or teachers but this does not appear to affect their overall attitudes to most teachers, whom they perceive as having inordinate power over them and generally disliking them. The attitude change which may result from participation in group work projects may lead individuals or small groups of children to see certain teachers as being well disposed to them and willing to treat them on a par with English children. These attitudes are not, however, generalized on to *school* – so that, although individual relationships may be good, general attitudes and behaviour may remain unchanged. Since the total school environment is perceived as unhelpful, this is to be expected.

Relationships are not stressed in Saturday schools – work is. If *or their parents*

anything, children are encouraged to ignore 'relationships' especially with friends who are not serious about work and might get them into trouble. It may be that in a voluntary situation the need to stress relationships does not exist – children come because they want to learn; teachers and other helpers because they care enough whether children learn to give up free time to teach them. In contrast, teachers in weekday schools who are committed to a 'relationship' based teaching style appear to need to stress relationships continually. One young teacher told me that 'it is impossible to teach these children (there were over 60 per cent West Indian boys in this school) unless you first have a relationship with them'. This is in a school with at least one suspension per week, and where even as he spoke we could hear masters literally screaming at boys and boys shouting back, teaching going on against a continual din and uproar – or so it seemed to me. Yet this teacher, just two years past his probationary year, firmly believed that he could only teach where a relationship already existed. In one day he might take three to four classes of 25–30 boys each. Was it possible to have 'a relationship' with each and every one of these boys? I asked. Was it necessary? He felt that not all boys needed a relationship every day or with the same intensity – a death in the family, father gone 'away' etc., could lead to the necessity to help that one boy on a particular day, but the basis for such help had to exist beforehand. Thus he felt that the teacher should aim at developing some kind of a relationship with all the pupils he teaches. His views appeared to be based on the teaching of Carl Rogers and, I suspect, were more in line with what he had learnt in college and what he believed to be ideal, rather than on what actually happened on a day-to-day basis in his school.

The problem is – how is the teacher to develop a relationship with children or groups of children he/she actually dislikes and who (because likes/dislikes tend to be mutual) also dislike the teacher? Is it really necessary to develop a 'relationship' with a child in order to teach it numeracy and literacy? What if one is a perfectly good mathematics teacher but hopeless at 'relationships'? Should one not be a teacher?

There may be a danger here of relationships assuming importance beyond anything that is useful or meaningful within the context of the provision of schooling for working-class and black children in contemporary British society. Irrespective of the theoretical or other weaknesses of the emotions/relationships approach to teaching in the classroom, it is clear that, given the negative feelings which both groups (teachers and pupils) generally have of each other, it would be unwise to allow emotions and relationships to assume major importance in urban schools. A black teacher told me that in her view left-wing radical teachers had done more harm to black children in schools than any other group. She said that the perfect teacher for West Indians was a traditional no-nonsense teacher who knew her subject and knew how to teach. 'Politics don't matter – unless the teacher is really right-wing, of course – NF or something like that – otherwise it's a non-issue.' Many community workers and youth workers also blame left-wing teachers for over-indulging black kids, letting them 'get away with anything so long as they had a good relationship with the child'. In my experience, this transcends political boundaries and is as common among liberal as among so-called radical black teachers.

What should be the aim of schooling for West Indian children? Historically, traditional liberal education theory has as its distinguishing characteristics belief in:

1. *The Integrative Function of Education.* The process whereby the young are integrated into the roles expected and required of them in adult society (Durkheim).
2. *The Egalitarian Function of Education.* Whereby society is serviced, governed and controlled by a meritocracy of intelligentsia drawn equally from all social classes and all groups, the only criteria being intelligence (Dewey).
3. *The Developmental Function of Education.* Whereby the process of education promotes in the individual autonomy, self-realization, self-actualization and self-understanding – the 'rational man'/person created as a result of exposure to liberal ideas and education.

Examined against these criteria the school system as a whole would seem to fail West Indian children on all counts.

Integrative schools are not 'integrative'. Increasingly West Indian youngsters are rejecting 'the roles expected and required of them by adult society'. They are refusing to do the menial jobs which their parents were glad to do; they call this 'shit work'.

Within the West Indian working class there has developed a distinct grouping of unemployed men and women, which increases at the end of every school year. It is not a reserve army of labour – that is to say, held in reserve to be called upon at the will of London Transport, Fords, night cleaning agencies, hospitals and all other employers of black immigrant labour. Call as they might, the youths have uncompromisingly refused to budge. It is an overwhelming refusal of shitwork (Race Today Collective, 1975).

The counter-culture developing amongst young blacks in Britain including membership of the Rastafarian religion and alternative lifestyles around it, clearly indicates an unwillingness on the part of young West Indians to accept the position offered to them in British society. Even though, to many observers, the alternatives they create for themselves appear equally unattractive and lead to equally bad results.

It follows from what has already been said that the egalitarian function of schooling too is a dream. As far as most West Indian parents and children are concerned, the schools do not even begin to offer anything like equal opportunity; they suffer all the disadvantages of the urban working-class and the additional ones of prejudice and racism. It was interesting to be told that all the most successful West Indians in this country were educated in the Caribbean, at least for most of their school life. Whether this is true or not I have no idea, but it is widely believed in the West Indian community. I was told by one West Indian Deputy Head that Britain is a long way from producing its first 'home-grown' black university lecturer! Whatever the reason, black children do not do well in schools and since the basis of the meritocracy is intelligence demonstrated by a suitable number of certificates and degrees, the school system clearly fails on that count as well.

What of the final criterion, the developmental function of education? From the data presented we saw that West Indian children in the total sample had average self-concept scores and average-to-high self-esteem and thus the need for self-concept enhancement for all West Indian children must be questioned.

Gramsci, in his *Notes from Prison*, argued against relationship-based teaching. He insisted on the value of hard work and discipline and for the need of the potential working-class intellectuals to acquire mastery over the knowledge and skills of the elite if they were to effect any change in their own class and position in society. However, Gramsci did not see social change simply in economic terms, indeed he believed in 'critical self-consciousness' as the means towards personal awareness resulting in cultural and intellectual change. He required education to 'produce people who could both master the skills of intellectual production and use them in engaging the forces of history in active critical self-consciousness'. But the self-awareness he stressed was not the reflexive self-indulgence of the highly individualistic, idealized, romantic liberals but part of a historical process whereby the individual knows herself as 'part of the historical process which has deposited in one an infinity of traces'. Gramsci argued against the developmental role of education because he knew that such emphasis would result in an almost totally ignorant and illiterate working class. He knew that for the working class to succeed they had to produce intellectuals capable of mastering elite culture and turning it to their own use – the working-class intellectual would have to develop and sustain, through the rigour of disciplined study, a coherent world-view.

> What is required then is that children be instructed in the often tedious rote learning of a whole intellectual tradition . . . it is through such a process that each child will be enabled to analyze and think on a par with those intellectual traditions he/she must overcome in order to take up his proper place in civil and political society.

In Gramsci's terms, such aims required that the traditional curricula provide both the historical forms of the various worlds as well as the intellectual rigour through which such worlds may be viewed. Professor Brian Simon (1976) has warned Marxists about the dangers of 'relativism' in these words:

> The 'radical' nature of this relativist ideological position, and the danger of taking it seriously, is shown in the practice of those young teachers who, accepting this view of knowledge, and in their sentimental generosity, identifying with their working-class pupils, begin to see their role as shielding them from the demands of formal schooling and acting more in the role of the social worker . . . rather than as teacher, with the specific function of inducting pupils into the knowledge, skills and abilities that derive from the objectives of an education appropriate to the mid-late twentieth century. The dangers are evident: it provides means . . . of denying to the working class access to knowledge, culture and science.

Another leading Marxist intellectual, Maurice Levitas, has also dissociated himself from the relativist position with regard to knowledge and has argued that the working class must first subject themselves to knowledge before they can master it.

We have seen that both in terms of the traditional liberal objectives based on the development role of education, and in terms of the supposedly radical phenomenological Marxist approach, the efforts meet with small returns. More fundamentally they appear to work against the interest of the working class as a whole.

Implications

Policy

Policy decisions should encourage teachers in urban schools to have as their primary objective the teaching of skills and knowledge and the development of associated abilities in children. Teacher training should emphasize that teachers' professional interest lies in 'the inducting of children into knowledge, skills and abilities' rather than in the provision of social work or therapy to children. Training courses could encourage teachers to consider the use of more formal methods of teaching which appear to have more overall parental support and which may be more effective for certain children.

Another observation concerns the disproportionate stress which has been placed on knowledge of the cultural and home background of 'immigrants' in teacher training. Since most British research and writing on West Indian family life is ethnocentric and portrays the West Indian family as a pathological variant of the European middle-class family it is very likely that the effect of much of it is counter-productive in terms of the schooling of West Indian children. It may reinforce already held stereotypes and not enable the teacher to regard black children as potential intellectuals, worthy of their best teaching effort, instead of potential clients for therapy.

If there is significant demand for Black or Ethnic Studies from the West Indian community, this would need to be examined sympathetically by the LEAs and DES – but it should not be assumed that the introduction of Black Studies programmes in schools will in itself have a notable effect on (a) the performance of West Indian children as a whole, or (b) reduce the tendency towards alienation, and the development of what have been termed (Willis, 1977) 'school counter culture' amongst West Indian adolescents. The issues are far too complex, and are tied in with other economic, social and political factors which schools in themselves can do little about.

Saturday schools

The DES, the ILEA and LEAs with numbers of West Indian children may be interested to find out more about the numbers of Saturday schools in their areas, the teaching methods they use and the success they have in increasing the attainment of West Indian children in schools. Since all official Saturday schools are known to the authorities, it should be possible to acquire this information using existing channels of communication and thus obviate the need for further academic research. Thus, project leaders could be asked to supply information on children attending their projects based on the use of attainment tests at six- or twelve-monthly intervals. Formal examination passes of children attending these schools could also be monitored over time. The information yielded would be far from perfect, but it could provide a useful beginning. By encouraging the Saturday schools to be self-monitoring, this could increase efficiency and help ongoing evaluation which could provide valuable feedback on performance etc., which more academic research might lack.

Any policy decision on the education and schooling of West Indian children might consider the giving of funds and other types of support to community-based cultural and educational projects. This would be in preference to extending the influence of the schools (via Black Studies, the use of Creole, steel bands etc.) into difficult and sensitive areas which are fraught with problems.

Theory and research

The findings have important implications for self-concept research and theory in relation to schooling. In particular the need to develop a substantive theory based on the use of both empirical and phenomenological research methods. Willis (1977) has drawn attention to the development of a particular kind of school counter-culture amongst young West Indians in the schools he studied. He has indicated that research in this area is urgently required and recommends that it should employ the methods of research he used with his sample of working-class boys, the Observer Participant method, which lays stress (almost exclusively) on the subjective reality of the actor and the actor's interpretation of his own world as the basis of social science research. Such research, if it were possible, would be helpful in clarifying issues of self-concept, impact of school-culture on West Indian children and their response to it. On a more practical level, research is needed to identify the process whereby the school system labels West Indian children as (a) maladjusted, (b) educationally subnormal and (c) emotionally disturbed, and thus consigns them in increasing numbers to special schools and treatment groups of one kind or another. It is clear that what Willis has labelled the school counter-culture, as well as being a response to a prospective wageless condition, is also a reaction by West Indian pupils to the violence which is done to them virtually from the moment they enter the formal school system. If research has a role to play it must be in helping the school system and educational authorities to be less racist and discriminatory in their practice. As far as self-concept research itself is concerned, it has yet to prove its relevance or usefulness in relation to the schooling of the black child in Britain. It may also be useful for social scientists, as well as identifying what they take to be the pathology of the black family and lifestyle, to devote some time to investigating the capacity for survival and cohesion amongst minority group families in the face of the oppressive and destructive forces which characterize British and American societies in their dealings with people of African descent.

Schools and teachers

Most self-concept theory and research appears to offer to teachers the opportunity of creating 'new selves' for children out of the raw material they were offered by parents. My belief is that schools should be places for acquiring skills and knowledge and developing abilities associated with these skills and knowledge. The teacher's job should be to teach children these skills and knowledge and encourage the development of general abilities.

Many (particularly young) teachers are put under enormous stress by the requirement to develop relationships as the basis of their teaching methods. This can lead to feelings of inadequacy and loss of enthusiasm for the job which they still have to continue to perform. If teachers felt sure that their primary aim is to teach one feels sure that this would lead to an easing of stress and consequent improvement in overall 'relationships'.

Schools and teachers must accept that West Indian parents care enormously about their children's education, and they must take some responsibility (at least) if parents hesitate to come to their schools or are hostile and unco-operative when they do. Schools and teachers should attempt to build on the obvious enthusiasm which West Indian parents have for education and resist the temptation to label as 'over-ambitious' or 'unrealistic' expectations which they would take for granted in white middle-class parents.

Although I have stressed the need for teachers to teach basic skills, this should not be taken as a desire for rigid traditional curricula – the curricula can only ultimately express the basic power relationships of society as a whole.

As Bourdieu (1977) has written, 'relationships of communication are always, and inescapably, power relations which depend for their form and content on the material or symbolic power accumulated by the agents (or institutions) engaged in these relations'. Although curricula can be mediated and modified by the teaching process itself and by the pupils to whom they are directed, they remain an expression of power and it seems that only by mastering the traditional curricula will more West Indian children have that basis of choice which many middle-class people take for granted.

We may gain some insight into the realities of the problem of 'choice' for working-class and 'immigrant' black children by reading what Kelvyn Richards wrote in an article on multi-racial schools about the 'ambivalence' of the school in helping youngsters decide about future careers and prospects:

> The ambivalent position of the school is more clearly illustrated if we consider careers guidance and placement. Many young Asians and West Indians aspire to jobs in the Civil Service, local government, or the professions. They are concerned to stay on at school, or to go to a college of further education, and gain as many qualifications as possible.
>
> On the other hand, careers teachers strongly advise these people to get a job, and to obtain training on the factory floor or an office; and criticize them for having aspirations beyond their abilities. Perhaps teachers must recognize that it is in the factory and the office that 'colour bar' and racialist sentiments are most openly expressed. We must counsel more carefully.

Richards also advises 'the multi-racial communities' that their demand for 'the best of British education' will have the inevitable consequence of the 'westernization' of their young people. This argument suggests that mastery of traditional curricula involves complete absorption into the dominant value system, resulting in higher levels of alienation due to raised expectations, better education etc. He writes:

> What are we really doing? Schools profess their aim to be equality of opportunity for all, and yet guide these non-white pupils into factory and office, where they are not really wanted. The factory owners say they welcome all, and yet employ predominantly white workers.
>
> The multi-racial communities demand the best of British education, and yet refuse to recognize that an inevitable consequence of this will be the 'westernization' of their young people.

But a feature of post-industrial society is the mobility of labour on an international scale, and it is possible that the mastery of traditional curricula may extend the choice of these young people in a way that would have been considered impossible a decade or two ago. They should at least have the choice.

Parents, children and the West Indian community

Parents, children and community leaders should press for a return to achievable goals by teachers; by the same token, the West Indian community itself must assume responsibility for keeping alive what elements of their own language and culture they think worth preserving. In that they will be in company with the Jews, Irish, Turks, Poles, Muslims and Hindus, who also constitute minority groups in this country, all of whom have established Saturday/Sunday schools and other supplementary education projects with the aim of preserving culture and language.

As well as this, the West Indian community must, for the forseeable future, continue to supplement the regular schooling which children receive in the weekday schools, but they must continue to press for better State education for their children, in the meantime making good, as far as possible, the deficit in basic skills of literacy and numeracy.

This study has very little direct information to offer on the issues which concern West Indian parents most – except perhaps to indicate some of the reasons why (some) schools fail (some) children; and the ways in which certain theories, ideas and research findings may have influenced the development of teaching styles and methods which are particularly unhelpful to West Indian children.

Conclusions

The conclusions of this study are that self-concept research and theory and teaching styles based on these ideas have little to contribute towards an understanding of how West Indian children in Britain should be educated, and may have contributed towards the low attainment of such children – because they stress affective goals of self-expression, self-fulfilment, happiness and so on as the basis of their teaching methods. It has been suggested that teaching methods associated with mastery of skills and knowledge and the development of abilities should be substituted for affective-type goals which are vague, and give teachers access to aspects of pupil personality which should be private, extending teacher control of areas of pupil personality which are unnecessary for instructional purposes. Whilst not decrying all attempts at curriculum innovation and creativity, the need for schools to retain a commitment to the mastery of basic intellectual skills and competencies by all children has been expressed.

References

Bennet, N. *et al.* (1976) *Teaching Styles and Pupil Progress*, Open Books.

Bourdieu, P. (1977) 'Symbolic Power' in Gleeson, D. (ed.) *Identity and Structure*, Nafferton Books.

Brittan, E. M. (1976) 'Multiracial Education 2 Pt II', *Educational Research*, 18/3.

Gramsci, A. (1971) *Selections from the Prison Notebooks*, Lawrence and Wishart.

Race Today Collective (1975) *The Police and the Black Wageless*, Race Today Pamphlet.

Richards, K. (1977) *Times Educational Supplement*, 9 December.

Simon, B. (1965) *Studies in the History of Education*, vols 1–11, Lawrence and Wishart.

Simon, B. (1976) 'Contemporary Problems in Educational Theory', *Marxism Today*, June.

Willis, P. (1977) *Learning to Labour*, Saxon House.

It has been suggested that teaching methods associated with mastery of skills & knowledge & the dev of abilities should be substituted for affective-type goals ...

CHAPTER 1.5

TEACHING RACE*
STUART HALL

What I broadly want to do is to address four sets of problems. First, I want to identify some of the pedagogic difficulties involved in teaching about race; then I want to say something about the economic, political and ideological aspects. These remarks are not directly addressed to the specific curriculum interests that might arise in schools or indeed the kinds of questions that might be posed in examinations. Instead, I have tried to organize them around the issues which one needs to engage when teaching in this area.

First of all there are pedagogic difficulties which are especially important because this is an area about which people feel very strongly indeed. One of the strategies which some teachers adopt is to try to side-step the explosive nature of the subject itself and walk around it trying to catch it unawares. (Except that it usually catches you unawares rather than the other way round.) It is not possible to do very much about race at a steadily high classroom temperature. You have to recognize the strong emotional ideological commitments people have to positions about race. This is a question which is very strongly charged, emotionally, and this fact has to be recognized and brought out. Whatever your own commitments and feelings about the area (and all of us have feelings about it), they have to be made clear in the way in which we handle the topic and the kinds of things we say about it. It's not a topic where an academic or intellectual neutrality is of much value. Nevertheless I do think you have to create an atmosphere which allows people to say unpopular things. I

* *Multiracial Education*, 1980, vol 9/1, pp. 3–13. Note: This is an edited transcript of an informal talk given to the London branch of the Association of Teachers of Social Science in April 1980. Copyright: National Association for Multiracial Education.

don't think it is at all valuable to have an atmosphere in the classroom which is so clearly, unmistakably anti-racist that the natural and 'commonsense' racism which is part of the ideological air that we all breathe is not allowed to come out and express itself. What I am talking about here are the problems of handling the racist time-bomb and doing so adequately so that we connect with our students' experience and can therefore be sure of defusing it. That experience has to surface in the classroom even if it is pretty horrendous to hear: better to hear it than not because what you don't hear you can't engage with. This is, after all, part of the very combustible material about which we are teaching. We are not talking about an abstract topic with which we are entertaining ourselves or over which we are stretching our minds. We are talking about very real concrete social, political and economic issues which touch the students' lives, which they experience directly. So we have to consider the problem of how to create an atmosphere in which those questions can be openly and honestly discussed; one in which your own position can emerge without people feeling over-weighted by its authority (although the teacher's authority is always exerted whether you are at the front or back of the class).

Now to move on to the empirical, conceptual and theoretical problems which are involved when teaching in this area. Because the subject is exceedingly complex it is very difficult to teach clearly. One of the curious paradoxes is that people know very simply what they feel about race and where they stand but when it comes to explaining the phenomena (i.e. relations between different ethnic groups, racist practices, racist beliefs, racial prejudice) it becomes a great deal more complex, because it requires putting together explanations from different areas of knowledge. All the attempts at a simple explanation are doomed to fail.

There are two obvious approaches to explaining racism. One is to argue that racism has to do with race, which actually is not quite as obvious as it sounds. Here the statement is taken in its own right in an attempt to explain social phenomena by applying single-mindedly the categorian criteria of relations between races. But, paradoxically, the category of 'race' alone cannot provide an adequate explanation of racism. The other approach which is a mirror reflection of the first is to say that the whole question of race is the phenomenon of more classical traditional kinds of structures and practices, especially economic and class ones and that one can dissolve questions of race by looking at them in terms of deeper economic relations and social and economic structures etc. of a more familiar kind. This will take you some, but it certainly won't take you all, the way. Without going into all the arguments, it doesn't seem to me that racism is wholly attributable in a simple way to capitalism, although it would be equally impossible to study racism in isolation from the economic and social structures of capitalism in which it now functions and operates.

It follows that one has to look at the articulations between different things which appear in our world closely linked (and are linked in important ways) but are not dissolvable into one another. In considering the relations between race and class, for example, we are concerned with complex social phenomena which are produced by different sets of determinations and which, though always linked, have different and in some ways distinct histories. This does not mean that we should isolate out ethnic relations from the other social relations and the social structures in which we find them. I am very much opposed to constituting race as a specialist area of social science – the 'race relations' problem, as it were. Race is a phenomenon which one only begins to understand when one sees it working within the different institutions, processes and practices of whole societies, in their full complexity; societies in which race becomes a determining aspect of the social structure, of the way in which its relations work and the way in which institutions are linked and connected with one another. Race and class relations will always be differently combined in different social formations as you will see if you compare the complexities of their combination in South Africa, say, and the US or Britain.

The first point that I'm making, then, is that there is something intrinsically difficult and complicated about understanding the dynamic of race in social structure. We all hope understanding race and racism will inform our ability to transform racist societies and racist situations. We have a kind of wager that if we understand things better we might be able to unlock or shift them. But we do have to recognize the complexity of the analytic and explanatory problems we confront in dealing with these phenomena, while at the same time trying to use them to connect back to questions of politics and practice. It is not possible in the end to deal with this issue in a wholly analytic way – that is to say, in a way which does not raise the question of changing the existing structures that we are examining.

I might have implied a moment ago that it doesn't matter how you set up the teaching situation, whether in terms of racism or ethnic relations or racial prejudice or discriminatory attitudes and practices. I do, however, think it matters crucially. There is a liberal commonsense way of approaching the topic which fastens on to questions of discriminatory attitudes between people from different ethnic populations, prejudicial actions, beliefs and opinions etc. One tendency in teaching is to take these immediate surface manifestations of the problem at face value and to look at how these prejudices arise through a kind of attitudinal or social psychological perspective. There is a second strategy which says that all of this is mere surface appearance and we must go to the structures which generate particular kinds of attitudes. I tend to favour the second of these alternatives.

We have to uncover for ourselves, in our own understanding, as well as for the students we are teaching, the deep structural factors which have a tendency persistently not only to generate racial practices and structures but to reproduce them through time; and which therefore account for their extraordinarily immovable character. One of the things I want to come back to when I talk about racism and ideology is the way in which racism is deeply resistant to attempts at amelioration, good feeling, gentle reform and so on. For that reason I turn to the structural dimensions first, although it would be a mistake not to bring explanations back to what a moment ago I called the surface phenomena. One has, after all, to explain what students will be most sensitive to – the interplay of feeling between the groups which are structured around the awareness of racial difference. No matter how deep you go into structural factors you need to show that they do generate particular relationships between groups of people. But first you have to be able to show that you can get a deeper understanding of what lies behind and determines those surface relations.

Teaching strategies which engage people's most obvious, uncomplicated, unreflexive apprehensions of a problem are important. But if, having engaged them at that level, you try to change attitudes and prejudices by putting good attitudes and good prejudices in their place, what you get is a total relativism: 'Well you believe that and I believe this, you see it that way and I see it this way'. It becomes extremely difficult to move on in any productive way. Social science is about deconstructing the obvious, it is about showing people that the things they immediately feel to be 'just like that' aren't quite like that. The really crucial question is how do you begin to make that move away from the level of obvious prejudice and belief. One needs to undermine the obvious. One has to show that these are social and historical processes; and they are not written in the stars, not handed down. They are deep conditions which are not going to change if we simply start tinkering around with our feelings. We must not give our students that kind of illusion. We can however begin the process of questioning what the structures are and how they work.

Let me say something more now about economic and industrial factors. Here again I issue a kind of warning or qualification. There is a tendency to think either that the structural economic features explain pretty much all that one needs to know: or, on the other hand, that to deal with the structural economic features is to collapse into an economistic account of a phenomenon which is more complex than that. I don't think that any structural or generative account of racism can afford to leave out the crucial level of economic determinations. Although economic factors are not a sufficient explanation of the phenomena they will take us a good deal further than anti-economistic or anti-reductionist sociologists would like to think. This is one area where the economic dimensions do explain a good deal. Suppose you are trying to answer the apparently simple question, 'why did they come here to work in the first place?' What you are trying to explain is the identifiable growth at a certain stage in the post-war period of a black Commonwealth migrant workforce. One can of course find black enclave populations in Britain centuries before that but what we are trying to explain from the early 1950s onwards is a qualitatively new phenomenon. It undoubtedly has a very close relationship to the high demand for labour in British industry at that particular period. It would be impossible to try to explain the full factors which opened the doors for working people from the Asian sub-continent, the Caribbean and parts of Africa without looking at the particular labour needs of British industry at that stage. Only if you go back to the debates about whether in fact the black overseas population should be recruited in that way will you see that paramount in people's minds at that time was the question of the relative shortage of labour. This provides a starting point not only to explain the general questions of the flow of people but also to explain internal movements in terms of the economic, the need for certain kinds of surplus labour. This will explain the particular clustering of the black working population in specific areas. It enables one to look at the way recruitment into particular industries, particular occupations and particular occupational levels clearly have a very strong economic substratum to them.

The real question is, how much are you going to try and explain in that way? You can attempt to match up in a very fine-tuned way either the rise in indigenous racism or the shifts in particular legislative policies with particular economic movements. For instance, what are the correlations between economic movements and, say, the introduction of the very early race legislation? How much was it due to the fact that at that stage already the demand for that kind of labour was beginning to tail off in the British economy? How relevant was it that already the first wave of black migration from the Caribbean was beginning to tail off before those economic dips became manifest? How important was the fact that already from the late 1950s, certainly from 1957 and 1958 onwards, there was beginning to be an explicit political and social problem around race which must have had its bearing on both the decision to legislate in the area, making it into a manifest political topic about which politicians were going to conduct a debate on how to legislate – all this obviously affecting the way in which those issues would be debated in the society as a whole?

I am not convinced that the question of economic determination can provide either adequate explanations or the sort of fine-tuned intermesh that I was talking about a minute ago. The economy is a necessary but not sufficient condition for understanding the post-war history of British racism. If, for instance, you try to explain the movements of black populations and their settlement and position in the British social structure it won't do. If you constitute the devilish collective mind of Capital, you could just imagine it meeting occasionally in committees and saying 'How much new labour do we need and where do we need them from?' – but your understanding will not progress. The contradictions built into what is happening economically and what is being legislated and discussed politically are too divergent to constitute anything like a neat functional fit between what capital needed, what the labour market provided and how the state legislated. The important questions concern the relationship between surplus populations and the dynamic movements of the economy. The questions of surplus populations and the notions of the surplus labour force or reserve army of labour are generative and productive ideas which move the relationship between the patterning of race and the dynamic of the economy on to a somewhat deeper and more adequate theoretical or explanatory level. The moment you make that move you are beginning to shift away from any sort of explanation which would identify race exclusively as the element which requires explanation. At that point you do, for matters of teaching strategy as well as for reasons of explanation, have to identify black migrant with other surplus or reserve populations including the native unemployed, women and the Irish, all three of whom in British history constituted and played something of the same role in relation to the attraction and expulsion of different labour forces in different phases of capitalist development. What this cannot explain is whether capital positively differentiates between these forces in terms of their cultural and social criteria – race, gender or nationality.

There are important senses in which one can speak of an Irish racism in Britain. Racism and sexism, as ideologies, are more comparable in some ways than are either with ideologies of class because both racism and sexism depend on the processes of naturalization. They tend more easily than class relations in terms of their ideological syntax to ground themselves to the evidence of nature. There is of course also that tendency in class to think that 'they' were really born that way but it is so much easier with racism or sexism to find a warrant for discrimination in biology. It is this transposition from historically and culturally created differences to fixed natural or biological or genetic differences which gives those two ideologies their deep-seated structure. Use the evidence of your eyes, vive la différence. I am not of course attempting to give race and sex privilege over class. I am trying to account for certain specific differences one can make in the functioning of different ideologies. One of the ways in which ideologies function is to 'natural-ize' and 'eternalize' themselves. They disguise the fact that they are historic and symbolic constructions by appearing to be simply part of what nature has ordained. Some ideological formations find it easier to make that move from history to nature, giving them a long and deep persistence. I am only comparing race and class ideologies here in terms of their power to disappear behind Nature and I am pointing to the striking similarities between sex and race in at least this respect. Slaves, degraded by historical and economic relations from men to 'goods and chattels', were then categorized physically and mentally as an inferior species. But it is also interesting that, as white men became criminals, they too tended to be depicted, more and more, like an inferior physical type – coming to look more like slaves and black primitives.

Now let me say something about the more political aspects. In the light of the earlier argument you can see why particular forms of migrant labour form a specially flexible reserve army especially in the early phases of migration when that black labour force came more or less fully reproduced. It was ready for work, composed largely of fit, able bodied adults; whereas in the next generation the labour force has to be reproduced socially as well as physically. You have them born and then grow them and teach them and educate them and train them and discipline them before you can work them: and by then there are actually no jobs for them to do. So then you have to look after them in unemployment, reproduce them through enforced leisure and police them; they are going to get old and go on living quite a long time. West Indian women particularly are strong and long survivors. So the reproduction costs of this labour force looked particularly attractive in 1951 and look particularly unattractive and expensive in 1981, when in any case you have less money in your pocket and fewer schools to reproduce them through and less places in the dole queue. The reproduction costs begin politically to turn back on you.

There is an argument that one of the ways to understand the legislative policies of race in Britain is that, as the cost of reproducing the black labour force has grown, as Britain had to take the fact seriously that they are here to stay and to settle throughout the full life cycle, so the legislation has tended to try to reconstitute that black population more as a really authentic migrant force, like Southern Italian labour whom you send back home for Christmas and deny the right to vote and so on. If you have tried to travel on the train from South to North Italy during the Swiss industrial holiday you will know who keeps those cuckoo clocks going. The reproduction costs of Western European 'guest workers' are partly borne in Calabria, the North Coast of Africa and the interior of Turkey. They have managed to maintain that system of continuous movement partly because of geographical proximity but partly also by making it difficult to bring families and making it unattractive for them to stay. This pattern was also quite common in a previous period of migration, that between the Caribbean and North America until it was limited by legislation during the latter part of the war. In the 1940s and 1950s there was a constant movement of migrant labour backwards and forwards from Jamaica to the Southern states of America and if they were able to stay for a substantial part of the year they took very substantial earnings to the family back home.

Part of the argument is that what is happening here is a retrospective political enforcement of migrant status on a settled black population.

This involves discouraging anybody else from coming in and especially discouraging the unification of divided Asian and black families, curtailing the non-labouring part of the population – the aged – and then encouraging repatriation ('after you've worked it out, shove off back where you came from!'), leaving the black population here not exactly like, but very much more like a long-term 'guest worker'. This is more appropriate in a political climate when there is no shortage of labour but growing unemployment coupled with economic recession, when there is the need to expand employment opportunities for the white population; tending therefore to generate much higher levels of unemployment among blacks in general and especially among black school-leavers. In this situation it makes sense politically to limit the growth and convert the black population into a more flexible and responsive labour force. One of the best statements of this argument, which is worth looking at, is Sivanandan's short pamphlet, *From Immigration Control to 'Induced Repatriation'* published by the Institute of Race Relations. This thesis seems to provide part of the explanation though it doesn't deal with other political and ideological factors attached to questions of race and racism in Britain which have to be introduced into the explanations to complete it.

I do want to say something briefly about the political level. I want to point, on the one hand, to the rise to visibility of the question of race as an indigenous theme of British political life and political relations. We have to examine how it happens, when it happens, in response to what factors and how it is brought about. 'Powellism', conceived as the politics of a single individual, is certainly not adequate. When attempting to explain the politics of race in Britain we have to pay attention to the institutional basis in which that politics has developed. We have to look at those particular sections of political leadership which have chosen not only to make statements about race but which have actually used race to open up a wide range of political contradictions, some of which had very little to do with race at all. We have to look at the rise of political movements which operate on the back of an indigenous racism and which try to awaken racist sentiments in society as part of a wider reactionary-populist politics. We have to look at the very real and growing importance of the media and especially of the press and above all the popular press in a quite specific campaigning role around issues of race, around primitive appeals to the notions of a 'British way of life', 'alien cultures' etc. The thematizing of social and economic contradictions through racist projections is a major political development of the last two decades.

Ideological questions are one of the most effective ways in which we can return to what we previously spoke of as attitudes, prejudices and beliefs. The difficulty with focusing on attitudes and beliefs is that you eventually come back to the notion that these are individual emanations of good and bad feelings and to do with the differential perceptions of other people. Before long you can fall into the commonsense argument, 'Don't we all make differences and jokes about people who are different from ourselves?' You begin to sketch out a world which ought to have eaten itself from end to end because of multiple 'racisms' based on brown and black hair, green and pink eyes etc. One really has to stop that runaway rout into 'mere difference' and ask why some of those differences have consistently become historically pertinent. It's along the specific line of 'difference' that populations divide, that societies structure themselves, that perceptions crystallize and that people bring out truncheons. We must beware of dissolving the question of race into an infinite scatter, an inventory of all the possible differences that people can make, and show that it has served a very powerful social and historical function in organizing and mobilizing different societies at different stages in history.

As far as questions of race are concerned what matters much more than differences are the already available languages which surround us from birth in this society: languages which are powerfully charged, well developed, which have consistently signified the historical relation between the people of this nation and other nations, this economy and other economies, in ways connected with race. The way in which we think and feel and perceive racially has a great deal to do with the available languages of racism available in societies like ours. The racist elements of those languages can be used to put together different racist formations. It isn't that anybody confuses in their head old-style imperialism with the indigenous racism of the 1970s and 1980s: but the old syntax is rich and the repertoire can be drawn on at different moments to provide racist definitions of the situation.

There is no sense in which you could try to explain the distribution of racist ideologies in a simply class structured way. There is no way in which relations between Britain, either as a slave-owning or as an imperial economic and political power, and the rest of the world could have been lived out over long periods of time leaving one whole class sector of the population saturated with racist ideas and the rest of the population totally free of them. It is an inconceivable notion, not only in terms of how ideologies penetrate societies but also when you look at actual ideological and political practices. Racism in our society is in part sustained by the defensive institutions of the working class as much as by the offensive institutions of the capitalist class. The fact that certain forms of working class and trade union racism differ in their extent, in their modality, in their grip on people's imaginations from other types, say National Front racism, is not the same thing as saying that it would be possible to discover a pure working class untouched by racism. Those differences have to be confronted because, if you go back to the politics of race and the resistance to racism, they have been one of the most pertinent factors which have consistently divided the working class politically within itself throughout the whole of the period that I am talking about. It has prevented the emergence of anything that even remotely resembled a mass anti-racist political organization or struggle, whose principal thrust would have been the internal unity of classes across the divide constituted by race. In fact the history of the period is the history of the continued internal segmentation of the labouring force and one of the principal ways in which that segmentation has expressed itself politically and ideologically is around questions of race. That has been one of its crucial political and ideological effects. In an increasingly non-expanding economic and political climate, racism of a virulent kind has been able to provide a sort of quasi-explanation, not only for people at the top of the society but also for people at the bottom of the society, as to what it is they are experiencing and why a kind of racist politics makes sense.

To paraphrase Powell (who should know) race is not safe but combustible material. If you try to stop the story about racial politics, racial divisions, racist ideologies short of confronting some of these difficult issues; if you present an idealized picture of a 'multi-cultural' or 'ethnically varied' society which doesn't look at the way in which racism has acted back inside the working class itself, the way in which racism has combined with, for example, sexism working back within the black population itself; if you try to tell the story as if somewhere around the corner some whole constituted class is waiting for a green light to advance and displace the racist enemy and constitute a non-racist society, you will have done absolutely nothing whatsoever for the political understanding of your students. Of course, you can also tell the story in a way which so undermines the possibility of building and developing social and political movements around those issues that the only conclusion is a deep pessimism. One has to walk a very fine line here. We want to change or transform the world as it is but that is something which has to be done, it isn't something which is written down and guaranteed by the conditions which we inherit. There are no guarantees against the growth of a popular racism, but there is always, in the factual everyday struggles of those who resist racism, the possibility of an anti-racist politics and pedagogy.

Somehow we have to tread that difficult line whilst not selling short the complexity of the issues with which we are dealing. Instead of thinking that confronting the questions of race is some sort of moral intellectual academic duty which white people with good feelings do for blacks, one has to remember that the issue of race provides one of the most important ways of understanding how this society actually works and how it has arrived where it is. It is one of the most important keys, not into the margins of the society, but to its dynamic centre. It is a very good way of getting hold of the political and social issues of contemporary Britain because it touches and connects with so many facets.

SECTION 2

LANGUAGE

CHAPTER 2.1

CHILDREN FROM FAMILIES OF OVERSEAS ORIGIN*

Since the mid-1950s schools in most large cities in England have received children whose parents are of overseas origin. The majority of these are children from the West Indies, India, Bangladesh and Pakistan, whose parents have come to seek work in Britain. Others are children of Italian, Spanish and Cypriot workers. In addition there is a scatter of Chinese children whose parents are engaged in the catering industry. There are considerable numbers of Asians from East Africa, including the refugees expelled from Uganda in the last two years. Some of the families have now been settled in Britain a decade or more, and their youngest members have been born in this country. The great majority of the children, born here or brought from overseas, have a big adjustment to make when entering school. For most of them this adjustment includes a linguistic factor, either that of learning English as a new language, or of learning Standard English as a new dialect. The children's linguistic adjustment relates in many ways to their educational progress, and it is to this issue that we turn in this chapter.

It is, of course, helpful to have some idea of the number of children of families of overseas origin at school in Britain, though there is considerable difficulty in arriving at useful statistics. In 1973, by the DES definition[1] then existing, there were 284,754 'immigrant children' in maintained primary and secondary schools in England and Wales, comprising 3·3 per cent of the total school population. More significantly, since immigrant populations are concentrated largely upon Greater London and industrial cities in the Midlands and North, individual local

* Bullock Report, chapter 20, *A Language for Life*, 1975, HMSO, pp 284–95. Reproduced with the permission of the Controller of Her Majesty's Stationery Office.

education authorities can have as high a proportion of immigrant children on roll as 27 per cent. Raw statistics such as these help to show why such a large measure of attention has to be paid in some areas, much more than in others, to the educational needs of the children labelled 'immigrant'. Obviously what is needed is as sharp a measure as possible of these special educational needs. An immigrant child does not present problems to a school simply because he is an immigrant child. Centrally collected figures cannot, for instance, indicate exactly the numbers of children with linguistic needs nor give any measure of these needs. The only people who can do this satisfactorily are the people on the spot, the teachers in the schools and the local education authorities. A few authorities have already had considerable practice in making such assessments. Bradford is notable in having carried out for several years an annual survey of immigrant children in its schools, distinguishing between their different ethnic origins, identifying their levels of proficiency in English, and making flexible educational arrangements accordingly. We recommend that all authorities with immigrant children should make similar surveys regularly, in order to achieve a greater refinement in their educational arrangements. Now that the NFER's English language tests[2] are available, it should be possible to give an accurate assessment of proficiency in understanding, speaking, reading and writing English on the part of children for whom it is not their native language. It is clear from the available reports that comparatively little provision is made in some areas, that the education of children of overseas parentage is given a low priority, and that many of the existing arrangements do little more than meet the initial language and adjustment needs of new arrivals. It is, of course, at that point that the need for intervention is most sharply felt in the schools, but the adjustment of immigrant children to their new environment and to learning elementary English is only the beginning of what for most is a long process. It is a process that consists primarily of learning to live in or between two cultures, and of learning to handle two languages or dialects.

The term 'immigrant' is sometimes used in a very general sense, often to mean anyone of overseas parentage, or with a black skin. It is not uncommon to meet teachers and members of the public to whom all Asian immigrants are the same, irrespective of their country of origin, and for whom there is no difference between India and the West Indies. It goes without saying that teachers and others should have an informed and sympathetic understanding of the children's different origins, the cultures of their homes, and the very real link between some of their countries and

Britain. No-one should accept a stereotype of 'the immigrant child', but should acknowledge the very great differences there are between children who fall into this general category. There are differences not only of language and culture, but in the manner in which families succeed or fail in settling here, and in providing a secure home for the children. Many immigrant children come from stable supportive families in which the relative affluence of the parents is evident; others face grave problems of insecurity and hardship, and in many respects resemble some of the indigenous families in the same inner city area.

In urging a greater measure of attention to the education of immigrant children, we want to emphasize the long-term nature of the issues involved. The inflow of newcomers and their families has slowed down considerably in the 1970s, but the needs of the children who are already here are continuing ones. They cannot be dealt with briefly and then forgotten. Although there has been little sustained research describing the comparative performance of children of minority groups at school in Britain, there is enough to show a disturbingly low pattern of attainment. The Community Relations Commission underlined this in its evidence to the Committee, and in its report to the Home Secretary,[3] as did ILEA in the details provided of the 1968 Literacy Survey in its schools. This survey included a census of the reading attainment of eight year old children in ILEA primary schools, and it is worth remarking that in 1972 23·3 per cent of the immigrant children in school in England and Wales were concentrated in ILEA. The evidence as we received it made no distinction between children of West Indian and Asian origin, and it is clear that there are special reasons for the failings of both groups. The figures are disturbing in showing the markedly lower reading standards of immigrants. A high proportion come into the category of poor readers: 28·5 per cent as compared with 14·8 per cent of non-immigrants. Conversely there is a low proportion in the category of good readers: 3·5 per cent as compared with 11·4 per cent non-immigrants. An unpublished analysis of all ILEA pupils transferring to secondary schools (quoted in the Community Relations Commission report referred to above) indicates that of immigrant children who have received their full education in this country, those of Asian origin are in fact performing at a level comparable with the indigenous population. Pupils of West Indian origin, on the other hand, are performing well below average. The EPA study in Birmingham was another source of disturbing results, and a good deal of publicity has been given to the high proportion of West Indian children in ESN schools in

London. This is partly attributable to their poor performance in primary schools, particularly in the skills of reading and writing. Further evidence, relating to the nation at large, comes from NFER studies, which show the generally low placement of West Indian pupils in streamed schools (lower than that of Indian and Pakistani pupils), and a low transfer rate to selective schools: four per cent for West Indians, nine per cent for Pakistanis, 25 per cent for non-immigrants. In common with the Asians the majority of West Indian pupils staying on for fifth and sixth form courses tend to take either low-level examinations or no examinations at all; only a small proportion of West Indian pupils take 'A' levels, a disturbing fact again in view of the long-term needs of the community.

Immigrant children's attainment in tests and at school in general is related not only to language but to several other issues, particularly those of cultural identity and cultural knowledge. No child should be expected to cast off the language and culture of the home as he crosses the school threshold, nor to live and act as though school and home represent two totally separate and different cultures which have to be kept firmly apart. The curriculum should reflect many elements of that part of his life which a child lives outside school. Some schools and authorities are already dealing wisely and boldly with these matters, and there are interesting examples in the recent Schools Council Working Paper, 'Multiracial education: need and innovation'.[4] But many more schools in multi-racial areas turn a blind eye to the fact that the community they serve has radically altered over the last ten years and is now one in which new cultures are represented. We see implications here for the education of all children, not just those of families of overseas origin. One aspect of the question which we believe merits urgent attention is the nature of the reading material that is used in schools. In their verbal representation of society, and in their visual content, books do a great deal to shape children's attitudes. We would urge that teachers and librarians should have this in mind when selecting books for schools. If the school serves a multi-racial society, does it have books about the homelands of its immigrant families, about their religions and cultures and their experiences in this country? The Library Association catalogue[5] of books for the multi-racial classroom makes some useful suggestions of titles. Even more important, has the school removed from its shelves books which have a strong ethnocentric bias and contain outdated or insulting views of people of other cultures? These questions are relevant across the entire age range. The reading material used in infant schools should be truthful and unsentimental in its visual and verbal content. Equally, the social studies texts in the secondary school should place in fair perspective the events and movements in history which have affected the peoples from whom the immigrant families spring. A survey[6] of children's books revealed much inaccurate, thoughtless and downright offensive writing about people from other countries. We strongly recommend the report of this survey, published by The Institute of Race Relations, to all who have responsibility for book selection in multi-racial schools. Similar surveys could be carried out by groups of teachers, who would be providing a useful practical service while developing their own sensitivity to the issues involved. These and related questions should also enter the initial training of teachers, for whether or not they go to teach in schools with immigrant children it is right that they should have this kind of awareness. This is an appropriate point to record our conclusion that there are not enough books available which represent children of overseas backgrounds in the ways we have been describing. We address this observation to publishers, whose contribution in this whole area is potentially very considerable.

In discussing the language needs of immigrant children it is important to distinguish between two broad groups. The first consists of families from the Caribbean, whose mother tongue is English – even if in several respects it differs from the kind of English spoken in England. The second group is made up of those whose mother tongue is a totally different language and who speak little or no English on arrival. We will consider these in turn. The 1972 DES statistics revealed that there were 101,898 children of West Indian origin (including Guyana) in the schools. Other evidence suggests that about half of these were from Jamaica, the remainder from the smaller islands in the group. For most of them the language of childhood and of the home is an English-based Creole, a variety or dialect of English. Jamaican Creole has been extensively studied and described over the last twenty years. It is recognized by linguists as being a well-developed language, with a sound system, grammar, and vocabulary of its own, and capable – like other varieties of English – of being used expressively and richly. However, the West Indian situation is very complex, since in most schools in the islands a standard form of English, very close to Standard English in England, is the medium for formal education and is the language the children are expected to read and write. There are already, then, linguistic difficulties for pupils and teachers alike in the schools of Jamaica and other Caribbean islands; and there are difficulties, if of a rather different order, for the West Indian children at school in Britain. For most of them the language of infancy and of the home will almost certainly be a form of dialect, though some members of the family will be able to switch to a more standard dialect for certain purposes. The child attending school will be likely to have teachers who know no Creole at all and who will expect him to understand and respond to a dialect that may at first be very strange to him . The teacher's ignorance of Creole, and perhaps his traditional attitudes to non-standard forms of English, will tend to make him dismiss Creole features in the West Indian child's speech as incorrect or 'sloppy' English. The issue of dialect thus raises many problems. It is clearly important that teachers should be fully aware of these and that they should recognize dialects for what they are. In assisting children to master Standard English, which in effect is the dialect of school, they should do so without making children feel marked out by the form of language they bring with them and to which they revert outside class. A positive attitude to West Indian dialect – as to West Indian culture – would help teachers and children alike in multi-racial city schools. This area of study should therefore receive attention in both initial and in-service teacher training. Useful support for this work can be derived from the findings of the Schools Council project on the teaching of English to West Indian children,[7] and we would draw attention to the strong interest in Creole language studies in several university departments of linguistics in this country. The information and expert guidance is available for those willing to draw upon it.

The Schools Council project carried out tests which showed that dialect impeded the children's learning of English in the areas of oral comprehension, spoken intelligibility, reading, writing and spelling. It also developed some material to help teachers counter the effect of dialect interference in children's written work. The main effort, however, was directed to materials for promoting communication skills in the multi-racial class, and neither this project nor any other as far as we know has studied the specific problems experienced by West Indian children in learning to read. It is reasonable to assume that if these problems were better understood by teachers there would be a general improvement in the literacy skills of West Indian children, with possibly far-reaching implications for their all-round performance at school and their social adjustment. There is urgent need for work of this kind to be carried out and for its results to be disseminated on a wide scale, and we believe that support should be given to appropriate research and development projects.

Little evidence was received about positive measures carried out in schools or centres to help West Indian children develop their language skills. However, we were impressed by what we heard of one outer London borough which has organized a 'supplementary service' for West Indian pupils. The children are selected according to need and taught in small groups for an hour a day, considerable emphasis being placed upon language. They are helped to distinguish Standard English from other forms, and to practise those English structures where there is most interference from dialect. This part of the teaching is fairly formal. The children are also encouraged to talk about themselves, and they have books and pictures in which black children figure as well as white. An important part of the work is helping children to have a positive attitude to themselves and to school, and West Indian teachers are among those who teach the groups. The scheme operates flexibly, with the teachers meeting once a week to discuss their work and plan materials. Similar schemes could be operated in other authorities where there are concentrations of West Indian pupils. Schools should also be encouraged to try different approaches, and to share their findings with one another. Work relating both to dialect and to improving the ability to communicate should be encouraged on a much larger scale. In our visits to primary schools we saw some good use of the Schools Council project materials referred to above. One component of these, 'The Dialect Unit', can give teachers insights into some Creole speakers' problems in writing Standard English, and it can also provide a springboard for further work initiated by teachers and children themselves. In some cases it is said that West Indian parents resent their children being singled out for special attention, and also resent the implication that 'they do not speak proper English'. But many West Indian parents are concerned about their children's progress and, from their own experience of learning to switch dialects in the West Indies, can understand the present difficulties of their children in this country. Consultation with them can often result in new approaches being developed to help their children, and schools should look for opportunities to draw on the support that parents and community can give. By getting to know some of the minority bookshops that now exist in London and elsewhere, and by using some of the excellent resource centres of local Community Relations Councils, teachers can obtain books and papers published in the Caribbean. They will find that these can provide stimulating new material for use in school, and at the same time give a useful insight into Caribbean life. We reaffirm that in order to teach West

Indian children effectively teachers need to have an understanding of their dialect and culture.

There is general agreement that at first sight the language problems of non-English speaking children are easier to deal with than those of the dialect or Creole speakers. They have to learn English as a second or even a third language, but what they know, namely their original language, and what they need to learn, are clearly distinguished in the teacher's mind. There is by now a considerable body of methodology available and some very useful materials, at least for the initial stage of learning English as a second language. The different types of organization set up in LEAs are fully documented in the Schools Council Working Paper[8] and the Townsend study.[9] In some of the large authorities with immigrant populations there are flourishing teachers' centres and a strong system of support and in-service training for teachers of English as a second language. Considerable practical knowledge has been contributed to the field by teachers and college lecturers returning from teaching posts overseas. However, these teachers tend to move on again, and there is in any case a high staff turnover in the inner city schools where most of the work is done. These factors contribute to a shortage of teachers able to teach English as a second language and of people to train them, a problem noted by the Parliamentary Select Committee.[10] There are, of course, no easy remedies to teacher shortages of this kind, though more should certainly be done to make it easier for teachers returning from overseas postings to be recruited into language teaching for immigrant children.

The organization of this teaching within a school and within an authority should measure up to the demand. The situation can be summed up as one in which the teaching often starts too late and ends too soon. In some areas even the provision of places for the limited number of new entrants in a special class or language centre is inadequate. Children may consequently have to wait several months to begin to be taught English; in a few places not even this provision exists. This cannot be justified on the ground that the children will pick up English anyway and that special language teaching is unnecessary. We believe that it *is* necessary, and that it must be provided. It is outside the scope of this Report to examine the advantages and disadvantages of the different types of provision made for teaching English as a second language. Common sense would suggest that the best arrangement is usually one where the immigrant children are not cut off from the social and educational life of a normal school. The money spent on transporting children to other schools or centres, or peripatetic teachers from school to school, might sometimes be much better allocated to the appointment of full-time language experts to the schools where the children are on roll. Where there is a very small number of such children in several schools, then bringing them together for sessions of specialist teaching may be more practicable. Some of the special centres set up for this purpose provide highly professional language teaching. We are, however, aware that this teaching is often carried out in complete isolation from the child's school, and that his other teachers, including the head, may be unaware of what he is learning and of the methods used to teach him. Specialist language teachers need to work in close liaison with other teachers. In whatever circumstances they operate, they should be given time to consult with these teachers in the schools and to be in touch with the child's education as a whole.

Another worrying aspect of this *initial* provision is the fact that it absorbs almost all the trained teachers who know anything about the teaching of English as a second language. Very few are to be found giving sustained language help to immigrant language learners *beyond* the initial stage. In statements of policy LEAs often claim that the aim of initial language teaching is to bring the immigrant child to the level of English at which he can profit from the normal school curriculum in company with his English-speaking peer-group. This generally means a year or less, or at most eighteen months. In most cases, however, it is unrealistic to think that the immigrant can reach that level of proficiency in English in eighteen months or less. His whole experience of English, the language and the culture, has more or less to be mediated through school. The Indian child virtually goes home to India every night. His participation in mixed social activities outside school is limited, and this is particularly true in the case of girls. Weekends and holidays are times when the child may hear next to no English spoken at all. Although after a year he may seem able to follow the normal school curriculum, especially where oral work is concerned, the limitations to his English may be disguised; they become immediately apparent when he reads and writes. He reads slowly, and often without a full understanding of vocabulary and syntax, let alone the nuances of expression. His writing betrays his lack of grasp of the subject and a very unsteady control of syntax and style. His mistakes, or deviations from Standard English, often bear a superficial resemblance to those of the slow-learning native speaker, whom he resembles in his limited range of expression. But many of the mistakes are essentially those of the second-language learner, such as a failure to use articles in a way that comes automatically to the native speaker, or inaccurate verb forms and confused morphology. Coupled with this, his handwriting is often that of someone who has never been taught systematically how to form and link the letters of the Roman alphabet in an acceptable cursive style. We regard it as a grave disservice to such children to deprive them of sustained language teaching after they have been learning English for only a comparatively short time. In our view they need far more intensive help with language in English lessons. This should be the task of a specialist language teacher, whose aim should be to help them achieve fluency in all the language skills. In oral work the emphasis might be on expression, on vocabulary extension, on finding the right style for the right occasion, and on achieving an acceptable pronunciation. In reading and writing teachers need to follow a developmental programme, using a graded language scheme or following a planned course. Non-native speakers are known to experience difficulty in reading extensively and at a reasonable speed. This indicates the need for a planned reading curriculum, in which texts are used with appropriately graded language and content. But there was little evidence in the schools and centres we visited of really advanced English language work of this nature, and of a good supply of well chosen books which were contributing to children's language development.

It is also clear that the children need linguistic help right across the curriculum, and that here the language specialist's task in the secondary school merges with that of the subject specialists. Broadly speaking, all subject teachers need to be much more aware of the linguistic demands their specializations make on pupils. It is no easy task to help teachers to this awareness, and co-operation and experiment are called for within and between schools. We were impressed by the efforts of schools we visited in Bolton[11] and Bradford, where the specially appointed language specialists had devised a flexible co-operative system within the school. They functioned both as teachers and consultants, sitting in on subject classes, analyzing the linguistic demands made on immigrant learners in different areas of the curriculum, and offering running help to the children as the class proceeded. This is a much more effective way of working than dealing with pupils in comparative seclusion, which is bad both linguistically and socially. It is feasible for language experts to work in this fashion not simply with second-language learners but also with Creole-speaking children. Arrangements of the kind we have described demand trust and co-operation between language specialist and subject staff, and the role of the head and of heads of departments is obviously vital in creating the right atmosphere. There should be more initiatives to establish a new role for the language teacher in a multi-racial school, one of consultant and adviser across the curriculum rather than of teacher confined to a single room. As a matter of urgency teachers able to work in this way should be appointed extra to complement wherever secondary schools have on roll a significant number of children who are no longer classed as initial language learners but need linguistic help. We recognize that this recommendation would be costly to implement in some authorities, and we acknowledge the difficulty of recruiting teachers with the appropriate skill and experience. Nevertheless, we see no other realistic solution for the linguistic and social problems posed by the presence of large numbers of second-stage language learners in schools.

We have suggested that those authorities with areas of immigrant settlement should maintain a continuous assessment of the language needs of immigrant pupils in their schools. For the most part these are not accurately assessed unless there is a member of the advisory staff with a major responsibility for immigrant education in the authority. We would strongly urge the appointment of advisers with special responsibility for the language development of immigrant children, able to provide suitable and sustained in-service training and to support groups of teachers in their response to local problems. Needless to say, it is as important for these advisers to liaise with the authority's other advisers as it is for the language specialists in a school to co-operate with other teachers. They should certainly work in close association with their colleagues responsible for advisory work in English. The specialist adviser needs to have a clear view not only of what is required, but of the way in which existing strengths can best be used. For instance, some trained teachers of English as a second language could profitably be deflected from initial language work in a reception centre to dealing with the more complex needs of second stage language learners. Unless there is a person responsible within the authority such informed use of resources tends not to occur.

A special word needs to be added about children of overseas parentage in infant and nursery classes. In the first place we see the provision of nursery classes in inner city areas as having great importance for the early language development of immigrant children. This is true both for those from non-English speaking homes and for those from West Indian homes. It is known that many West Indian parents leave children with child minders in circumstances which encourage passive response from the children and which must often have harmful effects on their development, both linguistic and general. It is often reported that they find it difficult to adjust to the informal environment of the nursery or infant reception class, that they are bewildered rather than delighted by the variety of activities offered them, and that they find it hard to concentrate even for a short period on any single activity. There are special difficulties, too, for very young children from non-English speaking families, children born in Britain but brought up in homes where neither the language in use nor the culture is English. Teachers of these young children have shown reluctance to do any 'formal' language work with them, usually on the ground that in the good infant or nursery class they would learn to speak English anyway, without any intervention on the teacher's part. But these children, after a full two years in infant classes, often reach junior school seriously lacking in fluency in English. To meet the special needs of these children, teachers in nursery and infant classes should be willing to modify their traditional organization. The child bewildered by a choice of activities might be given a more limited number of alternatives. For children with language difficulties it is essential that for a short period every day a teacher should sit with individuals or small groups and talk with them. The experiments conducted in the pre-school and infant centres and classes of Bradford and other towns have already shown that special language tuition can be provided early and saves time and trouble later. There is nothing to suggest that it need in any way be too formal, nor need it take much time from the other important learning opportunities that nursery and infant classes would normally want to provide. Valuable guidance for language work with non-English speaking infants is contained in a forthcoming Schools Council publication in the *Scope*[12] series. Another recent development is the extension of the work of the Schools Council project 'Communication Skills in Early Childhood' to nursery classes in which there are children of families of overseas origin. Both these sources of information should help nursery and infant teachers to focus on priority areas of language and deliberately extend the young child's use of English.

Until now there has been a shortage of nursery provision in many of the areas where there are large numbers of overseas families. The promised expansion of nursery education will do something to remedy this, but there are two important points to be made. First, it is clear that the conventional training of nursery and infant teachers has normally lacked a component that will help them understand the specific language difficulties and cultural values of children from families of overseas origin. There is a need for both these aspects to be taken into account in teacher-training programmes and in-service education. Secondly, new approaches may be necessary if these children are to be reached in their early years. The links of such families with the existing schools are often tenuous. Mothers may be at work all day, or live in purdah, or speak no English; fathers may be permanently on night shift. Notices sent from school are sometimes not read, or are misinterpreted. The parents sometimes want to delegate to the school full responsibility for social training. In some instances they know nothing of the possibilities of nursery education and feel unable to take advantage of it where it exists. In the case of many of these families the conventional channels of communication between school and home do not function, and quite different strategies are needed.

There are good arguments for a more sustained and systematic service linking home and school, especially in the areas of intensive immigrant settlement. In some areas there is evidence of good results ensuing from various systems of home visiting, sometimes involving a teaching member of a school staff, himself a member of an immigrant community, sometimes the provision of social welfare assistants attached to infant schools. In the West Riding, after the success of the home visiting scheme in the EPA project, there has been a development whereby a home visitor teaches a little English to housebound Pakistani mothers and to their young children through the medium of simple educational toys. In a summer holiday project students worked on a one-to-one basis with immigrant school children, and one of the most profitable achievements was to build up a pre-reception class for rising-fives, immigrant children unable to speak English but due to enter school the following autumn. There were three weeks of small-group and individual play involving a great deal of language interaction with willing student teachers and an experienced infant teacher in charge. The result was that the children developed the confidence to speak English and became familiar with the apparatus and activities of an infant class. An additional benefit was the informal contact between teacher and parent, a valuable foundation for the coming school year. Obviously, none of these approaches provides a complete answer and all of them need adequate financing. Professional advice should be available for the personnel involved, whether they be trained teachers or nursery helpers, social workers, home visitors, or student volunteers. Members of the advisory service should provide them with training in language development and in understanding the social and cultural values of families of overseas origin; and the role of members of the minority communities themselves is obviously vital in this work of mediating between the different communities. Children of overseas origin should see people of their own communities in the role of teacher and helper. LEAs should be alert to the needs of providing training, or retraining, to immigrants who will be able to perform this important function.

The importance of bilingualism, both in education and for society in general, has been increasingly recognized in Europe and in the USA. We believe that its implications for Britain should receive equally serious study. When bilingualism in Britain is discussed it is seldom if ever with reference to the inner city immigrant populations, yet over half the immigrant pupils in our schools have a mother-tongue which is not English, and in some schools this means over 75 per cent of the total number on roll. The language of the home and of a great deal of the central experience of their life is one of the Indian languages, or Greek, Turkish, Italian or Spanish. These children are genuine bilinguals, but this fact is often ignored or unrecognized by the schools. Their bilingualism is of great importance to the children and their families, and also to society as a whole. In a linguistically conscious nation in the modern world we should see it as an asset, as something to be nurtured, and one of the agencies which should nurture it is the school. Certainly the school should adopt a positive attitude to its pupils' bilingualism and wherever possible should help maintain and deepen their knowledge of their mother-tongues. The school that really welcomes its immigrant parents must also be prepared to welcome their languages, to display notices and other materials written in them, and even to adopt some of the rhymes and songs learnt by the young children at home. At least one authority is experimenting with an even greater investment in bilingualism by encouraging pre-reading experiences and early play in the language of the home in pre-school and infant classes. Confidence and ability in this language will help the children to the same qualities in their second language, English. Schools in neighbourhoods where many languages are spoken, as in North London, would find suggestions of this kind impracticable, but there is every reason for adopting them in areas where there is a fairly homogeneous language situation. In any event, bilingual pupils should be encouraged to maintain their mother-tongue throughout their schooling. There is a great deal to be said for their entering for 'O' and 'A' level examinations in their first language. The Townsend study[13] shows that though schools often encourage this, few if any actually give tuition in any Indian language. The immigrant communities themselves are reported as teaching their own languages, and the range encompasses Greek, Punjabi, Urdu, Gujurati, Hindi, Italian, Polish, Arabic and a cluster of others. Little is known about the effectiveness of such provision, and we recommend that further study should be made of this and other aspects of bilingualism in schools. It has an important contribution to make to what we suggest is the central recommendation of this chapter: a sensitivity and openness to language in all its forms.

References

1. The Department of Education and Science used the following definition in its Form 7(i) when collecting annual statistics of immigrant children until 1973: (i) children born outside the British Isles who have come to this country with, or to join, parents or guardians whose countries of origin were abroad and (ii) children born in the United Kingdom to parents whose countries of origin were abroad and who came to the United Kingdom on or after 1 January ten years before the collection of the information.
2. *Tests of Proficiency in English*, NFER, Ginn, 1973.
3. *Educational Needs of Children from Minority Groups*, Community Relations Commission, 1974.
4. *Multiracial education: need and innovation*, Schools Council Working Paper 50, Evans/Methuen Educational, 1973.
5. J. Elkin *et al.*, *Books for the Multiracial Classroom*, a select List of Children's Books, showing the backgrounds of India, Pakistan, and the West Indies: The Library Association Youth Libraries Group, 1971.
6. J. Hill, *et al.*, *Books for Children, The Homelands of Immigrants in Britain*, Institute of Race Relations, 1971.
7. *Teaching English to West Indian Children*, Schools Council Working Paper 29, Evans/Methuen Educational, 1970.
8. *English for the Children of Immigrants*, Schools Council Working Paper 13, HMSO, 1967.
9. H. E. R. Townsend, *Immigrant Pupils in England*, NFER, 1971.
10. Select Committee on Race Relations and Immigration, Session, 1972/73, *Education, Vol 1*, Report, HMSO.
11. A film depicting the co-operative system at Deane High School, Bolton, is available on loan from The Central Film Library, Government Film Building, Bromyard Avenue, Acton, London, W.3. The title is *English as a Second Language: first and second phase teaching*.
12. *English for Immigrant Children in the Infant School*, Scope Handbook 3, Longman, 1981.
13. H. E. R. Townsend, *op. cit.*

CHAPTER 2.2

DIALECT IN THE CLASSROOM*
JOHN RICHMOND

A bit of autobiography. Five years ago I went to teach English in a girls' comprehensive school in South London. At that time about 50 per cent of the school population was second generation Jamaican. That figure has steadily risen to the point where about 80 per cent of this year's first-year intake is second generation Jamaican. The main reason for this trend is that the traditional white working-class population of Vauxhall and Kennington, where the split-site school is situated, has increasingly moved away from the area to the outer suburbs of London or to new towns. Thus it is that, within a three mile southerly radius from, say, Lambeth Bridge, you now get a mixture of the really quite wealthy, and of those who are as poor as it is possible to be in modern, industrial, welfare-state Britain.

The really quite wealthy are professional people who decided that if they were going to live in England they might as well live in London, and who, starting in the early 1960s, were attracted by the then relatively cheap price of property in the area, and had the money to buy houses from private tenement landlords, and then convert them into single family dwellings, or into two or three self-contained flats. As this tendency developed through the 1960s and into this decade, the price of houses in the area increased dramatically, so that it is now impossible to buy property in certain parts of Kennington and Vauxhall unless you are earning a good deal more than the average teacher does. The Prince of Wales owns property in the area, including the Kennington Oval and a rather chic private estate about 300 yards from the upper building of the school, where he numbers the former prime minister among his tenants.

* *The English Magazine*, vol 2, Autumn 1979, pp. 18–23. Published by the ILEA English Centre.

Somehow, we don't see many of the children of these people. I suppose they must go to private schools, or at least to one or other of the church voluntary-aided schools in the area.

The children we do see are from the council estates, or from the few remaining streets of two-up two-down Victorian artisans' cottages, many of which are multiple owned by private landlords. These are largely the children of parents who came to this country between 1950 and 1965 from the Caribbean, and in the case of this particular district of south London, very largely from Jamaica. The reasons why they came are now well known. They came in response to the British Ministry of Labour's urgent request for man- and woman-power to work the service industries of British cities, and to do unskilled work in factories. They were enticed by offers of good pay, decent housing, and the wonders of the British education system for their children. At the same time in the Caribbean (and for that matter in India and Pakistan), the withdrawal of colonial investment was the cause of massive unemployment, slump, and lack of prospects. They came. They brought with them, among other things, their language. Fifteen or twenty years later, a few people in British education are waking up to the remarkable fact that the people of the Caribbean brought their language with them when they came, and that that has crucially important implications for, at the very least, curriculum and assessment in schools where their children go to learn.

The history of Jamaican Creole

I want to say a few sentences about the history of Jamaican Creole, because that's the Caribbean language I know most about. I don't suppose there are many people reading this who would want to describe Jamaican Creole (JC) as 'a kind of broken English'. Unfortunately, there are still plenty of people in quite powerful positions in education who do think that that is what JC is, even though they're usually too sensible to say it in public. Even more unfortunately but more understandably, there are many Jamaican parents who regard JC as 'bad talk', and would think of an article written by a teacher about the excellence of 'bad talk' as the ultimate piece of sinister hypocrisy. The reason why so many skilled and expressive middle-generation speakers of JC have such a low opinion of their language, is partly the same reason why many Cockney or Birmingham speakers regard their speech with such ambiguity. The reason is the generations and centuries of sociolinguistic conditioning from the top, which have persuaded many people that certain ways of speaking are associated with poverty, lack of education, and cultural limitation, and that a certain other way of speaking is associated with social and material success, and an educated understanding of the world.

The position of JC is one stage more complicated than this, however, because of the racial history of the island in the last 300 years. For, having dismissed the idea that JC is 'broken English' or 'bad talk', we come to the much more plausible notion that JC is 'a rather broad dialect of English'. The word 'dialect' is now such a popular term that it's almost necessary to define it every time we use it. A definition of 'dialect' might be: a variant of a language produced by social or geographical conditions, with significant distinctions from the other variants of that language, but maintaining sufficient phonological, grammatical and lexical similarities with those other variants to be obviously within the scope of definition of that language. On that definition, it's a toss-up whether JC is a dialect of English or a language by itself which has been strongly influenced by English. I would favour the second description myself, for reasons we shall come to shortly. Of course, the judgement one finally makes depends on the sentences one chooses to analyze. If we take the sentence –

Mi a taak wid unnu pickney

– we can recognize the words 'Mi', 'taak' and 'wid' as versions of Standard English (SE) 'me', 'talk' and 'with' in a sentence which SE would render as 'I was talking with you children' or 'I am talking with you children', depending on context. Then we have 'unnu', a word from the West African language Ibo, meaning 'you' plural. 'Pickney' is originally from Portuguese, and means 'child' or 'children'. JC likes to distinguish between 'you' singular and 'you' plural in a way that SE doesn't bother to any more. The probable reason for this is the importance of the 'you' singular/'you' plural distinction in most of the West African languages. On the other hand, JC isn't much worried about varying its personal pronouns for case or gender (neither are most of the West African languages), and is quite happy for 'mi' to stand as subject or object first person singular pronoun, where SE must distinguish between 'I' and 'me'. The 'a taak' construction to indicate a progressive verb – 'am talking' or 'was talking' – is quite different from any British English progressive verb construction, and probably comes from Twi, another West African language, where it is an emphatic particle meaning 'it is' or 'they are'. JC regards the presence of 'unnu' as sufficient indication of the plural, so doesn't need to inflect 'pickney' in this instance, where SE needs to inflect 'child' to 'children'. In a sentence without the 'unnu' clue or any other plural indication, JC would use the plural form 'pickney-dem'. Finally, the characteristic sound system of this sentence when spoken is widely different from any British English dialect.

West African languages

There are different individual sources of the various features I've mentioned, but the general truth is that JC is founded on a West African grammatical and phonological system, to which have been grafted large amounts of European (principally English) vocabulary, with a wide range of smaller influences from other sources. There are two main reasons for this.

First, there were many skilled linguists living in West Africa before the arrival of the Europeans. The Niger-Congo family of languages numbers many hundreds, of which the majority have quite small speech-communities. In the fifteenth century, several peoples, each of whose mother-tongue was different, might be living very close to each other. As is usually the case with closely related languages, the most significant distinctions between each language lay in vocabulary. In terms of sound-systems and grammar, the similarities outweighed the differences. Thus it was common enough for people to speak several languages besides their mother-tongue, grafting new vocabulary onto a familiar grammatical base, using a word from the mother-tongue if they hadn't learnt its equivalent in the neighbouring language. When the Europeans arrived, and the necessity for trading communication arose, it seemed the sensible thing to the leaders of the native peoples who had to deal with the strangers, to take over as much, say, English vocabulary as possible, in order to understand and be understood. The West Africans were better linguists than the monoglot island race. Not for the last time, they performed a major linguistic shift. Thus it was that English trading pidgins, based on the languages of the Western Sudanic sub-groups of the Niger-Congo family, were established on the west coast of Africa before the Europeans' cultural superiority in the use of arms and gunpowder established the slave trade.

The second reason for the basic character of JC is more familiar. The slave-traders and slave-owners in the Caribbean recognized the danger of allowing over-large groups of Africans who spoke the same language to remain together. So they divided and ruled to the point where individual families were split up and sent to different islands. They forbad the slaves to speak their own language to those remaining who might understand them. Such a grotesque ban was presumably impossible to enforce completely, but nevertheless all the slaves' utterances to the white man or to each other in situations where the white man could or might hear, had to include elements of the language (and vocabulary is of course the most obtrusive element) which the master understood and approved. With wonderful speed, flexibility and skill, the slaves did this, making a new language out of the most diverse elements in the most appalling human circumstances. This is the language, remember, that some people call 'broken English'.

The twentieth century in Jamaica

An express time-train through Jamaican history from the middle of the seventeenth to the middle of the twentieth century shows the period of actual slavery giving way to economic virtual slavery. It shows JC remaining remarkably stable during that time, changing much less than one might expect of a new language, changing less than the English masters. The rise of SE in England in the eighteenth century, and the coming of compulsory state education in England in 1870, with its single-minded admiration of SE and its despair at the intellectual incompetence of those children who seemed unable or unwilling to speak it; these important developments had their effect in Jamaica, as elementary education and then a small amount of fee-paying or scholarship-entrance secondary education was introduced for black children. It was quite clear to the educators that the English of the classroom must be 'correct English', and not the 'country talk' they overheard in the fields and the streets. So they enforced this, and children 'talking bad' inside the classroom were beaten. I've already mentioned what effect this had on many Jamaicans' view of their own language.

Beyond education, the twentieth century in Jamaica, like everywhere else, has seen the rise of bureaucracy, the world of the official and the clerk, an increased need for things to be managed, approved and organized, rather than simply done. The world has got more complicated. The closer black people got to the centres of power, business and administration, the greater the need became to approximate as closely as possible to the language of the manipulators of those centres – to the white man's language. There's nothing unusual in that, of course. The same thing happens in any hierarchial society, whether race intervenes or not.

Hence arose what has come to be known as 'the Creole continuum' in Jamaica, as throughout the Caribbean. A spectrum of language, with full JC at one end, and full 'educated', 'civil service' SE at the other. Such simple models should never be trusted too much, and there are plenty of minor quirks, oddities and contradictions along the spectrum's length. But it'll do for the minute. Jamaican people found it not just useful but essential to be able to move back and forth along that spectrum, depending on who they were talking to, where, and for what purpose. The boy with a good job in an office in Kingston would not speak to his boss in the same way as he spoke to his mother when he went to visit her in the country. The girl about to take the Common Entrance Examination knew that if she passed it, she'd be spending the next few years, and maybe the rest of her life, in a different part of the spectrum than if she failed it. Or if she didn't know it yet, her mother did.

In spite of the imposed sociolinguistic prejudice which we've noted against the Creole end of the continuum, a much healthier and equally strong counter-instinct prevailed among many Jamaican people, and survives today in the attitudes of many of the children at the school where I teach. Whether it's a result of the extraordinary circumstances of Jamaican and pre-Jamaican linguistic history, I don't know. But the counter-instinct is a respect for range. It recognizes that different kinds of language seem appropriate for different audiences and environments. It understands the range. And it has a great respect for people who can operate that range as widely as possible.

The language of black south Londoners

It's at this point that we come back to the London postal districts of SW8 and SE11 where we began. It's also at this point that the spectrum model becomes more or less useless, because of the intervention of London vernacular speech (and you can substitute the local vernaculars of other British cities as appropriate). Jamaican children growing up in south London take on most, if not all, of the characteristics of the indigenous speech of the area, and so can no longer be seen as sliding up and down the single plane of one spectrum, but switching, sliding and mixing between any of Jamaican Jamaican, Jamaican Creole, London Jamaican, south London vernacular, and SE. So it's quite wrong to think of Jamaican, or any West Indian, children in British cities speaking one kind of language; in common with first, second or third generation immigrant groups the world over, their linguistic situation is very complex, because of the complex nature of their historical experience. I believe that schools and teachers have a vital and overriding responsibility to recognize, accept and encourage the language which children bring to school, however complex or varied that may be, and however it may be different from the language of the school as an institution or from the language of individual teachers.

Dialect as part of the work of the English classroom

My own interest in the power, beauty and subtlety of JC was largely provoked by *Brixton Blues,* an improvized play done by a third-year class of mine in September 1976, which relies heavily on JC speech forms. That play caused something of a stir in the school, and provoked a range of responses, from massive enthusiasm on the part of the girls who watched the videotape, or read and acted out the transcript of the videotape, to deep suspicion on the part of some staff that this kind of thing was going on as part of the curriculum of the school. One of the play's most creative effects, in my view, was that it set the precedent that this very important area of the language range of many of the children was actually admitted to exist in one small corner of one subject of the secondary curriculum. The play started a tradition of dialect plays, poems and stories in English lessons. We didn't make a great fuss of it. No one was ever forced to write in dialect, though I have several times been accused of 'teaching these children patois'. It was simply known that those who wanted to, and knew how to, use dialect as part of their English work, were welcome to.

Here are two examples of the tradition. The poem is by Julie Roberts, the story by Sandra Herridge.

No justice

We nah get justice inna dis ya
Babylon.
We h'affee seek ah justice outta
Babylon,
We mus' return to Africa our
righteous blessed land,
Cause Babylonians present system
ah get way outta han',
Dem always accusing we fah wat
we nevva don'
Trying fe teach WE! right fram
wrang,

We tell dem seh we innocent
but deh dou't our word,
Dem tek us inna court an'
mek we look absurd,
We try tell dem seh Rasta no tief,
But dey dou't us still, dem
still don't beleev!

Mouta Massey

It was the day when the Common Entrance Examination results were coming out. Most of the people in Sherwood were hurrying to the Post Office to buy a newspaper.

Miss May flicked the latch of her gate, stole a last glance at herself through the glass of her bedroom window and then started her way to Sherwood crossroads, where the Post Office was. On her way there she met Miss Maty, one of Sherwood's commonest chatter boxes.

Unlike Miss May, who was well spoken and who looked quite neat, Miss Maty mixed her English with her own Jamaican way of speaking. She was wearing a pink roll-sleeve blouse, a yellow pleated skirt, that had banana stain all over the front, and a kata on her head. She was carrying a bucket of water, but when she saw Miss May she put it down on the roadside, leaving only the kata on her head. She was preparing to gossip.

People in the district teased her by saying that the quickest way to spread news around the place was to tell Miss Maty. Because of her great liking to exercise her lips, they nicknamed her 'Mouta Massey'.

Her excuse for being so nosey was that she lived all by herself and so, when she gets an opportunity to gossip there wasn't any harm in that. But the gossiping lips of Miss Maty often got her in difficult situations. That morning when she met Miss May was one of the many occasions.

Miss May: Good morning Miss Maty, how are you this morning?

Miss Maty: Mi aright May. Wey yuh going?

Miss May: I'm just going to the Post Office to buy a glena.

Miss Maty: Eh! eh! Yuh ton big shot ova night. Is only backra readings glena nowadays.

Miss May: Don't be like that Miss Maty, I'm a working woman and I have all the rights in the world to read the papers when I want to!

Miss Maty: Sarry Mis May, but mi neva know dat yuh read al papers. Mi shoudve guessed – anyway, yuh are de posh type, only chat like mi when yuh angry.

Miss May: I don't always read the papers, but today is special, you know, the results of the Common Entrance exam are coming out. I wonder if Sonia passed? She worked hard and the teacher told me that she have a good chance.

Miss Maty: Tek mi advice, if shi pass nuh mek she goh to the same school as Jeanie gal Donna. Mi hear dat she bright in har lessons, but she don't have any manners whatsoever. Your pickney will have a good chance as long as shi nuh mingle wid dat gal. All shi tink about is ramping an' enjoying harself. An' har poor Muma, boy, sometimes mi heart grief fi de woman. Yuh know har pregnant sister was like dat. Every single night ena row shi used to go dance hall, an' stay till late. An' what about Jeanie's sister? Mi hear dat shi runnaway from home . . . An' . . . an' . . .

Miss May: Aright! Aright!!! Aright Miss Maty. Yuh making yuh mouth fly like cabbage ena put! Cho man! people dont have no secret in disa place. You know more bout people's background than dem know demselves. I don't have time to labrish[4] wid yuh! Mi gane!

Miss Maty: Wait fi mi! Mi deh com wid yuh!

Miss May: I do not wish to talk or walk with you Miss Maty. All a person need to lose their dignity is a bit of your lips, and anyway I haven't got time to wait until you go home and change.

Miss Maty: But mi not going home, mi coming like this.

Miss May: What?! People don't go to Sherwood crossroads like that!

Miss Maty: But mi not going to Sherwood crossroads. Mi will turn back half way, mi upset yuh, so mie will com and just keep you company.

Miss May: It's really nice of you Miss Maty, but you really don't have to.

Miss Maty: But I want to Miss May.

It wasn't until that moment that Miss May looked down. 'What are you going to do with the bucket? Miss Maty! look at your feet! Them dying to wash! You can't come to Sherwood crossroads like that surely. Look how the mud peeping from between your toes like peeping tam.' 'Oh no! I forgot to wash off mi feet. Mi slipped in a puddle when mi was helping up the bucket,' said Miss Maty.

A sudden, but somehow splendid idea flashed into Miss Maty's head. She ran to a nearby banana tree, tore a dry banana leaf from it and used the water from the bucket, with the leaf, to wash her muddy feet.

She followed behind Miss May, telling her how sorry she was for making her lose her temper. She told Miss May that when she was a little girl her mother used to give her pepper and rice to stop her from chatting so much. Then she suddenly confessed that what she told Miss May about Miss Jeanie's daughter wasn't positively true. 'Mi tink Melva tell mi, mi not sure, but you know she don't like Jeanie already. They did fight at pipeside an' tore off each other's blouses. It was a shame to see two grown women going on like dat. Mind yuh, mi wasn't there. I went to market, but from what I hears it was disgraceful,' remarked Miss Maty.

'Miss Maty, your lips are drifting again. If Jeanie and Melva had a fight, that's none of your business! No wonder people call you 'Mouta Massy'. Anyway, we soon reach Sherwood crossroads, aren't you turning back?' asked Miss May. 'Mi reach too far already, soh I might as well come all the way. Mi will go an' visit Miss Margaret, we haven't chat fi ages,' answered Miss Maty.

When they reached Sherwood Content (another name for the cross-roads) Miss May went to get the newspaper and Miss Maty wandered off to gossip with a group of women whose daughters failed the exam. She talked and talked; one by one the people were leaving. Before long Miss Maty was standing barefooted, alone and sad on the piping hot Post Office step. Miss May was nowhere to be seen so Miss Maty went home sadly.

Sonia did pass the exam and so did Donna. They were both sent to a nearby school in Falmouth. Both Miss May and Miss Jeanie were very proud of their daughters. As for Miss Maty, she continued to be a gossiper and found herself in many other embarassing situations.

The end

The intervention of non-standard grammar in mainstream school writing

I come now to a more complicated question, and one which is separate from the matter of the conscious use and enjoyment of dialect as part of the work of some children, principally in English classes. In spite of what I've said, and believe to be true, about the crucial importance of accepting and encouraging children's language as it is, the fact remains that the whole state education system, and the secondary curriculum in particular, is predicated on British SE. That assumption works from the cradle at five, to – often – the grave at sixteen. This puts sensitive teachers into a terrible dilemma, and I include here not just teachers of West Indian children, but teachers of all children whose language differs from the prestige dialect in which text-books are written, which teachers for the most part use themselves, and by which children's whole lives and futures will be judged in public examinations. How do you satisfy these implacable demands, combined often with the demands of parents and of children themselves to be taught to write the language which is the key to success in this society, and at the same time maintain one's belief that the acceptance of the child's language is both ideologically desirable and pragmatically essential?

First of all we need to dispose of one generalization which is both unhelpful and untrue. That is, that children always write the way they talk. They don't. There are plenty of children (just as, I expect, there are plenty of readers of this for whom it was true when they were at school) who move from the language they normally speak and possibly think in, to the language which they shrewdly regard as appropriate for school writing. It's called code-switching, and a lot of children do it without any trouble, do it unconsciously.

However, there are other children, I believe the majority, for whom code-switching constitutes a problem, an obstacle, a barrier to success. Somehow, every time they do a piece of writing for a teacher, it comes back covered in impatient red marks. That's very discouraging for them. It's also discouraging and irritating for the hard-worked teacher, conscientiously marking the writing, to find the same 'mistakes' cropping up again and again. Why does it happen? Let's look at a piece of writing done for me by Pat Cummings two years ago, when she was in one of my third-year English classes. The important thing to know about Pat is that she's always been extremely school-motivated. She came into the first year of the school in 1974, finding that reading and writing were hard and problematical activities. She's in her fifth year now and many, though not all, of her problems have been solved. That has happened largely through her own determination. She's never been interested in dialect writing. In the piece which follows we see a second-generation Jamaican girl, aged fourteen, writing for teacher. The piece is reproduced exactly as I first received it from her.

At night club

'One night I was invited to a night club with some of My friends. At 11.00 I got ready to go to the night club. My friends boyfriend pick me up. We got to the night club at 11.30. My friends boyfriend pour me a glass of sherry and left me all by myself. I stood around doing nothing, no one ask me for a dance I go so board that I went outside to get some freshair and came back on. Later on I went into the changing to get ready to go home. I open the changing room door and I left it open. then suddenly door slammed so hard that it frightened the life out of me. I felt so scared, I didn't want to go in the hall and asked Someone to stay with me. because it might sound stupid for me to asked. I stayed and went to the mirror to put some powder on my face, and as I was putting some powder on my face I felt a Black shadow coming up to me than all of a sudden the window slam I felt so scared that I started to scream. Then a girl came in and calm me down. I was so scared that couldn't open my mouth 15 minutes later I felt much better so I told the girl my story. When I was finish what I was saying to her. She told me that there was a young girl who died in this changing room. She said to me the girl was only in the changing room for 15 mintues "was she a nice girl?" She was all right I didn't know her much. I wonder why she wants to haunt this place." don't aske me because I don't nothing." how did you feel when the Black Shadow was coming up to you" I felt as if someone was coming up to me and lean their hand on to me. I felt funny inside of my body" I think I better I hope we meet again." "Mary where is tom" "we've been looking for you what have you been it's a long story let's get in the car and I will tell you all about it.'

The teacher's reaction to a piece of writing like this should be: how do I offer practical help with this? Technically, there's quite a lot wrong with it. Responses like 'slovenly', 'careless', which are always unhelpful, are particularly inappropriate here. The story was offered in earnest good faith. One valid response, it occurred to me, which might help Pat and me, would be to make an organized list of all the features in the writing which I might want to comment on, or correct, or bear in mind for future comment and correction. I did this, and it immediately and permanently became clear that never again could I do a blanket correcting job on a pupil's writing as if all 'mistakes' came from the same source and could be treated in the same way. To begin with, those features normally regarded as straightforward errors divided quite definitely into mistakes in the strict sense, where Pat knew what was correct but hadn't managed to transfer that knowledge accurately to the page, and examples of lack of proficiency in certain written conventions which mature writers generally regard as being useful. Presumably that distinction (represented by sections A and B in the list below) implies a different kind of handling on the part of the teacher who wants to make a helpful response. More importantly from the point of view of this article, I found that Pat was producing features in her writing which represented the grammars of non-standard dialects which, quite properly, form a part of her language competence. I use the plural 'grammars' and 'dialects' because 3. of section C is more likely to be a London vernacular influence than a JC influence. Here is the organized list I made. I'm afraid that it may seem to some readers to be stating the obvious, but I console myself with the thought that two years ago the list, once made, together with its implications, were a revelation to me.

A. Mistakes in 'At the Night Club'

1. Misspellings: 'board'/'bored'
   'mintues'/'minutes'
   'aske'/'ask'
2. Omissions: 'into the changing (room) to get ready'
   'that (I) couldn't open my mouth'
   'I don't (know) nothing'
   'say no more about (it)'
   'don't you think you (should) go home'
   'what have you been (doing)'

B. Examples of lack of proficiency in written conventions generally accepted as being useful:

1. Omission of full stops: e.g. 'Then a girl came in and calm me down I was so scard that (I) couldn't open my mouth 15 minutes later . . .'
2. Omission of capital letter at beginning of sentence: e.g. '. . . came back in. later on . . .'
3. Omission of apostrophe: e.g. 'My friends boyfriend'.
4. Omission of speech marks: e.g. 'She was alright I didn't know her much. I wonder why she wants to haunt this place"' (These two sentences are spoken by different people.)
5. Omission of question mark: e.g. 'don't you think you (should) go home'.

C. Examples of dialect features:
1. Non-use of SE – ed inflection to signal simple past; use of context or temporal phrase:
   a. 'My friends boyfriend **pick** me up'
   b. 'My friends boyfriend **pour** me a glass'
   c. 'No one **ask** me for a dance'
   d. 'I **open** the changing room door'
   e. 'all of a sudden the window **slam**'
   f. 'a girl **came** in and **calm** me down'; the standard irregular past form is used (correctly), but the present is maintained with 'calm', which has a regular past form.
2. Use of generalized singular noun form in plural sense:
   a. 'With some of my friend' (SE – 'friends')
3. Use of double negative:
   a. 'I think you do **not** want to say **no** more about (it).

D. Examples of features which may be related to dialect:
1. 'I didn't want to go in the hall and **asked** someone to stay with me. because it might sound stupid for me to **asked**.' Pat would never use 'asked' in either of these contexts in speech; they are not natural dialect features at all. They seem to be an overreaction to an awareness that the '–ed' verb ending represents a frequently occurring distinction between vernacular speech and school writing.
2. 'was coming up to me and **lean** their hand on to me'; it might be argued that 'lean' and the omission of '–ing' is an inconsistency unrelated to dialect. It is possible, however, that a preference for the simple present to the '–ing' form in Pat's speech means that the distance between 'was' and 'lean' has caused her to revert to the simple form; i.e. 'was' is not powerful enough to influence 'lean' at that distance.

I think Pat's position here is a very common one. There are many Jamaican, Caribbean, and for that matter indigenous London, Birmingham or Newcastle speakers, who to a greater or less extent than Pat are representing the grammars involved in the language they speak, in their writing. One of those grammars is SE, of course. It's foolish to say that Pat is being inconsistent because she sometimes puts –ed on the end of past tense verbs and sometimes doesn't. You wouldn't expect her to be 'consistent', given the variety of linguistic influences on her, or, to take the other sociolinguistic view, given that inherent variability is an element of the dialects of all of us.

A necessary myth and a possible strategy

What do I think should be done about it? My opinion divides into two sections, plan A and plan B. Plan A is cloud-cuckooish and Utopian, but worth mentioning nevertheless. Given that all linguists agree that all dialects of English are equally efficient, complex and rule-governed systems, and given that we now understand the historical reasons why the prestige dialect misleadingly known as SE has achieved its dominant position, the public examination boards, universities and other arbiters of linguistic and academic standards should simply cease to penalize pupils and students who represent, in their writing, features of the non-standard grammars in the language they speak. If the will existed for that to happen, it could happen very quickly, and it would be a radical change indeed. It would certainly make our lives as teachers, and the lives of our pupils, easier and more successful than they are at the moment. It would probably raise academic standards generally, since teachers and learners would have more time and energy to really engage with knowledge rather than tilt at windmills of standard and non-standard features in writing.

However, I'm aware that we don't live in the world of plan A, and that the educational wind at the moment is blowing away from rather than towards that world. I'm also aware that plan B, the plan for the real world, is a compromise, and less than satisfactory in a number of respects. But I think it's the best we shall manage.

The first thing is that there should be a policy, understood and agreed by all the staff in the school, on dialect features in writing. The way to decide on and implement that policy will vary from school to school, but a way of starting might be to collect examples of writing done by several pupils across a range of subjects, and analyze them in a similar fashion to what I did with Pat's piece. The ideal group to do that would themselves represent several major areas of the curriculum.

I'm going to stick my neck out and say what I think that policy should be. Readers may disagree with me about the emphasis, the tone of voice, or perhaps the timing of what I suggest, but I hope the principle will be recognized. I believe that up to the end of the third year in secondary school, teachers should not attempt to standardize non-standard features in children's writing. That, of course, assumes that teachers know the difference between a non-standard feature and a mistake in the first place.

The damage done to children's confidence and fluency as writers by the early and sometimes constant rejection of their language is considerable. And however kind or sensitive the teacher may be, I think it's unfair to ask most children below the age of fourteen to perform such an abstraction which most middle class children are never called upon to perform. Up to the end of the third year in secondary school, there's plenty to work on in helping children to improve their writing in ways not related to dialect.

In the fourth and fifth years of secondary school, if it's obvious that some children are producing non-standard features in their writing for which they will be penalized in examinations, teachers should point out to them, preferably individually and at the most in small groups, what those features are, and what their standard equivalents are. That's also the time when work on dialect as such can be most useful and enjoyable, and link in with advice of this kind. It may well be that the specific features in question are rather few in number. The task is often not as frightening as it sounds; fifteen- and sixteen-year-old children are increasingly making self-reflective judgements, and many of them will see the short-term sense of the advice as regards the exams.

I'm not happy with the previous paragraph. In some way it's a shoddy compromise. But in the extremely imperfect educational world where we work, we have to avoid brutality and ignorance on the one hand, and (too much) star gazing on the other.

Thanks to Julie Roberts, Sandra Herridge and Pat Cummings for allowing me to quote from their writings, and to David Sutcliffe for several of the insights about the early history of JC.

CHAPTER 2.3

HOW DO YOU SPELL GUJERATI, SIR?*
JANE MILLER

Kulvinder is five and halfway through her first year of primary school. Her teacher sometimes feels concerned that Kulvinder doesn't speak at school, but she lets herself be reassured by the child's bright watchfulness and by the alacrity with which she always does what she is told. Besides, Kulvinder's mother and father are so keen for their daughter to speak good English that they have given up speaking Punjabi at home and speak only English now. Kulvinder doesn't say much at home either, but perhaps that will change when her parents have learned more English themselves.

Andreas lives in East London, and he goes to the nearest school, though his father worried at first about sending him there. He had heard that over half the children were black and that the school had gone downhill since it became comprehensive and some of the Jewish families round there began to send their sons to fee-paying schools. Andreas is tall for twelve, one of the tallest in the second year, and he seems to like school, though his father is never sure that he's learning anything. This week he's been teaching his class some Greek, in English lessons if you please. He began with the alphabet, writing it up on the board. Then he made the class work out the words 'West Ham for the Cup', which he'd writen in Greek letters. He could tell they'd got it when they jeered. His father has written a funny poem which Andreas will give them tomorrow, though he'll have to help them translate it. It's good the way Mr. Orme lets the boys be teachers sometimes. They're learning all about the history of writing and alphabets with him. Andreas finds it strange that some people hate writing, can't see the point.

* *The State of the Language*, eds. L. Michaels and C. Ricks, University of California Press, 1980, pp. 140–51. Copyright 1980 by The Regents of the University of California, reprinted by permission of the University of California Press.

Michelle is twelve too. There was a lady in her English lesson today who asked them all what languages they knew. They thought at first she meant French, which they started last year with Mrs. Brooke. But it turned out that she meant things like Indian and Brok French. Michelle was really surprised that apart from her there were five others in the class who spoke Brok French. She'd thought Nadia was Indian, but she speaks the sort of French they speak in Mauritius. By the end of the lesson they'd discovered that besides English, which everybody speaks, there were children who knew Egyptian, Greek, Urdu, Spanish and Italian, as well as Jamaican language and French Creole. The lady said that their French teacher might be interested that six of her pupils spoke French patois. Michelle nearly told her that Mrs. Brooke never seemed interested in anything much except getting your homework in on time.

Three voices, one of them inaudible, must be allowed to speak for themselves out of what is variously regarded as a Babel or a resource for teaching of unimaginable richness. A recent survey of just over three thousand children in their first year at eighteen London secondary schools turned up fifty-three overseas dialects of English and nearly as many home-based ones. Among the three hundred children in their first year of just one of those schools, twenty-eight languages were spoken apart from English.[1] London schools are often in the news for doing worst in tests set for the whole country, worse even than Glasgow schools. There was a time when researchers got used to urban children doing better than rural ones.[2] Children living in towns were expected to be better off, more ambitious and sophisticated. All this has changed, and London is suffering from that worldwide complaint, the inner-city crisis. It would be easy to blame that on all those languages, but mistaken. They aren't spoken in the schools, after all. There are some English teachers who say that the children in their classes have too little language, not too much, and that what there is is usually bad, in every sense.

In Andreas's class they had a lesson last week from one of the boys, on Korean, and how you write it in different directions to show whether you're talking about the past or the future. That was amazing. Mr. Orme did Ancient Greek when he was young and he wanted to find out whether that helps at all with Modern Greek. He's impressed by all the languages his pupils speak. One boy, who speaks Urdu, Punjabi and Hindi, can read and write in Urdu and Punjabi and is learning to read Hindi at after-school classes. It has taken him only four years to sound like a native Cockney speaker and his writing is good too. Mr. Orme is rather a rarity. He has gone to the trouble of finding out what languages the boys speak at home, and because a lot of them are from Jamaican families he has learned to speak their language and can discuss in detail the differences between Kingston Jamaican, London Jamaican and the sort of English he speaks. Some teachers think he's wasting his time, that he'd have to agree that since the children live in England and will probably stay for the rest of their lives, teaching them the sort of English which helps them to pass exams and get jobs is what he's there for. Mr. Orme does agree, though he finds it harder and harder to be sure that he knows what sort of English that would actually be. When he was a boy he won a place at a grammar school in Durham. All the boys spoke with an accent, even used different words, but their English teacher saw to it that they didn't speak sloppily with him. So that for a long time Mr. Orme had believed that you couldn't expect even to spell properly if you didn't talk like the BBC. Wouldn't all those rules for doubling letters, spelling the *or* sound and silent *e*'s be much easier to get right if you talked posh? He remembered one of his mates saying that squeezing up the vowels and making a big thing of the consonants was the way to get on. Mr. Orme's ideas have changed since then. He likes the way his pupils speak and he even likes his own accent now; still 'rough', as he thinks of it, after all these years in London. When he talks about these things with his friends they think he's a bit sentimental or just making the best of a bad job. It is difficult enough to explain, let alone to justify, his conviction that his being interested in the languages his pupils speak does actually help them to write English of several sorts and to speak more confidently in class. It isn't as if he knew all those languages himself, though: Yoruba, Arabic, Cantonese, Gujerati. He often wishes he did when he's teaching his examination classes. He can't even find good dictionaries for most of the languages, let alone science textbooks or novels.

For a long time research into bilingualism operated within the assumption that bilingual children were likely to have problems at school. Welsh-speaking children in Wales[3] and French-speaking children in Canada[4] did less well than their monolingual (English-speaking) counterparts. In the way of so much of that kind of research, most of it had, by the sixties, been queried and even contradicted on the grounds that the tests which were used to establish the inferior attainment of bilingual children ignored both the social factors underlying the bilingual ones and the effects on a child of speaking one language at home while learning (and being tested) in another one at school. There had, as well, always been some people in Wales who were prepared to concede that knowing Welsh as well as English might be seen as providing the benefits of a cheap classical education; benefits, by the way, which were not queried. For that is one of the anomalies about attitudes to bilingualism. Whereas learning a foreign language and even one or two dead ones as well has always been the *sine qua non* of a 'good' education, and whereas a child who picks up fluent French and Italian, say, because her father has been posted abroad, is likely to be thought fortunate, at an advantage, even 'finished,' a child with two or three non-European languages, in some of which he may be literate, could be regarded as quite literally languageless when he arrives in an English school, where 'not a word of English' can often imply 'not a word'. Partly, this is a matter of the history which has made of English a *lingua franca*. I should want to suggest, however, that it also has a good deal to do with the view that English as a school subject is bound to concentrate exclusively on its written form. It is not that there need be any argument with the tradition which makes schools the promoters of literacy, but that the written form and its intimate relation with Standard English speech can be made to exclude the realities of the language as it is spoken. Many children spend a larger proportion of their day in school on writing than on reading, speaking or listening. Even tests which are intended to assess oral comprehension, reading competence and response to literature are made to depend on the child's knowing how to write a certain sort of English prose. That is the sort of English Mr. Orme *should* be teaching his pupils, and it is not a form easily learned by anyone whose own speech is under suspicion. The best examples of expository or imaginative prose draw vitally upon the spoken language. The belief that a child can learn to produce even the most modest versions of such prose while his speech is dismissed, even perhaps excoriated, is likely to be doomed, and we can't, surely, be wanting children to 'talk like a book'.

To be genuinely multi-lingual or multi-dialectal in contemporary Britain is allowed, then, to be a drawback. It is still thought 'useful' to know some Latin, while knowledge of Standard Tamil, say, and one of its dialects is thought 'confusing'. There is, of course, a special kind of usefulness in knowing something of a language from which English partly derives and which has certainly mattered to English literature, just as there is another kind of usefulness in speaking your mother tongue. Other claims have been made for the learning of a second language, however, beyond these sorts of usefulness. One would be that another language embodies as it expresses another culture, and that another culture introduces the possibility of critical detachment about one's own. Another would be that there are aspects of the nature of language itself, which are often more easily learned through an encounter with a second language. Connected with this is the notion that the conscious mastery of a language is an intellectual discipline in itself. Recent research on bilingual Hebrew/English children[5] draws attention to those things which these children do better than their monolingual peers. Because they are earlier able to separate meaning from sound, they are also able to develop earlier what Margaret Donaldson has called 'a reflective awareness of language as a symbolic system',[6] which is a prerequisite for developing abstract thought. Perhaps because the learning of language has required more effort of them, these children are often more sensitive to the appropriateness of their speech and to the effect it produces on hearers of it. They also become aware earlier than most children of the structures within one particular language system which contrast with those of the other one. Even at those points where one language might be expected to interfere with the other, to overlap or create confusion, possibilities for particular insights were noticed, so that fusion rather than confusion worked to produce at an earlier age a sense of what languages generally consist of, get up to, are used for.

What, it might be asked, is the hurry? Many monolingual children will develop that kind of awareness of language too, in time. But since learning to read depends on this ability to stand back from language, to hear it and watch it function, as it were, and since learning to read quickly and successfully can determine a child's whole school experience, it is important that teachers exploit what may be real advantages for the bilingual child. There are teachers who have done so. A fifteen-year-old bilingual Turkish boy, for instance, was asked to translate into written English a story told by his mother in Turkish to her three-year-old daughter. He was able to discover for himself, and partly to solve, the problems of turning into written English an oral story in another language intended for a young child and told by a woman who was elaborating a narrative out of a real experience. Then two thirteen-year-old Jamaican girls improvized a play in patois on videotape. Because they wanted to transcribe their play, in order to develop and improve it, they decided to transcribe its present version. They found themselves having to invent an orthography and a way of representing their own speech which would allow a reader to 'hear' it as far as possible. The exercise was useful on several counts, not the least important being that it introduced one of the girls, who had barely been able to read and write until then, to the nature of written language and to the purposes there might be for her in learning to write. It is the kind of exercise which would be hard to match in a language for which conventional spelling already existed.

In one sense, it is all quite simple. Where a child grows up speaking more than one language or dialect, and those languages or dialects have equivalent status in his own and in other people's eyes, and where the connections between those languages and their differences are made explicit, multi-lingualism can be an unqualified good. Mr. Orme's pupil, Andreas, is in that rare position. He still visits Cyprus. English people know about Greek, even hear it spoken on their holidays. Andreas speaks Greek for most of the time at home, but other members of his family speak English too; and he is not aware of making conscious decisions about which language to speak to whom, about what or where. He could read and write in Greek before he arrived in England,[7] and he learned English in a school where it was assumed, rightly, that he was competent linguistically even if he didn't know English, and where they had come to rely on and to admire his success. He was lucky too to embark on the second of his languages before he was too old to do so easily and to learn it principally through using it with children of his own age. As an example of bilingual advantages he is ideal, though hardly typical.

It is a characteristic irony that while the learning of languages can be an expensive business, nearly all those people in the world who grow up bilingual do so because their mother tongue or dialect has associations with poverty which make it likely to be thought inappropriate for education and some kinds of employment. Many of the people who have come to live in England during the last twenty-five years are in the position of speaking either a dialect of English or another language altogether, which they are encouraged, and in some cases are themselves all too ready, to relinquish. What will happen to Kulvinder between now and her first letter of application for a job? Her parents' refusal to use their own language may have implications about their view of themselves which go well beyond the danger of depriving their daughter of a language which is hers as well as theirs. Kulvinder's watchfulness has something of the look which children acquire when they are brought up by deaf parents. Modern language teaching often makes good use of a temporary outlawing of the mother tongue. It is a strategy which assumes that sheer need to communicate is sure to power the acquisition of a new language, as it has been thought, simplistically, to power the acquisition of the first. For a child in Kulvinder's circumstances the refusal to speak Punjabi is probably disastrous. Certainly she has proved that her need to communicate is not as powerful as all that.[8]

The variety of ways in which multi-lingualism is experienced by children is probably infinite, ranging from a kind of 'anomie' at one extreme to a quite special flexibility and effectiveness as a language user at the other. Somewhere between are all those children who leave their mother tongue at home and learn 'English' at school. This can produce a damaging dividedness, particularly when it is not discussed, shared or understood. A second language learned and used only in school can feel like a language for passivity, acceptance, attention, listening and Kulvinder's obedience. Its use will be constrained by rules and prohibitions, its vitality and subtleties hidden. Similarly, the home language may be relegated to the terrain of childhood, interesting only as the expression of a vestigial folk culture. The life of action and feeling, of first experiences and what is directly known can become divorced from the world where language has become an instrument for generalization, organization and the assimilating of new ideas and knowledge. There is a danger of that happening to any child, but the danger is a much greater one if the two selves, so to speak, talk different languages. Cultural values can be distorted, polarized into what is quaint, half extinguished, and what is practical, modern and remunerated. Many children are marooned between languages and between cultures, forgetting one more rapidly than they acquire another; and meanwhile they may be regarded by teachers and by other children – ultimately, perhaps, by themselves – as bereft of all the things language stands for: intelligence, humour, daring, inventiveness, enthusiasm, discrimination and curiosity. And without those qualities it is not easy to learn the new language which might enable you to regain them. A child's first sorting out of its impressions of the world, of its own place there, and of noises which are meaningful from those which are not came with a particular language, which is now forced underground, made inaudible, unintelligible. Learning a second language is bound to be a matter of attaching it to the meanings which will always adhere in a special way to the first one. The confidence which allows us to use our language to make jokes and tell stories, let alone to answer a court charge or infer something of motive and intention from another person's speech, is not gained by dismissing as irrelevant the language which both produced and expressed the child's first thoughts.

Michelle's parents came to London from St. Lucia before she was born. They still speak French patois at home, and though she thinks her parents' English absurd she herself knew some English by the time she was five and went to primary school. Most of the time she speaks like the other children in her class, a non-standard London dialect. When she is with her West Indian friends she shifts into London Jamaican as they do. She says she has never spoken patois outside her home and that 'most West Indian people say that patois is bad for young children to speak.' That may be why her parents sent her to a school where there are relatively few West Indian children. That, at any rate, is what Michelle believes. When she recalls, and mimics, her first teacher at primary school telling her, 'You're talking bad language, bad English,' she assumes that her teacher meant that there was something wrong with her accent. She is also able fiercely to say, 'You should be able to speak patois, Jamaican or English.' When Michelle assents to the disapproval her speech can elicit while defending her right to speak as she wants to and needs to, she is expressing the sort of ambivalence many dialect speakers grow up with. Her English teacher has no views about her language except that her writing is 'weak in sentence structure.' Neither this teacher's comment nor that earlier one about 'bad language' has been substantiated or explained to Michelle. She speaks, in fact, three languages:[9] French patois, non-Standard English and London Jamaican. She is fluent and effective in all three, makes easy shifts between them, stylish use of the incongruities the shifts can produce,[10] and is able, as well, to do an excellent imitation of Mrs. Thatcher. It is worth remembering, I think, that whereas all non-Standard English speakers are compelled to understand and sometimes to assume Standard speech patterns, Standard English speakers are rarely required to do the reverse. Yet in spite of this rich language repertoire, Michelle, at twelve, has already been made aware that neither her speech nor her writing will quite do.

That many of the difficulties which exist for a multi-lingual child also exist for a multi-dialectal one is due to their being the product of attitudes to languages generally, and to particular languages, rather than to their being inherent in multi-lingualism itself. They are especially difficult attitudes to grapple with because they are about class and race and status, though they masquerade as value judgements about language and fine (even musical) discriminations.

There is nothing new about multi-lingualism, or about the passions or the prejudices it provokes. Language has always been felt as a measure of identity, by individuals and by whole communities. The certainties which wiped out Gaelic in the Scottish Highlands and deplored Scots in the Lowlands have been relaxed, so that it is now respectable for plays on television to be in dialect and for novelists and poets to use the language of their childhood. It is, therefore, all the more surprising that no such welcome has been given by schools to the mother tongues and dialects of children. This may have something to do with the teacherly obsession with something called 'correct' language, and with correcting, in red ink, children's writing. It is an obsession which is encouraged and applauded by many people who would themselves find it hard to say what they meant by 'correct'. Children are famously less responsive to the thorough sub-editing job done on their writing – which can look at times like no more than a display of credentials – than to more positive ways of suggesting how a piece of written or spoken language might be made more effective, clear or truthful. That sort of approach, to be successful, relies on a sense of language being complex and diverse and its 'correctness' being no more than one aspect of what children need to know about it. Official documents are circulated, it is true, which preach the virtues of 'mother tongue maintenance', without specifying how this is to happen, let alone mean very much, if the examinations which are still allowed to validate all schooling continue to rely on a definition of English so exiguous as to exclude not just dialect but speech of any kind.

In America attention is focused at the moment on the predicament of Spanish–speaking and Indian children,[11] and there have been schemes to promote mother-tongue literacy before school and the use of the mother tongues as the language of instruction in school. These are brave moves, though it is not clear that they have managed to change the attitudes which have made such schemes essential and which still undermine them. In this country, where a request for a modest central government grant towards the funding of bilingual education in Wales can still produce an angry letter to The Times,[12] what little mother-tongue teaching goes on is undertaken by members of particular language communities, and only in a handful of cases with help from schools or local authorities.[13] There have been, no doubt, some successes, though all the schemes are on a small scale and necessarily dependent on a voluntary commitment to them. They may also encourage minorities to feel defensive about a culture and a language which are plainly not valued by the majority if they are excluded from school. The tragedy is that schools themselves see their role here as so confined, and the English language as so inflexibly unresilient, as to reject the value of their pupils' languages to themselves, to the curriculum and to the community to which the school belongs. Kulvinder could be beginning an education which allows her to feel proud of her language and of the special knowledge she brings to the learning of English. She could as easily remain in a state of profound bewilderment, fearful of having another language snatched from her, struggling not toward an English which she can take on positively as her own but towards something which, at best, will enable her to spell her employer's letters correctly, at worst, will get her a job where speech, and indeed thought, are not required of her.

Any normal child has mastered by the age of five an elaborate symbolic system and internalized its rules. This is true for any child learning any language. Through speech, and through learning to read and write, the child will 'learn to turn language and thought in upon themselves,'[14] so that he can talk about language and think about thinking. Children with more than one language are well placed to do this. Teachers in multi-lingual classrooms have at their disposal resources for introducing all their pupils to the nature of language, to the quality and the implications of linguistic and cultural diversity, and, thereby, to an outlook on knowledge built upon the kind of relativism which produces both intellectual rigor and intellectual openness. The best teaching always moves from a sensitive awareness of what the learner already knows to what is new; and the best users of English, speakers and writers, plunder the tensions and the variety which English has always so vigorously incorporated. If children are to become powerful users of language for their own purposes, and responsive to the subtleties and the excitements of what has been done, and can be done, with language, teachers would do well to begin from an appreciation of the strengths, the highly developed social and linguistic skills, children bring with them when they come to school. And that means all children. There is more and more evidence that children who are 'weak in sentence structure' or possessed of 'limited vocabularies' are encountered with unusual frequency by some teachers and most researchers.[15] Perhaps it is because such teachers and researchers are the only people given to asking children questions to which they don't really want answers, and to engaging children in conversation about matters of interest to neither party. They might try listening more to children talking their own language to their own friends about things they urgently want to talk about and find out about.

It is time to make use of language diversity; not just the diversity as between one school and another, or between one child and another, but the diversity within each individual child and within the use of language itself.

This respect for diversity would, after all, make of an examination or a letter of application no more than single items in a genuine language repertoire, one for use not one up for judgement.

Notes

1. These figures are drawn from the interim report of the survey of linguistic diversity in ILEA secondary schools (1978) by Professor Harold Rosen and Tony Burgess of the English Department, University of London Institute of Education.
2. See, for example, W. R. Jones, *Bilingualism and Intelligence* (Cardiff, 1959).
3. Jones, *Bilingualism*.
4. W. E. Lambert, 'A Social Psychology of Bilingualism' (1967), in J. B. Pride and Janet Holmes, eds., *Sociolinguistics* (London, 1972).
5. Sandra Ben-Zeev, 'Mechanisms by which Childhood Bilingualism Affects Understanding of Language and Cognitive Structures,' in P. A. Hornby, ed., *Bilingualism: Psychological, Social and Educational Implications* (New York, 1977).
6. Margaret Donaldson, *Children's Minds* (London, 1978).
7. Chester C. Christian, 'Social and Psychological Implications of Bilingual Literacy,' in António Simôes, Jr., ed., *The Bilingual Child* (New York, 1976). This article describes a project undertaken in the US and based on the belief that preschool literacy in the mother tongue is an advantage to the second-language learner.
8. It is now accepted that there is much more than a need to communicate involved in a child's learning to speak. For a fascinating illustration of this see A. R. Luria and F. Ia. Yudovich, *Speech and the Development of Mental Processes in the Child* (London, 1973).
9. There are drawbacks to using the word *language* for the dialect of a language. I do use it here, not because Michelle's dialect is so aberrant as to seem something quite different from English, but because it works as a complete and coherent system for her, which cannot simply be judged in terms of its divergences from Standard English. A blurring of the distinction between 'language' and 'dialect' is also appropriate here, in my view, because the problems they pose for the child in school have so much in common.
10. This capacity to shift between two or more dialects of English is at last being recognized; and some superb documentation is coming out of London schools at the moment. For examples of this, see John Richmond, *Brixton Blues* (London, 1976) and *Dialect* (London, 1977).
11. Muriel Saville-Troike, *Bilingual Children* (Resource Document prepared for the Centre for Applied Linguistics, Arlington, Virginia, 1973).
12. Letter from Walter Clegg, MP for North Fylde, to *The Times*, 18 August 1978.
13. John Wright, *Bilingualism and Schooling in Multilingual Britain* (London, 1978). This article gives an excellent account, and evaluation, of the successes and failures of some schemes to improve the situation in Britain.

14. Margaret Donaldson, *Children's Minds* (London, 1978). For a brilliant and elaborate discussion of this point see L. S. Vygotsky, *Thought and Language* (Cambridge, Mass., 1962).
15. Courtney B. Cazden, 'How Knowledge About Language Helps the Classroom Teacher – Or Does It: A Personal Account,' *Urban Review* (1976).

SECTION 3

ATTAINMENT

CHAPTER 3.1

THE EDUCATIONAL PERFORMANCE OF ETHNIC MINORITY CHILDREN*
SALLY TOMLINSON

The issue of the performance and achievement of ethnic minority children in schools, particularly those of West Indian origin, continues to perplex practitioners, worry parents, and sporadically to engage the attention of educational researchers. It is important, in the interests of social and racial justice, to know just how the children of ethnic minority parents are situated within the various selective and classification processes in British education, and how they are performing and achieving academically, – particularly since educational credentials are crucial in providing for employment opportunity, job security and occupational and social mobility. As yet no overall systematic study has been undertaken in this area, but there are a variety of localized research studies which have been carried out during the past twenty years which provide some information. The results of some of these studies have become confused with comment and opinion about the findings, and have occasionally been used more to fuel political and ideological argument than to initiate debate on ways of improving education for minority group children.

This article attempts an overview of research studies concerning the ability, performance and achievement of minority group children, particularly those that have been carried out since 1966. In that year Goldman and Taylor published a survey of research on 'coloured immigrant children'.[1] As far as possible, comment about the research is avoided – the aim being to document who carried out the research, in what year, the sample size and characteristics of the children tested, the results of the research, and the explanations offered for the results by the researcher(s). As Bagley[2] has pointed out, two major types of studies can be identified,

* *New Community*, vol VIII/3, Winter 1980, pp. 213–34.

those using individual psychometric tests, ostensibly to measure 'ability' and those using group tests to measure performance. These latter are usually tests of verbal reasoning or reading skills, or teacher assessment of children's school performance. A few studies have examined success in public examinations and school-leaving qualifications, and official statistics and some research has indicated the position of minority children in school 'streams' and in 'special' education. The use of conventional psychometric tests for minority group children has been heavily criticized, usually on the grounds that the tests are culturally biased, and recently attempts have been made to develop new tests of potential 'learning ability'.[3] The debate over 'culture-fair' assessment is eschewed here, but Hegarty and Lucas[4] have provided a lucid discussion of this question. Studies using teacher assessment have also been criticized,[5] as they have usually been carried out without considering the effects of teacher expectation, and perceptions, of minority group children. Researchers have usually decided, on an ad hoc basis, that what they were measuring was the comparative performance of minority group children and indigenous (largely urban) children. Early studies compared 'immigrant' as against 'non-immigrant' children, and the length of time spent in UK education was considered to be an important variable in explaining performance. More recently studies have concentrated on measuring the comparative performance of indigenous 'white' children as against the (mainly British-born) children of Asian and West Indian origin – the latter group usually found to be performing and achieving least well. The assumption behind the studies is that the experiences of these different groups of children in the education system are more or less similar and comparison is possible. It may be useful to recall John Rex's comment in 1972 that 'What is necessary before we can draw conclusions about the performance of one group or another, is that we should understand on a meaningful level the type of relationship which the minority group has to the society'.[6]

Research pre-1966

In 1966 Goldman and Taylor[7] produced a useful survey of literature to that date on 'immigrant' children, documenting the general educational situation of the children and their perceived specific educational problems. They noted that up to that time studies which could be classed as research, rather than comment, were very few indeed. The pre-1966 studies reviewed here are all mentioned in Goldman and Taylor. Initially it is important to note a piece of comparative research[8] carried out by P. E. Vernon, a Canadian professor, during the early 1960s, which probably helped legitimate comparative studies of the educational perform-ance of minority children in Britain, since Vernon's work is well known internationally. Vernon compared 100 English boys from rural South-East England with 50 West Indian boys in Jamaica, matched for age and background. The boys were all tested on a variety of individual verbal, perceptual and performance tests (Vernon graded arithmetic test, NFER English attainment test, Mill Hill vocabulary test, Piaget battery of 31 items, Porteus maze, Kohs blocks, Goodenough draw-a-man test and others). The West Indian boys consistently scored lower than the English boys, although their performance varied between tests. Vernon explained their 'moderate degree of retardation' by handicaps created by the socio-economic, cultural and linguistic environment, family instability and poor educational facilities – all factors which have subsequently been used to explain the poorer performance of children of West Indian origin in Britain. Vernon later (1967) worked with data from the Inner London Education Authority's eleven-plus test results, examining the verbal reasoning, English and arithmetic scores of 1,200 'immigrant' children in London primary schools. The mean IQ score for immigrants was 76 against an 'English' norm of 100, rising to 91 for children with six or more years schooling in England. The score for West Indian immigrants was slightly lower than for other groups. Vernon explained improved scores in terms of better schooling and environmental conditions in London.[9]

Several pre-1966 studies were undertaken by post-graduate students. Alleyne (1962)[10] for a London University MA compared the IQ scores and school attainment of groups of children in London, Wales and Trinidad. The scores of the Trinidadian children were lowest, and explanations for this centred around test bias and bi-lingual problems. Saint (1963)[11] for a Birmingham University M.Ed tested 100 Punjabi boys attending Smethwick secondary schools, using Ravens progressive matrices – the result of which he converted to IQ scores. The mean score for the Indian boys was 84·5, as against an 'English' norm of 100. His explanation centred on the irrelevance of the previous educational experiences of the boys, as their scores did improve with length of schooling in Britain. He also noted the school problems of the Indian boys. 'The (white) Teddy boys do not like us, they spit and kick at us . . . and drag us out of lavatories' (Indian boy).

Houghton (1966)[12], another Canadian professor, studied children at eleven infant schools in an English local education authority. He was interested in possible racial differences in IQ scores. He tested 71 matched pairs of four to five year old white and Jamaican children, 36 girls and 35 boy–pairs, who had been at school less than ten weeks, using the Terman-Merrill forms L–M. The results showed a mean IQ score of 90 for the Jamaican children, 92 for the English children, not a significant difference. Jamaican girls scored 90 as against 89 for Jamaican boys, English girls scored 92 against 91 for English boys. The explanation offered for all the depressed scores was that of 'deprivation' in social, linguistic, environmental, maternal and paternal terms, but no conclusions were drawn as to 'racial' differences.

The ILEA Studies

The research which has probably had most impact on educational practitioners and on beliefs about the educational performance of minority group children in general was that undertaken by the Inner London Education Authority's Research and Statistics group between 1966–75. The authority had become concerned over the performance of 'immigrant' children during the early 1960s and had complaints from white parents that their children were 'held back' by the presence of immigrant children. A working party from the local inspectorate and the school psychological service was set up to inquire into the educational performance of immigrant and non-immigrant children. Their report was produced in 1967[13] and an article, based on the complex technical appendix to this report, appeared in *Race* (1968) by Little, Mabey and Whitaker,[14] director and researchers for the Research and Statistics group. The report and article documented research in a sample of 52 London primary schools in which 1,068 'immigrant' pupils were transferring to secondary school in September 1966 – they comprised a quarter of all ten to eleven year olds in the authority. Information on the children was collected by means of a questionnaire to head-teachers, and also a 'leavers schedule' for every child, to be filled by the head. The 'immigrant' children comprised West Indian, Indian, Pakistani, Greek and Turkish Cypriot and 'others'. The ILEA placed all its pupils in one of seven Profile Groups (one to seven) for scores on English, maths, and a specially-devised verbal reasoning test. The English and maths scores were based on teacher assessment. The results of this 1966 survey showed that while the 'average' ILEA child was placed in profile group four, the average 'immigrant' child was placed in group six. Only two per cent of immigrant pupils were placed in group one for any of the tests. Four-fifths of the immigrant children were rated as below the median of the authority's normal range of performance, as were half the non-immigrant children, and 85 per cent of West Indian children were placed in the lower half of profile group four or below. There was a marked improvement in the performance of immigrant children with increasing length of schooling in England but even with full English primary education the performance of immigrants was below that of non-immigrants. Depressed non-immigrant scores were attributed to large classes, teacher energy diverted to immigrants, lack of stimulus for non-immigrants and able white families leaving immigrant neighbourhoods. Poor immigrant performance was explained in terms of language, cultural, and family factors, patterns of immigration and poor home–school contacts. This study was reported in the *Financial Times* (10/5/68) as 'a most disturbing report' and this response and the methodology of the study have been criticized by Bagley.[15]

A further ILEA study examined the performance of 4,269 immigrant and 22,023 non-immigrant pupils aged eleven in 1968. This research is summarized by Little (1975[a]).[16] Again, immigrants were found to be more often placed in the lower profile groups with the West Indians doing worst. They were eleven times more likely to be placed in groups six or seven than one or two, although with a full English education they performed better. Asian pupils fully educated in English had a performance distribution very similar to the indigenous children. A table from this 1968 research was published in Little's 1975 article and reproduced again by Little (1978)[17] in a televised lecture. The use of ten-year-old data in this way may be one reason for the confusion surrounding reports about the current educational performance of minority children.

The Research and Statistics group at the ILEA also conducted a continuing literacy survey of 32,000 eight year old pupils who were in their second year at junior school in 1968. A sentence completion test devised by the NFER was used. This research is reported by Little and Mabey (in Donnison and Eversley, 1973)[18] and by Little (1975[a] and [b]).[19] The first literacy survey found that overall, London children had a reading age six months below their chronological age, immigrant children one year below. The West Indian immigrant groups had the lowest reading score. The majority of this cohort of children were tested again in 1971 and 1975, using slightly different versions of the NFER tests. Little (1978)[20] refers to the scores on these tests, but there does not appear to be further published work available on the literacy surveys. Unpublished

ILEA papers show that while the scores of indigenous children remain more or less the same over the years, the 'immigrant' scores decline slightly – the West Indian performance deteriorating most sharply. One of the conclusions Little arrived at concerning these ILEA studies was that 'it is the child from the West Indian background whose needs, in terms of basic skill performance, should be given highest priority'.[21]

Explanations for the performance of all the children in these London schools were sought in the concentration of immigrant children in the schools, in 'multiple deprivation', as measured by an index of social deprivation devised by the ILEA[22] and in the social and ethnic mix of the neighbourhoods.

The EPA research

A further piece of large-scale research which produced evidence concerning the lower test performance of immigrant, particularly West Indian, children, was the Educational Priority Area action–research project directed by A. H. Halsey at Oxford University.[23] This research was carried out in London (Deptford), Birmingham, Liverpool, the West Riding of Yorkshire and Dundee. The research had its origins in the recommendations of the Plowden report (1967)[24] which drew attention to 'disadvantaged' children. One criterion of disadvantage suggested by Plowden and reproduced in criteria for selection of EPA areas was a 'high concentration of immigrants'. Thus British-born children were considered to be disadvantaged if immigrant children were present in their schools. The children in the project areas of London and Birmingham included large enough 'immigrant' groups for test scores to be examined separately (Payne, 1974)[25] but not for differences between boys and girls to be noted. In Deptford 2,892 children at twelve primary schools were tested, of whom nineteen per cent were West Indian and 7·7 per cent 'other immigrant'. In Birmingham, 1,990 children at six primary schools were tested, fifteen per cent being West Indian, 24·8 per cent Asian and 3·3 per cent 'others'. The head-teachers of the schools 'decided' the country of origin of the children. The children were given the English picture vocabulary test, the SRA reading test and other tests of attainment. On the EPVT test, a test of listening vocabulary, the mean score for London indigenous children was 97·9, the mean score for West Indian 86·9, with twice as many West Indian children in the three bottom categories as in the overall national sample. The score for West Indian children in Birmingham was 81·6 and Asian children in Birmingham had an even lower EPVT score of 69·6, a score 'so strongly skewed as to bear no resemblance to the normal distribution of scores in the nationally representative sample'.[26] On the SRA reading test, a quarter of West Indian children in the London project areas and two-fifths of the Asian children 'obtained scores indicating an inability to read in English'.[27] The mean reading score for indigenous London children was 93, for West Indians 88. In Birmingham the mean West Indian score was 83·5 and the Asian score 78·4. An analysis made of test scores between ages five and eleven, showed that the test scores of West Indian EPA children began to fall off earlier than the scores of their non-immigrant class-mates and suggests that this may reflect a 'more general pattern in the performance of West Indian children'.[28] Reasons advanced for these lower scores include larger family size of immigrants, the use of Creole by West Indian children and the recent arrival in England of many of the Asian children. It was also hinted that the worsening performance of West Indian children in school might be the result of school processes. The test results collected by the London EPA project are further reported in Barnes (1973),[29] and are also used twice by Alan Little in his two 1975 articles as a 'comparison of immigrant school performance with underprivileged indigenous children'.[30] Thus information from the ILEA research group studies and the EPA London project appear in the same published articles.

Research 1967–1974

A number of smaller-scale studies on minority group 'ability' and performance were carried out from 1967. In that year Graham and Meadows[31] published a study primarily concerned with psychiatric disorder among children of West Indian origin. They studied 55 West Indian children referred as 'maladjusted' to a Brixton child guidance clinic between 1963–65. Of these 29 were boys, 26 girls, and all were first-generation immigrants. Fifty-five white children at the clinic were selected as a control group and the children were all given the Stanford Binet test, or the Weschler Intelligence scale for children (the scores of which were then converted to Stanford–Binet equivalent). The IQ of the West Indian boys was 97·6, that of the white boys 101·7. The IQ of the West Indian girls was 81·3 and that of the white girls 96·7. On a reading test the West Indian children scored a mean of 81·6, the white children 84, although all children showed some degree of reading retardation. The explanations offered for the poorer performance of West Indian children centred on the traumatic separation of children from their parents, and the difficulties of rejoining families – three sad case histories were appended to illustrate this explanation. The poorer performance of West Indian girls is explained by their greater domestic and child-minding responsibilities. 'Colour-prejudice' is also noted as an explanation, and the occupational social class of West Indian parents is shown to be lower than the whites.

A small study by Wiles (1968)[32] reported in the Institute of Race Relations newsletter, showed that in one inner London comprehensive school there were slightly more 'immigrant' children than white in the top streams of the school, and that the performance of the immigrant children equalled the whites when all the secondary education had been obtained in England. Wiles explained this by greater motivation on the part of the immigrant pupils.

A piece of research for which data was collected in 1969, but the results not published until 1979, was partially carried out by Phillips.[33] It is not always clear in the published article that this ten-year gap between data-collection and publication existed as the author interprets his findings with the hindsight of other studies done during the 1970s.

The Birmingham Centre for Child Study and a remedial education service in the West Midlands carried out a survey to identify poor readers in 1969. Two thousand four hundred children aged seven at 42 infant schools were tested on the EPVT test and the Southgate reading test. Equal numbers of boys and girls were involved, and 12·6 per cent of the children were classed as 'immigrants' (in this case West Indian or Asians). On the EPVT test, indigenous children had a score of 96·8, West Indians 78 and Asians, 65. West Indian girls did better on this test, scoring 79·4 against 76·6 for West Indian boys. Asian boys did slightly better than girls: 65·6 – boys, 65·5 – girls. On the reading test, indigenous children had a mean score of 85·6, West Indian 80·7 and Asians 78·4. Again West Indian girls did rather better, 82 as against 78 for the boys. On this test Asian boys did slightly better than Asian girls – 78 as against 77. Phillips goes on to claim that, although scoring below the mean for indigenous children on these tests, West Indian and Asian children are not 'under-achieving'. He introduces, but inadequately explains, the notion of D-Score (deviation from expectation) and computes a higher D-Score for West Indian and Asian children than for indigenous, to show that if matched for 'social and familial' factors the children score higher than white disadvantaged children. He claims that West Indian and Asian children, on average, acquire basic educational skills in British schools at least to the level of their abilities, when attainments and abilities are 'assessed on parameters which describe the indigenous population'. He concludes that there is no need to invoke explanations concerning teacher expectations or the alienation of non-white pupils, to explain their (poorer) performance. A further study reported in 1969 was carried out by Payne.[34] In this study 99 West Indian immigrant children, aged seven to eight years were matched with 99 British children. Four tests were given, Ravens coloured matrices, word reading test, Crichton vocabulary scale and a concept formation test. It was hypothesized that the West Indian children would do worse on all the tests except the concept formation test. In fact they did worse on all the tests. On the word-reading test however, West Indian girls and British girls respectively did better than West Indian boys and British boys. No explanations were offered. Two studies often quoted in brief reviews of literature on the performance of minority children are those of McFie and Thompson (1970)[35] and Ashby, Morrison and Butcher (1970).[36] McFie and Thompson studied 61 children of West Indian parentage referred to a London child guidance clinic between 1965–68, and aged between five and fifteen years. Fifty-one of these children were matched with an English control and tested on the Weschler intelligence scale for children and a Schonell reading test. The full IQ score of the West Indian children was 87, as against 98 for the English control group; the reading score was 77 for West Indians as against 82 for English children. The performance scores of the West Indian children, as measured by picture completion, block design, object assembly, etc. were as low as their vocabulary scores, leading the authors to conclude that teaching should focus on constructional and geometrical material as well as on language. McFie had previously worked with boys in Uganda and considered that both African and West Indian children would be handicapped in a 'European culture' if they could not deal with representational and mechanical materials. Ashby, Morrison and Butcher provided one of the first studies solely concentrating on Asian children. They tested 59 Indian and Pakistani children, 35 boys and 24 girls, aged between ten and seventeen years, and 150 Scottish children in five Glasgow schools. The children were tested on a Glasgow verbal reasoning test, a Moray-House V.R. Test, Ravens progressive matrices and the Goodenough draw-a-man test. The 'educational response' of the children was assessed from school record cards filled out by teachers, a five-point rating being given for oral English, reading, written English, formal arithmetic and problem arithmetic. The Asian children were divided into long-stay, medium-stay and short-stay groups. The results from the four tests of 'ability' showed that Scottish children scored higher than immigrant Asian children, but not always at a significant level. Thus long-stay Asian boys scored 104·8 on the Glasgow verbal reasoning test, as against 105·5 for the Scottish children. The ability of the immigrant Asian children was seen to improve with length of stay (on the Glasgow test, short-term immigrants only scored 84) and the Asian boys did better than the girls (on the Glasgow test they obtained a score of 93·9 against the boys' 96·1). On tests of attainment – how the children actually performed in school – there was a reversal in the scores for the long-term group. The mean attainment for the Scottish children in all subjects was lower than that of long-stay Asian immigrants, although they out-performed short-stay children. Asian girls did worse at arithmetic but as well at English as Asian boys. The authors sought an explanation in 'acculturation'. When families had been longer in Scotland and become more involved with the 'host culture' the children appeared to do better.

A study reported by Bhatnager (1970)[37] of 174 West Indian (90 boys and 84 girls) and 76 Cypriot (38 boys and 38 girls) children, with a control group of 100 English children, was primarily aimed at investigating the school adjustment of 'immigrant' children. However, the children, all attending a London secondary modern school, were given Ravens progressive matrices test to establish a (non-verbal) IQ score. The academic achievement of the children was also checked. The mean IQ of the West Indian children was 90, higher than that of the Cypriot children who scored 84, but lower than that of the English children who scored 102. West Indian boys scored higher than girls, 91 against 89 points.

Academic achievement was assessed by adding the children's grades in five subjects and assigning them an achievement score. The mean achievement score for all West Indians was 9·43, for Cypriots 9·46 and for the English 15·17. West Indian boys had a slightly higher achievement score than girls. The vocabulary of the children was also tested, and West Indian scores were lower than the English but slightly higher than the Cypriot score. Bhatnager explained his findings in terms of schools 'failing in their duty to the immigrant children'.

By the early 1970s the resurgence of explanations for the poorer test scores and educational performance of minority children in terms of innate racial differences[38] led to a more stringent focus on alternative explanations, particularly in terms of the lower socio-economic status of parents of black children. Bagley, in 1971,[39] undertook a partial replication of Houghton's (1966) study. Using two London primary schools he matched

50 West Indian children, fully educated in Britain, with 50 English children hypothesizing that black children from stable working class or lower middle class homes would not be intellectually disadvantaged. The children were tested on the Terman-Merrill revision of the Stanford-Binet test, and both groups achieved higher scores than the national norm of 100, the West Indian children having slightly higher scores than the English – 105 to 103. Bagley suggested that social class factors rather than race were important in explaining underachievement. A further piece of work undertaken by Bagley (1975)[40] supported this explanation. Fifty-nine children, aged eight to ten of West Indian and African origin and attending three London primary schools, were tested using the revised Stanford-Binet test again. Children in the study, who were considered by independent judges to be of 'wholly African ancestry' scored higher than the other children. However the majority of these children had middle-class parents.

Research published 1975–80

In 1970, Michael Rutter, a professor of psychiatry, together with a number of colleagues, tested the total population of ten year old children attending local authority schools in a London borough.[41] Teachers gave the place of birth of the children, which was later checked with parents' reports and found to be 97 per cent accurate. The total number of children was 2,281, of which 74 per cent were indigenous and 26 per cent children of immigrant parentage. Of the 354 children of West Indian origin in this study, 207 had been born in the UK. All the children were tested with the NFER test NV5, a non-verbal IQ test, and the SRA reading test. The children's teachers also completed a behaviour rating scale. Selected children were given individual tests (a short form of the Weschler intelligence scale for children, and Neale's analysis of reading ability). One hundred children of West Indian origin were selected for individual testing, 51 having been born in the UK and 49 outside the UK, and 105 'indigenous' children were individually tested as a control group. The mean non-verbal IQ score on the group test was 92 for 'indigenous' children and 82 for children of West Indian origin – of these, UK born children scored 85, immigrant West Indian children scored 76, Greek Cypriot children scored 85 and Turkish Cypriot children, 82. On the group reading test, the score for indigenous children was 86, for West Indians and Cypriots 84. Rutter concluded that 'children from immigrant families score well below children from non-immigrant or indigenous families'. On a comparison of the 105 indigenous children with the 100 children of West Indian origin tested individually, the indigenous children scored significantly higher than the West Indian children – the 'indigenous' verbal IQ score being 101 and performance IQ score being 103, the 'West Indian' scores being 86·9 and 90 respectively. On the individual reading test the West Indian group had a reading age one year below the indigenous children. The UK born 'West Indian' children scored well above those born in the West Indies, the UK born verbal IQ score being 89 as against 85 for the West Indian born, and the reading scores being 107 months as against 97 months, respectively. Thus, in 1970 'West Indian' children born in the UK achieved significantly higher scores than those born in the West Indies. Rutter explained the better scores of UK born 'West Indian' children largely in terms of school experiences, and expressed concern that children of West Indian origin were more likely to attend schools with characteristics associated with poor attainment generally. He also explained the findings in terms of 'adverse social circumstances' of West Indian families, and the early life-experiences of children of West Indian origin.

Data for an intensive study of language proficiency in multi-racial junior schools was collected in 1973 by McEwan, Gipps and Sumner, and published in 1975,[42] using a battery of tests developed at the NFER to check 'English proficiency'. Teachers in a national sample of 127 schools administered tests of listening, reading, writing and speaking, and sent the results to the NFER. In all 1,116 'Asian' children, 521 'European' children, 650 'West Indian' children and 785 'English' children completed the tests. The results showed that the English children performed at significantly higher levels than the minority group children although children born in the UK performed better –even those who had not had special language help. The authors expressed surprise that West Indian children only performed slightly better than Asian children and explained the findings in terms of use of dialect by West Indian children. Asian children who spoke English at home did better than those where mother-tongue only was used at home. Pre-school education did not appear to increase 'immigrant' language proficiency, and English children in schools with high proportions of immigrant children performed as well as those with few immigrant children.

Edwards (1976)[43] assessed the reading comprehension scores of 40 English and 40 West Indian children matched for age, social class and ability. The children were aged eleven to twelve years and the Neale

Analysis of Reading ability test was used. The results showed that even among good and average readers, the comprehension scores of West Indian children were significantly lower than those of whites. Edwards explained the lower scores in terms of 'dialect interference'.

A study also by Edwards (1978/79)[44] on language should perhaps also be noted here, as although it is not strictly research on the actual performance of any particular groups of children, it provides indications as to the way teachers perceived the possible academic performance of children of West Indian origin. Edwards asked twenty student-teachers to evaluate four recorded speakers – a middle-class boy, working-class boy, a bidialectal Barbadian girl and a recently arrived Jamaican girl using Creole features in her language. The student teachers' order of preference of speech was middle-class, working-class, West Indian. When asked how far they thought the four speakers would get in schools, (CSE/O Level/A Level) the student teachers considered the children of West Indian origin, purely on the basis of recorded language, to have the least potential. Edwards concluded that teachers do have stereotypes about children of West Indian origin which may partially stem from negative feelings about their speech and language.

P. Jones, in the course of study on the sporting activities of West Indian children,[45] studied two London comprehensive schools, where 635 English girls, 645 English boys, 144 West Indian girls and 188 West Indian boys were checked for achievement at O/CSE level and reading ability. Jones found that in both schools, significantly more West Indian children were in lower streams, 33 per cent of whites, 52 per cent of blacks. Girls for both groups had higher all-round achievement than boys, and overall, black children did less well than whites.

A study which was published and re-printed twice in 1978 was carried out jointly by Redbridge Black People's Progressive Association and the Redbridge Community Relations Council.[46] These groups had established a working party on West Indian pupils, as they were concerned at the apparent low level of achievement of the 800-odd pupils of West Indian origin in this outer London borough. They had found 'remarkably little concrete statistical evidence available on the performance of West Indian children, either at national or local level'. The working party studied a large comprehensive school in the borough which had one-third minority group pupils. The education authority provided the results of a survey in eight local multi-racial primary schools where the children had been given the NFER 'Junior-four' tests of verbal reasoning, English and maths. The results of this survey showed that at age eleven, the white indigenous children at these schools scored an average 97·7 for verbal reasoning, 98·7 for English and 99·0 for maths. The children from the Indian sub-continent scored 91·9 for VR, 92·6 for English and 93·9 for maths. 'African Asian' children scored 90, 89 and 92·4, and West Indian children scored lowest of all with 85, 88 and 86. At the comprehensive school in 1977, 27 per cent of all first year pupils received remedial help, but 46 per cent of West Indian pupils received such help. Average passes at CSE and 'O' level was 0·7 for the whole school and 0·3 for West Indian pupils; numbers of passes in these exams was 4·2 for all children and 1·0 for West Indian pupils; no West Indian child passed a single 'A' level in 1977 although West Indian children represented ten per cent of the school population. The working party suggested a variety of reasons for the poorer performance of West Indian children: 'self-identity and the effects of a hostile society' on the children was considered to be 'the core of the problem of underachievement'; teacher attitudes and expectations, criticism of dialect speech and cultural factors were also important; social class and deprivation were felt to play a small part; but innately lower intelligence, West Indian family structure and migration effects were discounted as possible explanations.

A small study was published in 1978 by Ward[47] who followed the progress of 22 'immigrant' children and 22 indigenous children in primary schools in an inner and outer London borough for a year, making systematic visits to the classrooms of the children. The 'immigrant' children comprised both recently arrived and 'born here' children, and were from the West Indies, 'Asia' and the 'Mediterranean lands'. The children were individually tested on the Weschler Intelligence scale for children, Ravens Matrices, the Harris draw-a-person test, and on arithmetic and reading tests. In the first testing, children born to immigrant parents in the UK only achieved a score of 74, but this climbed to 92 in subsequent testing. The newly arrived immigrant children at first scored only 63 but their score improved slightly with 'exposure to an English environment'. Language attainment scores of both immigrant and 'born here' children improved through the year, but in number attainment all the 'immigrant' children achieved and maintained the same standard as the English control group of children.

By the late 1970s some research studies were indicating that blanket statements concerning the underachievement of minority group children were untenable. Some children from minority groups were performing and achieving adequately within the education system. Bagley, Bart and Wong (1979)[48] noted that there had been little research emphasis, either in America or Britain, on why some black children succeed in school. They carried out a study of 150 black children aged ten to eleven years in four London schools in working-class areas. The children were scored on the Schonell silent reading test, classroom performance and teacher perceptions of academic potential. They also completed attitude scales concerning parents, home, school, and work and their parents were interviewed. As a control group, 151 white English children were also tested and they scored significantly higher than the black children overall on the reading test. A general correlational analysis was carried out to isolate the factors which might be associated with the poorer black performance. The authors reported that parental authoritarianism, shared housing, lack of home ownership, use of Creole at home, and poor levels of schooling of parents, were factors associated with the under-achievement of the black children.

West Indian parents who were highly critical of English culture and the English education system, who were bilingual, better educated and in adequate material circumstances, were more likely to have children with above average achievement in school, a positive attitude to school and a positive self image.

A study reported by Stones (1975, 1979)[49] indicated that the performance of West Indian children does not differ from that of English children providing they are given relevant experience in concept learning. Thirty West Indian and 30 white children aged ten and eleven, fifteen boys and girls in each group, from two Midlands inner-city junior schools were tested on Ravens progressive matrices test, and then given tests of conceptual learning originally devised by Vigotsky. On the Ravens Matrices Test, the West Indian score was 24, compared to an English score of 23, and there was no difference in their conceptual learning ability. A replication of this study was carried out with 23 Pakistani and 23 English children aged thirteen to fourteen, at a Midlands secondary school. On the Ravens Matrices test the English score was slightly higher at 43·5, compared to the Pakistani score at 41, but again, there was no difference in conceptual learning ability.

However, other research in the later 1970s was still indicating that, in some schools at least, minority children performed less well than their white peers. A study by Robinson (1980)[50] of Asian children from eight different birthplaces in the Asian sub-continent and Africa, compared reading scores of Pakistani, Indian, and African-Asian children. In all, 627 children, of whom 227 were 'Asian', in twelve primary schools, were tested on the GAP word recognition test and the CS maths test. The average age of the children was ten years ten months, and the schools' location varied from inner city to outer suburb. The mean reading age for the white children was ten years six months, for the Asians nine years and four months. The Asian children scored lower than recently arrived Irish children and the explanation offered for this was poorer language acquisition – 'limited opportunities for interaction brought about by living in a voluntarily segregated colony inevitably restrict the natural and casual learning of English'. In general, those Asian children whose parents spoke English scored higher. Of these, children of Pakistani parents scored highest at nine years six months, children of African Asian parents next at nine years three months, and children of Indian parentage lowest at eight years eight months. A similar pattern emerged with the maths score – the average white score being 92·8, the average Asian score 86·04. The author concluded that 'Asian under-achievement is restricted to . . . the low-status section of the community characterized by Asians with little education, restricted aspirations and poorly-paid employment'.

Data from the National Child Development Study (a study following the progress from birth to maturity of all children born 3–9 March 1958 in England, Scotland and Wales), concerning the school performance of immigrant children was reported by Essen and Ghodsian (1979).[51] Here 7,185 indigenous children and 1,045 immigrant children, including West Indian, Asian, Irish and European 'immigrants' of the first and second generation, were tested at sixteen years on two NFER tests of reading and maths. Test scores were transformed to a mean of zero and a standard deviation of one. The results showed that all the 'second-generation' groups had higher scores than 'first-generation' immigrant children – the Asians became the highest scorers in the 'second-generation'. The mean scores for the West Indian children were lower than for other groups. 'Second-generation' West Indian children scored minus 0·5 for maths and minus 0·6 for reading as against the indigenous children's scores of 0·05 and 0·06. However when allowance was made for social and home circumstances the differences in test scores were reduced. The authors concluded that poorer school performance is generally found among 'first-generation' immigrants but children of West Indian origin still do rather worse at 'second-generation' level. The findings for first-generation performance are explained in terms of language and culture-shock.

Bagley (1980)[52] has undertaken a detailed analysis of data on ethnic minorities in the National Childrens Bureau Survey. This shows that on the majority of tests of educational performance, and in teachers' judgements, West Indian children are under-performing. They are also over-represented in ESN-M schools. However, the one exception is the score on the draw-a-man test – the test selected by the NCB to identify 'gifted' children. Three times as many West Indian children were included in the 'gifted' group on this test as English children.

Selection, streaming and school-leaving qualifications

The first evidence on a national scale for the under-representation of minority group children in selective schools (grammar and technical) was provided by Townsend (1971).[53]

Figures supplied by the Department of Education and Science and published by Townsend showed that in 1970, nationally, twenty per cent of non-immigrant children transferred to grammar schools, whereas only 3·9 per cent of Indian, 2·4 per cent of Pakistani and 1·5 per cent of West Indian children did so. In a more intensive study of 260 multi-racial schools in 1971–72[54] a higher percentage of all children were found to have transferred to grammar schools – 25 per cent of indigenous children, nine per cent Indian and Pakistani and four per cent West Indian. Townsend considered that the cultural bias of selection tests and language problems might account for this. The DES statistics also recorded that in 1970 only six per cent of Asian and West Indian pupils were taking 'O' level courses, as against 42 per cent of indigenous children, and whereas only three per cent of indigenous pupils were taking non-exam courses, 23 per cent West Indian, 26 per cent Indian and 32 per cent Pakistani children were so occupied.[55]

The under-representation of minority group children in selective schooling appears to have continued throughout the 1970s. In 1976, Rex and Tomlinson[56] found that in Birmingham, the children of West Indian and Asian immigrant parentage were less likely to be attending selective schools than indigenous children. Out of a total of 1,526 pupils, children of householders in Handsworth, seven per cent of indigenous children, as against 1·5 per cent West Indian and 1·2 per cent Asian children were attending one of the city's seven remaining grammar schools.

On the question of streaming, a DES survey 1969–70[57] of 54 multi-racial secondary schools in sixteen local authorities noted that of the immigrant pupils in the schools 'a third were in upper streams, and four out of ten in lower streams', but makes no further comment.

Townsend's study of multi-racial schools[58] provided evidence that 'immigrant' children tended to be clustered in the lower streams of schools that organized by ability levels. Of the 28 primary schools who reported streaming, seventeen noted that West Indian pupils were clustered in lower streams, and nine reported Indian and Pakistani pupils in lower streams. Of the 72 secondary schools that streamed, those with less than 20 per cent 'immigrant' children reported both West Indian and Asian children clustered in lower streams. In schools with over twenty per cent 'immigrant' children the Asian children were more evenly distributed between streams, but the West Indian children tended to be slightly more concentrated in lower streams. A study by Taylor[59] of 67 Asian boys who left schools in Newcastle between 1962–67 also reported a tendency for English boys to be 'selected' more than Asians to attend the city grammar and technical schools, but the Asians tended to stay at school longer than the English boys. Of 53 Asian and 56 English boys studied in depth, five Asian boys obtained CSEs, two 'O' levels and one an 'A' level. Of the English boys three obtained CSEs, three 'O' levels, five 'O' and CSEs, and one an 'A' level. The others obtained no school qualifications, but eighteen of the Asian boys, as against four of the English, moved into further education, and nine Asians, as against two English, eventually moved to higher education.

Current debate on the educational performance of minority group children now centres largely around the acquisition of school-leaving qualifications. The few localized research studies done in this area suggest that minority group pupils, particularly Asian pupils, are acquiring some CSE, 'O' and 'A' levels, but some minority pupils tend to acquire them at a later age than indigenous pupils. The assumption that the acquisition of certificates by minority group children must always be compared to the number of certificates acquired by indigenous children in the same schools, may be a source of some confusion. Local studies may be more representative of factors associated with individual schools (teaching, organization, numbers of children entered for exams) than of the potentiality of either minority group or indigenous children to pass public examinations.

Several studies which provide evidence of school-leaving qualifications have been undertaken in the context of discovering the employment situation of minority and 'white' young people. Allen and Smith in 1972[60] interviewed 368 school-leavers in Bradford and 300 in Sheffield, in a study designed to examine entry into employment. 'White indigenous', 'East European', Asian and West Indian young people were interviewed. The 'educational exposure' was documented thus: in Bradford, eighteen white boys and eighteen girls, and eight European boys, reached 'A' level standard, but no Asian or West Indians; at 'O' level/CSE standard, 36 white boys and 30 girls, 20 East European boys and girls, sixteen Pakistani boys, two Pakistani girls, twelve Indian boys and ten Indian girls, and three West Indian boys and seven girls were recorded as passing; in Sheffield, 29 white boys, 29 white girls and four Europeans had reached 'A' level standard, but again no Asians or West Indians. Thirty each of white boys and girls, four European boys and six girls had reached 'O' level/CSE standard, but only five Pakistani and two Indian boys, seven West Indian boys and fifteen West Indian girls. Overall, whites achieved a mean of 2·8 passes in 'O' and CSE, blacks a mean of 1·9 passes. The authors note the school explanations for this poorer performance – linguistic problems, family background, lack of parental interest and pupil application – and offer an alternative explanation that the lack of educational success may legitimate the use of 'immigrant' children as unskilled labour.

Rex and Tomlinson[61] interviewed 25 young West Indians and 25 Asians who had recently left school. Of these fourteen West Indians had acquired 63 CSEs, and eleven of the Asians had 51 CSE passes, four 'O' levels and three 'A' levels. The West Indians reported some resentment that their teachers had not encouraged them to take 'O' levels. Fowler, Littlewood and Madigan (1977)[62] interviewed 54 Asian and 56 Glaswegian boys in Glasgow in 1972–73. In terms of 'O' level and Scottish 'highers' the Asian boys were marginally ahead, when first interviewed after leaving school. Twenty Asians had no certificates, but 33 had 'O' levels and 24 had 'highers', 22 Glaswegian boys had no certificates, but 33 had 'O' levels, and twenty had 'highers'. The Asian boys tended to be older, some leaving school at nineteen or twenty. A year later 32 Glaswegian boys were in work compared to thirteen Asian boys and 21 of the Asians had gone into further education or back to school.

A further study of Asian attainment is provided by Brooks and Singh (1978)[63] in studies of school-leavers in Walsall (by Brooks) and Leicester (by Singh). In the Walsall study interviews and a postal questionnaire to 54 Asians, (23 boys and 31 girls,) and 113 'whites' (54 boys and 59 girls), provided evidence on their attainment at CSE and 'O' level. Here 52 per cent of the white boys and 85 per cent of the white girls had no 'O' level passes, seventeen per cent of white boys and 38 per cent of white girls had no CSE passes. Seventy per cent of Asian boys and 87 per cent of Asian girls had no 'O' level passes, seventeen per cent of Asian boys and ten per cent of Asian girls had no CSE passes. The average number of 'O' level passes for those who did take the exams was (on the questionnaire) 3·4 for white boys, 4·1 for white girls, 3·6 for Asian boys, 4·3 for Asian girls. Thus although Asians were less likely to take any 'O' levels, they obtained slightly more passes. The author writes that 'it is the similarities between white and Asian educational performance which are impressive, rather than any differences'. In Leicester, over half the Asian pupils leaving ten schools in the main areas of Asian settlement were interviewed in 1976, a year after they had left (secondary modern) school at sixteen. Here 283 Asian pupils (161 boys and 122 girls) and 66 'whites' (44 boys and 22 girls) reported their school-leaving qualifications. Fifty-two of the Asian boys and 24 Asian girls took 'O' levels and nearly two-thirds of these passed in only one subject. A handful of Asian boys and girls passed in up to five subjects. Altogether sixteen per cent of both samples passed one or more 'O' level. The white sample tended to obtain higher CSE grades than Asians, 66 per cent of white boys and girls achieved CSE grade three as against 38 per cent Asian boys and 46 per cent Asian girls. There was a marked difference between the two samples in further education. Fifty-five per cent of Asian school leavers went on to full-time further education, mainly studying for 'O' levels. Eight per cent of whites were in full-time further education. Whites on part-time courses tended to be on block release linked to their employment, Asians studying part-time tended to be unemployed. The authors conclude that the Asians' belief in the importance of formal qualifications, and their higher unemployment, makes it more likely they would seek further education, but that 'the courses which they are on are often of dubious value to potential employers'.

Driver, an anthropologist by training, undertook an ethnographic study of a West Midlands multi-racial school (Driver, 1977).[64] He was partially concerned to offer explanations for the lower school achievement of West Indian pupils. In the 'school form' he studied in depth, English boys who took CSE exams obtained 12·3 CSE passes, English girls 11·6, Asian boys 12·7, Asian girls 6·8, West Indian boys 7·6, West Indian girls 7·1. Although 'there are the substantially lower results obtained by West Indian boys and girls' to be considered, Driver notes the greater persistence of West Indian girls over boys. Seventy-four per cent of West Indian girls got some sort of CSE result, against only 23 per cent of West Indian boys. Driver points to teacher 'failure to appreciate what the boys and their families expected of them' and peer group pressure, as explanations for poor West Indian male performance.

Driver and Ballard (1979)[65] reported on the performance of 'South Asian' and white pupils in 'O' level and CSE, in three inner-city secondary schools. The exam results of 276 Asian boys, 173 Asian girls, 358 English boys, and 305 English girls, school-leavers between 1975 and 1977, were noted. A 'scale of achievement' was constructed, allotting three units to an 'O' level pass or CSE grade one/two, two units to a CSE pass grade three/four, one unit to a CSE grade five pass, and statistics for each year in school were separately presented. Thus in 1975, at school A, the mean overall achievement score was $6 \cdot 8$ for Asian boys, $8 \cdot 5$ for Asian girls, $5 \cdot 1$ for English boys, $5 \cdot 8$ for English girls, at school D, the score was $8 \cdot 3$ for Asian boys, $6 \cdot 1$ for Asian girls, $7 \cdot 9$ for English boys, $5 \cdot 7$ for English girls.[66] The Asian pupils tended to score lower for English language than the whites. The authors conclude that 'Asian pupils achieve higher average results than do English pupils attending the same schools' with the qualification that the mean level of achievement remained low when set against the global standards of the British educational system. They postulate that Asian pupils in inner-city areas are less likely to be 'socialized for failure' than their English peers. Asian girls had a better record of 'school persistence' than the boys or English girls and the authors conclude that they are 'by no means so cowed and downtrodden as is often supposed'.

Driver (1979, 1980)[67] reported on the comparative performance of children of West Indian origin and whites at five inner-city multi-racial schools, including the three used in the Driver-Ballard analysis above. The examination results for those of 2,300 school-leavers who took public examinations in the years 1974–77 were examined, 590 of them being 'West Indian' pupils. In his 1979 article Driver reported that although the test results of West Indian children at eleven-plus tended to be lower than whites (at school B in 1976 a non-verbal test score at eleven-plus resulted in a score of $94 \cdot 6$ for English boys, $86 \cdot 6$ for West Indian boys), during their secondary school career, West Indian pupils 'pull ahead' and, overall, achieve better school-leaving qualifications ('O' level and CSE) than English pupils (although the published work does not make clear how many). West Indian girls tend to do better than West Indian boys, while English boys tend to do better than the girls. Thus, a rank overall achievement order at the five schools for the years 1975–77 show West Indian girls coming first six times, West Indian boys first twice, English boys first twice and English girls never first. English girls appear to do better at English language, appearing first on a rank order table four times, as against West Indian girls appearing first five times, English boys twice and West Indian boys once. Driver also records a higher persistence for West Indian boys and girls in staying on to take examinations. He explains his findings in terms of deterioration in the performance of English children in inner-city schools. The West Indian girls' better performance is explained in terms of family organization allotting 'power, property and decision-making' to women.

Bagley and Verma[68] have undertaken a further piece of research, as yet unpublished, which shows West Indian girls performing slightly better on the Brimer wide-span reading than West Indian boys, but all performing below the level of English pupils. The reading study was carried out in 39 secondary schools in urban areas – 29 West Indian boys, 35 girls, 416 English boys, 388 girls, and 35 Asian boys and fourteen girls were tested. The English scores were 18·3 for boys, 21·4 for girls. The West Indian scores were 15·5 for boys, 16·6 for girls. The Asian scored lowest – 10·2 for boys, 13·0 for girls.

Educational sub-normality

A major focus of concern over the past fifteen years has been the 'selection' out of the normal education system into schools for educationally subnormal children of a larger proportion of West Indian children than their presence in the total school population would warrant. The issue became of symbolic significance to the West Indian community, as it symbolized the general underachievement of their children in the school system.[69] However, there is very little actual research on the issue. Two ILEA reports,[70] official DES statistics,[71] Townsend's study of local education authorities[72] and Bernard Coard's short book,[73] which was a polemic, not research, form the basis of information about West Indian children and ESN-M schooling. The 1966 ILEA Inspectorate Report noted that while 13·2 per cent of children in inner London primary and secondary schools were defined as 'immigrant' 23·3 per cent of children in ESN schools were so defined. By September 1967 this figure had risen to 28·4 per cent. The ILEA undertook a survey of 22 ESN schools in May 1967, and the head teachers of these schools considered that it was four times as likely that an 'immigrant' child would be 'misplaced' in ESN school, than an indigenous child. The heads accounted for the over-referral of children of West Indian origin in terms of their behaviour in normal schools.

Townsend reproduced DES statistics for 1970 which showed that while 0·68 of all non-immigrant children in England attended ESN school, the figure for West Indian children was 2·33 but Indian and Pakistani pupils were 'under-represented' at 0·32 and 0·44 respectively. In Townsend's own research 68 LEAs answered a question as to whether they thought the proportion of 'immigrant' children in their ESN school was higher or lower than the overall proportion of immigrants in their schools. Authorities with over 30 per cent West Indian pupils answered 'higher' to this question. Townsend explained these findings in terms of the problem of assessment and lack of 'culture-fair' tests. Bernard Coard, then an ILEA teacher, later Minister for Education in Grenada in the West Indies, suggested that not only unsuitable tests, but also low teacher expectations, teacher stereotyping, cultural bias and the low self-esteem and self- concept of black children in a hostile society, could account for the official statistics. Tomlinson[74] in a study interviewing 120 professional people (teachers, psychologists, doctors etc.) who had made a decision on 40 children passing through the assessment processes for ESN-M education, found that the perceptions of head teachers of referring schools of the 'problems' of West Indian children, and their general referral criteria for ESN-M schooling, were almost identical, and that all professionals made decisions more speedily on 'immigrant' than indigenous children. It took an indigenous child two years, on average, to reach ESN-M school, passing through the assessment procedures; it only took an 'immigrant' child 11·4 months on average. Although suggestions for monitoring numbers of children in ESN-M schools have been made, no figures are available since 1972. However, Tomlinson estimates that while the proportion of children in the school population in ESN-M school is 0·5, the proportion for West Indian children is 2·5.

The 'ESN issue' has currently been overtaken by the issue of an over-representation of West Indian children in the variety of disruptive units, withdrawal classes and guidance units which have developed on an ad hoc basis during the 1970s. While there is much comment and speculation on this there is as yet no actual research. However at one such unit visited by Tomlinson in the course of her research, the population of West Indian pupils was 57 per cent, as against 42 per cent of children of Irish parentage and six per cent English parentage.[75]

Conclusion

As a great many commentators have noted, both small and large-scale studies using individual and group tests indicate that the performance of 'immigrant' children tends to be lower than indigenous, that 'immigrant' tests scores improve with length of schooling in Britain, that children born in Britain and receiving all their education in the UK perform better than 'immigrant' children, and that West Indian scores tend to be the lowest of all ethnic minority group scorers.

Of the 33 studies of West Indian educational performance reported here, 26 show the children to score lower than white children on individual or group tests or to be over-represented in ESN schools and under-represented in higher school streams. Five studies indicate that on certain tests (for example, the draw-a-man) or under certain conditions (for example, having 'middle-class' parents) West Indian children do as well as whites, and two studies indicate that at O/CSE level, performance may be equal to whites, or better, in urban schools. Of the nineteen studies of Asian educational performance, twelve indicate a lower score than whites on individual or group tests, or under-representation in selective schooling, or slightly fewer O/CSE passes than whites. Four studies indicate that on certain tests (for example, number tests) or under certain conditions (for example, length of schooling in Britain) Asian children do as well as, or better than white. Three studies suggest that at O/CSE level Asian performance is at least equal to white in urban schools.

The explanations offered for these research results range through disadvantage, socio-economic class, migration shock, family difference and organization, cultural factors, child-minding, school and teacher expectations, stereotyping, female dominance, self-esteem and identity problems and racial hostility.

It is not the purpose of this article to comment on results or explanations or on the value of continuing to make comparisons between ethnic groups and indigenous children based on individual or group tests. However, it is encouraging to note that despite minority under-representation in selective education and over-representation in lower 'streams' and special schools, on the basis of school-leaving qualifications – perhaps the most realistic measure of performance – some Asian and West Indian pupils are achieving 'O' levels and CSEs at least on a par with indigenous school-leavers in inner-city schools, although there is, to date, no evidence the 'A' level performance will allow ethnic minority children to move into higher education or professional training 'equally' with indigenous children. Research could now perhaps focus on factors which make for 'success' in the educational performance of minority group children.

Acknowledgement

With thanks to Chris Bagley, University of Surrey, who kindly read this article over to check for errors and omissions.

References

1. Goldman, R. J. and Taylor, F. 1966, 'Coloured Immigrant Children. A survey of research studies and literature on their educational problems and potential – in Britain', *Educational Research* Vol 8, no 3.
2. Bagley, C. 1979, 'A Comparative Perspective on the Education of Black Children in Britain', *Comparative Education* Vol 15, no 1, March.
3. Hegarty, S. 1978, *Manual for the N.F.E.R. Tests of Learning Ability* (individual form) NFER see also Haynes, J. 1971. *Educational Assessment of Immigrant Pupils* NFER, Stones, E. 1979. 'The Colour of Conceptual Learning' in (eds) Verma, G. K. and Bagley, C. *Race Education and Identity*, MacMillan.
4. Hegarty, S. and Lucas, D. 1979, *Able to Learn – the pursuit of culture – fair assessment*, NFER.
5. Bagley, C. 1979, op. cit.
6. Rex, J. 1972, 'Nature versus Nurture – the Significance of the Revived Debate', in (eds) Richardson, K. and Spears, D. *Race Culture and Intelligence*, Penguin.
7. Goldman and Taylor, 1966, op. cit.
8. Vernon, P. E. 1965, 'Environmental Handicaps and Intellectual Development', *Brit. J. of Educational Psychology* 35, parts 1 and 2.
9. Reported in DES 1971, *The Education of Immigrants*, Education Survey 13, HMSO.
10. Alleyne, M. H. 1962, 'The Teaching of Bilingual Children: Intelligence and Attainment of Children in London, Wales and Trinidad whose Mother Tongue is not English', unpub MA diss, University of London.
11. Saint, C. K. 1963, 'Scholastic and Sociological Adjustment Problems of Punjabi-speaking Children in Smethwick', unpub? M.Ed. diss. University of Birmingham.
12. Houghton, V. P. 1966, 'A Report on the Scores of West Indian Immigrant Children and English Children on an Individually Administered Test', *Race*, Vol 8, no 1, IRR.
13. ILEA 959, *The Education of Immigrant Pupils in Primary Schools* – report of a working party of members of the inspectorate and schools psychological service, 1967.

14. Little, A., Mabey, C. and Whitacker, G. 1968, 'The Education of Immigrant Pupils in Inner London Primary Schools', *Race,* vol 9, no 4.
15. Bagley, C. 1968, 'The Educational Performance of Immigrant Children', *Race,* Vol 10, no 1. Also see the Introduction to *Race Education and Identity* (eds) Verma, G. K. and Bagley, C. 1979.
16. Little, A. 1975, (a) 'Performance of Children from Ethnic Minority Backgrounds in Primary Schools', *Oxford Review of Education,* Vol 1, no 2.
17. Little, A. 1978, 'Schools and Race' in *Five Views of Multi-Racial Britain,* Commission for Racial Equality.
18. Little, A. and Mabey, C. 1973, 'The Inner City' in (eds) Donnison, D. and Eveneley, D, London. *Urban patterns, problems and policies,* Heinemann.
19. Little, A. 1975, (a) op. cit. *Oxford Review of Education,* Vol 1, no 2.
    Little, A. 1975, (b) 'The Educational Achievement of Ethnic Minority Children in London Schools', in (eds) Verma, G. K. and Bagley, C. *Race and Education across Cultures,* Heinemann.
20. Little, A. 1978, op. cit.
21. See Little, A. 1975, (a).
22. See Little, A. N. and Mabey, C. in (eds) Shonfield, A. and Shaw, S. *Social Indicators and Social Policy,* Heinemann 1972.
23. Halsey, A. H. 1972, *Educational Priority EPA Problems and Policies,* Vol 1, HMSO.
24. *Children and Their Primary Schools,* 1967, HMSO.
25. Payne, J. (ed) 1974, *Educational Priority – EPA Surveys and Statistics,* Vol 2, HMSO.
26. Payne, 1974, ibid, p. 8.
27. Payne, 1974, op. cit., p. 12.
28. Payne, 1974, op. cit., p. 21.
29. Barnes, J. 1973, *Educational Priority – curriculum innovation in London EPAs,* HMSO.
30. Little, A. 1975, (a) and (b) op. cit.
31. Graham, P. J. and Meadows, C. E. 1967, 'Psychiatric Disorders in the Children of West Indian Immigrants', *Journal of Child Psychology and Psychiatry,* Vol 8.
32. Wiles, S. 1968, 'Children from Overseas', IRR Newsletter, Feb/June.
33. Phillips, C. 1979, 'Educational Under-Achievement in Different Ethnic Groups', *Education Research,* Vol 21, no 2.
34. Payne, J. 1969, 'A Comparative Study of the Mental Ability of 7 and 8 year old British and West Indian Children in a West Midlands Town', *British J. of Educational Psychology,* Vol 39.
35. McFie, J. and Thompson, J. 1970, 'The Intellectual Abilities of Immigrant Children', *British J. of Educational psychology,* Vol 40.
36. Ashby, B., Morrison, A. and Butcher, H. 1970, 'The Abilities and Attainments of Immigrant Children', *Research in Education,* no 4.
37. Bhatnagar, J. 1970, *Immigrants at School,* Cornmarket Press.
38. See Blok and Dworkin (eds) 1976, *The IQ Controversy,* Quartet Books.
39. Bagley, C. 1971, 'Social Environment and Intelligence in West Indian Children in London', *Social and Economic Studies,* 20.

40. Bagley, C. 1975, 'On the Intellectual Equality of the Races', in (ed) Verma, G. K. and Bagley, C, *Race and Education Across Cultures*, Heinemann.
41. Yule, W., Berger, M., Rutter, M. and Yule, B. 1975, 'Children of West Indian Immigrants. Intellectual Performance and Reading Attainment', *J. Child Psychology and Psychiatry*, Vol 16.
42. McEwan, E. C., Gipps, C. V. and Sumner, R. 1975, *Language Proficiency in the Multi-Racial Junior School*, NFER.
43. Edwards, V. K. 1976, 'Effects of Dialect on the Comprehension of West Indian Children', *Educational Research*, Vol 18, no 2.
44. Edwards, V. K. 1978, 'Language Attitudes and Under-performance in West Indian Children', *Educational Review*, Vol 30, no 1.
    Edwards, V. K. 1979, *The West Indian Language Issue in British Schools*, RKP.
45. Jones, P. J. 1979, 'An Evaluation of the Effect of Sport on the Integration of West Indian School Children', Unpublished PhD. thesis, University of Surrey.
46. Black People's Progressive Association and Redbridge Community Relations Council 1978, *Cause For Concern – West Indian Pupils in Redbridge*.
47. Ward, J. 1978, 'An Observational Study of Interaction and Progress for the Immigrant in School', *Educational Studies*, Vol 4, no 2.
48. Bagley, C., Bart, M. and Wong, J. 1979, 'Antecedents of Scholastic Success in West Indian Ten-Year-Olds in London', in (eds) Verma, G. K. and Bagley, C. *Race Education and Identity*, MacMillan.
49. Stones, E. 1975, 'The Colour of Conceptual Learning', *Research Intelligence*, BERA, Bulletin, Vol 1, no 2.
    also Stones, E. 1979, 'The Colour of Conceptual Learning' in (eds) Verma, G. K. and Bagley, C. *Race Education and Identity*, Heinemann.
50. Robinson, V. 1980, 'The Achievement of Asian Children', *Educational Research*, Vol 22, no 2.
51. Essen, J. and Ghodsian, M. 1979, 'The Children of Immigrants: School Performance', *New Community*, Vol VII, no 3.
52. Bagley, C. 1980, 'Behaviour and Achievement in Ethnic Minority Children in a National, Longitudinal Survey', in (eds) Verma, G. K. and Bagley, C. *Self-Esteem, Achievement and Multi-Cultural Education*, MacMillan.
53. Townsend, H. E. R. 1971, *Immigrant Pupils in England – the LEA Response*, NFER.
54. Townsend, H. E. R. and Brittan, E. 1972, *Organisation in Multi- Racial Schools*, NFER.
55. DES 1970, *Statistics in Education*, A convenient table of DES 1970 Statistics is published by Edwards, V. K. 1979. p. 3, op. cit.
56. Rex, J. and Tomlinson, S. 1979, *Colonial Immigrants in a British City*, RKP.
57. DES 1972, *The Continuing Needs of Immigrants*, Education Survey 14, HMSO.
58. Townsend, H. E. R. and Brittan, E. 1972, op. cit.
59. Taylor, J. H. 1976, *The Half-Way Generation*, NFER.
60. Allen, S. and Smith, C. 1975, 'Minority Group Experience of the Transition from Education to Work', in (ed) P. Brannen *Entering the World of Work*, HMSO.
61. Rex, J. and Tomlinson, S. 1979, op. cit. Chapter 7.

62. Fowler, R., Littlewood, B. and Madigan, R. 1977, 'Immigrant School Leavers and the Search for Work', *Sociology*, Vol 11, no 1.
63. Brooks, D. and Singh, K. 1978, *Aspirations Versus Opportunities – Asian and White School-leavers in the Midlands*, Walsall, CRC, Leicester CRC.
64. Driver, G. 1977, 'Cultural Competence' Social Power and School Achievement: West Indian Secondary School Pupils in the West Midlands', *New Community*, Vol V, no 4, 1977.
65. Driver, G. and Ballard, R. 1979, 'Comparing Performance in Multi-Racial Schools – South Asian Pupils at 16 Plus'. *New Community*, Vol VII, no 2.
66. See Driver and Ballard, ibid. 1979, the appendices to the article.
67. Driver, G. 1979, 'How West Indians do Better at School (Especially the Girls)', *New Society*, 17/1/80.
    Driver, G. 1980, *Beyond Underachievement*, Commission for Racial Equality.
68. Bagley, C. and Verma, G. K. 1980, 'Brimer Wide-Span Reading Scores in Pupils aged 14–16 years in 39 English Secondary Schools', unpublished paper.
69. See Tomlinson, S. 1978, 'West Indian Children and ESN Schooling', *New Community*, Vol VI, no 3.
70. ILEA report No. 959. (1966).
    ILEA report No. 657. (1967).
71. DES *Statistics in Education. Vols 1 Schools* 1967–72.
72. Townsend, H. E. R. 1971, op. cit.
73. Coard, B. 1971, *How the West Indian Child is made ESN in the British School System*, New Beacon Books.
74. Tomlinson, S. 1981, *Educational Subnormality: A Study in Decision-Making*, RKP (forthcoming).
75. Tomlinson, S. 1981, ibid. Chapter 7.

CHAPTER 3.2

COMPARING PERFORMANCE IN MULTIRACIAL SCHOOLS: SOUTH ASIAN PUPILS AT 16-PLUS*
GEOFFREY DRIVER AND ROGER BALLARD

South Asian educational achievement: previous evidence

Despite the frequent assumption that ethnic minority children generally pose major problems for educators, even casual conversation with teachers in multiracial schools reveals that, by the end of their school career, South Asian boys and girls tend to achieve results which are at least equal to, and often considerably better than, those of their English classmates. Indeed these same teachers often comment on the striking over-representation of South Asian children in their sixth forms.

This view of South Asian school success has been substantiated in recent research by Taylor[1] and Singh.[2] Taylor announces quite simply that 'Asians do better', but his generalization needs to be carefully qualified. His data base was confined to 67 boys who left schools serving the Elswick district of Newcastle upon Tyne between 1962 and 1967. His sample was restricted to boys only, and the size of the local minority settlement was so small that there were on average less than two male South Asian pupils in each year of the five schools which the great majority of his respondents attended. Their experiences were thus effectively that of a dispersed population, and so rather different from those of South Asian pupils in most other British cities. Yet within these limitations Taylor shows that both educational achievement and commitment to educational success was a great deal higher amongst his South Asian respondents than it was amongst a matched sample of English boys.

* Appendix 1 to *Beyond Underachievement*, 1980, Commission for Racial Equality, pp. 58–70. By permission of the Social Science Research Council and Macmillan, London and Basingstoke.

Karamjit Singh has provided more up-to-date evidence in his study of South Asian school leavers in 1975 in Leicester. This time both sexes were included, and the study was conducted in a city with a much larger minority population. Twenty per cent of the sixteen-plus cohort in Leicester schools in 1975 were pupils of South Asian origin, so their concentration in the schools he studied was obviously a good deal higher. Nevertheless, patterns essentially similar to those described by Taylor emerge. The overwhelming majority of Singh's South Asian subjects attended secondary modern schools (his figures were collected in the last year before a comprehensive system was introduced), but their achievements in sixteen-plus examinations seem to have been no worse than their 'white' peers, despite the fact that 42 per cent of his Asian sample had not received their primary education in Britain. Moreover, a very much higher proportion of 'Asian' than 'white' pupils transferred to grammar schools to take sixth form courses at sixteen-plus, and of those who left school, more than half enrolled for courses at colleges of further education.

Yet there are major problems in assessing the significance of Singh's data, let alone for using it as a basis for generalization. He concerns himself with school-leavers alone, and so his results are not representative of the whole age-cohort. The response rate which he achieved from both his 'Asian' sample and his 'white' control group was low, and for girls among the latter unacceptably so. He aggregates information across different schools in a way which, as we argue later, cannot be regarded as statistically satisfactory. Finally the number of 'white' pupils with which his 'Asian' sample is compared is so small (on average four boys and two girls per school) that statistical comparison cannot be reliable. Yet despite these cautionary comments, the underlying pattern of Singh's results does seem to be very similar to that reported by Taylor. Finally it is also worth referring to a much smaller survey by Brooks, reported in the same pamphlet as Singh's work. As a result of a study of South Asian school-leavers in Walsall, Brooks concludes that 'it is the similarities between white and Asian educational performances which are impressive, rather than any differences'.[3]

In view of the heat which has been generated in the debate on education and the ethnic minorities, it is striking that there are virtually no studies of the educational achievements of South Asian pupils in British schools other than those reported above. A few studies have been carried out using psychometric tests, but we would agree with Taylor that, in the long run:

performance in such concrete terms as certificates obtained, terminal age of full-time education and admission to higher education is harder evidence than either (teacher) assessment or test scores.[4]

Examination performance by school-leavers: 1975–7

It is in this context that the statistical information presented in this paper should be viewed. The data were collected during 1978, in the course of a broad survey of the sixteen-plus examination performance of minority and majority school-leavers in Britain between 1975 and 1977. Driver's interest was in differences in the performance of West Indian boys and girls, the results of which are reported elsewhere.[5] A great deal of information on the performance of South Asian pupils was, however, collected at the same time, and it is that which will be discussed here.

The original plan was to survey local authority schools in different parts of the country, but it eventually only proved possible to gain access to schools in five LEAs. Each of these schools contained substantial numbers of West Indian pupils, but only three contained sufficient numbers of South Asian pupils to make statistical analysis worthwhile. The figures presented here thus concern only three of the original five schools.

In each school surveyed records concerning all pupils in two or three of the most recent generations of pupils reaching sixteen-plus were examined, and their results in 'O' level and CSE examinations were noted. Teachers who had known the pupils well were asked to classify them on an ethnic basis. The categories available were South Asian, West Indian, other ethnic minorities, and English, as explained in Driver's report.[6] The statistics presented here concern the examination results of 1,523 individuals, of whom 276 were South Asian boys, 173 were South Asian girls, 358 were English boys and 305 were English girls. Information concerning a further 411 pupils at these three schools, most of whom were categorized as West Indian, has not been included here.

It is, alas, too simplistic to approach these data as if they referred to a homogenous population. If it were possible to compute together the results of pupils from different age grades and schools, it would make the computation a very staightforward matter. However, such a procedure is technically unacceptable, since it involves the summing of unlike unit-scores of achievement. Pupils attending different schools, and indeed those in each year in each school, face different curricular structures, from which different kinds of assessment, based on different course work taught by different teachers have evolved. Given these unique qualities, direct cross-computations between years and schools must be regarded as unsafe. To avoid these difficulties, statistics for each year in each school have been separately presented.

Acceptable scales of achievement are also notoriously difficult to construct, and all measures necessarily contain an element of arbitrary weighting. The system used here is one in which 'O' level and CSE passes in different subjects were scored as follows:

For an 'O' level pass, or for CSE Grades 1 and 2	—	**3 units**
For CSE Grades 3 and 4	—	**2 units**
For CSE Grade 5	—	**1 unit**
For a pupil absent, unplaced or not entered	—	**0 units**

The scores which each pupil obtained in each examination were then added together, giving each individual an overall sixteen-plus result. Since individuals were identified as belonging to pupil-categories arranged by sex and ethnicity, average results for each category could be obtained. These average results were then placed in rank order for each school-leaving generation, and the levels of achievement for each pupil-category, relative one to another, shown.

The results of this process are set out in Tables 1 and 2 (see at end). While Table 1 gives the mean results, readers are warned that no comparison is possible between the immediate results for categories in different schools and generations. To avoid the pitfalls of such unwise use of statistics, it is recommended that the relative performance of pupil-categories, as represented by the rank-order tabulations in Table 2, be used to make comparisons between populations of school-leavers in different years and different schools. The tabulation of resulting position points gives some indication of the *consistency* of achievement by pupils in the four different categories across the school-leaving generations investigated. The figures broadly indicate that there is a fairly wide, and certainly a very consistent difference in mean levels of achievement between South Asian and English pupils in the set of seven school-leaving generations. When these ethnic categories are further divided by sex, it is evident that, while English boys obtained higher mean results than English girls, this tendency was reversed (although in a less clear-cut way) amongst South Asian boys and girls.

There are also differences between pupil categories in terms of their academic persistence. The fraction of course entrants at fourteen-plus who actually stayed on to achieve a result of some sort at sixteen-plus provides a convenient measure of school persistence. From Table 3 it can be seen that South Asian pupils, and especially the girls, got consistently high persistence scores, while there was a much higher drop-out rate amongst English pupils. English girls showed a particularly strong tendency to drop out of school.

These differences suggest a possible qualification to the trend indicated in Table 2. Can the superiority of South Asian pupils in mean performance be explained simply in terms of their greater persistence, rather than the achievement of better results among those who stayed the course? As Table 4 indicates, when examinees alone are considered, a consistent difference between South Asian and English achievement remains. Alongside this it is also evident that the gap between English boys and girls is reduced, while South Asian boys appear to move above South Asian girls. It may be that South Asian girls have more persistence than their brothers, but do not necessarily achieve quite such high average results if they stay on. On the English side, these figures seem to reflect the strong propensity of girls in these schools to drop out or to leave school without achieving anything more than minimal qualifications.

Patterns of achievement

The data available also allow us to analyze patterns of achievement subject by subject. Quite clearly English Language is an area of critical importance but, as Table 5 shows, South Asian pupils have no clear overall lead in this subject.

On the other hand it needs to be stressed that their achievement was in no way inferior either, despite the probability that for many of them English would not have been their first language. It is also clear that English language is one of the few subjects in which the performance of English girls emerges as superior to that of English boys.

It is evident that, as far as South Asian pupils in these schools are concerned, any handicap in school achievement arising from the fact that English is not their mother tongue has largely been overcome, at least in comparison with their English class-mates, by the age of sixteen-plus. It thus seems probable that the South Asian pupils whose achievements are reported here made dramatic progress in the course of their secondary school careers. The clue to this may be provided by the figures in Table 6. By good fortune, records of pupils' reading ages at thirteen-plus for one age-cohort (that represented by column A3) were discovered at one school.

From this admittedly very limited set of figures it would appear that, for this particular group of pupils, an important transformation may have taken place in their final years at school. While at thirteen-plus the South Asian children came a full year behind the English children in mean reading age, with the South Asian boys as back markers, by sixteen-plus the situation had changed completely. That group of South Asian pupils achieved higher mean examination results than the English pupils behind whom they had formerly lagged.

Having made this general point, it must be stressed that it is not here suggested that there are no problems at all in the sphere of English language as far as South Asian pupils are concerned. In the statistics which have been presented so far care has been taken not to compare mean levels of achievement either across schools, or against any absolute standard, for our concern has been to explore differential patterns of achievement within particular age-cohorts. Yet when pupils move on to take a job, or enrol for a further qualification, their achievements will be measured against more universal standards. The precise nature of the standards employed may vary a good deal, but possession of 'O' level English language or its near equivalent at CSE is invariably a component part of the threshold demanded. In fact only thirteen per cent of the pupils whose results are discussed here cleared that hurdle. This figure reflects the low levels of academic achievement which are very often found in inner city schools, whether or not they contain minority ethnic pupils. By the standards of such schools, the performance of South Asian pupils in our survey was not poor, and they certainly could not be said to be holding back their English counterparts. The general standard of achievement in these schools is, however, almost certainly lower than in schools in general. Given this situation, the challenge for educational policy lies in improving the educational performance of *all* the pupils who attend them, not just those who are drawn from the ethnic minorities.

It seems probable that the South Asian children in our sample were far from reaching their full potential in English language, for they consistently out-performed their English classmates in other critical subjects. In mathematics, for instance (see Table 7), their superiority could hardly have been more marked. South Asian children also performed well in physics and biology (in schools A and E) as well as in integrated science (as these subjects were taught in school D). The figures which are set out in detail in Tables 8, 9 and 10 also reveal some striking differences between the sexes. Amongst English pupils, biology was, along with English language, one of the few areas in which girls achieved higher mean results than the boys, while in physics, traditionally a 'male' subject, the boys were consistently ahead of the girls. South Asian pupils, on the evidence of the results shown here, seem to be much less strongly affected by these essentially English stereotypes of the different sciences. South Asian girls did less well in physics, where they were overtaken by English boys. Otherwise the differential in performance between South Asian boys and girls seems narrower and less clear-cut than it is among English boys and girls.

Discussion

What are the general implications of these findings? In the first place it is clear that we can confirm Taylor's general conclusion, but on the basis of a much larger and more up-to-date sample. Asian pupils achieve higher average results than do English pupils attending the same secondary schools. This does, however, need to be hedged about with a few important qualifications. The schools from which data were collected were by no means representative of secondary schools in general. They were chosen precisely because they were multiracial in character, and in fact just under half of the children in the age-cohorts discussed here were identified as being South Asian or West Indian. All three schools were located in inner urban areas, but there is no reason to suppose that the patterns of achievement recorded for English pupils in this study are markedly different from those that might have been found in non-multiracial schools in similar environmental and social contexts. We are, however, fully aware of the wide disparities in achievement which can be observed in different schools, as recently shown by Rutter et al.,[7] and that disparities often exist between inner-urban schools and those which are located in more socially prestigious suburbs. It seems that South Asian pupils made more effective use of the educational resources available to them than did their English class mates, even if the mean level of achievement still remained low when set against the global standards of the British educational system.

The statistics presented here are the outcome of a small project with limited aims, in which no attempt was made to examine patterns of performance in non-multiracial schools, or those located in suburban areas. Furthermore, attention was focused on sixteen-plus results, principally because these mark the final and comprehensive assessment made of all pupils at the end of their period of compulsory education.

Comparison of educational achievements across broad population categories at later stages in the educational process is much more problematic,
because participation is voluntary. Nevertheless post-secondary qualifications are now a prerequisite for entry into virtually all professional and
technical occupations, and this prompts the posing of a further set of
questions. How strong are aspirations to achieve post-secondary qualifications amongst members of different population categories? How well have
members of such groups been equipped during their secondary education
to embark on such courses? And finally, how successful have they been in
gaining the qualifications to which they aspire?

The South Asian population in Britain is of course extremely diverse,
but some common features can be detected. Although some migrants,
such as doctors, have come to Britain with considerable educational
qualifications, the great majority of immigrants were from rural areas, and
had little or no formal education. Their principal concern was to earn and
save money rapidly, so they tended to withdraw their children from school
at the earliest opportunity so their earnings could begin to contribute to
the family income. None the less, Ballard's recent ethnographic evidence
suggests that, once having settled down in Britain, members of many
South Asian families have begun to develop much higher educational and
occupational aspirations for their children. Not only have they encouraged
them to work hard at school, but they have generally been prepared to
extend considerable support to their children's efforts to gain further
qualifications in the tertiary sector.

Even though the South Asian pupils in our survey were relatively
successful, this does not necessarily mean that many of them were actually
equipped with the minimum requirements for entry into more advanced
training courses. It is here that the rather broader scope of Taylor and
Singh's work is of particular value, for they considered the activities of
South Asian students at college as well as at school. Both studies show how
South Asians have used Colleges of Further Education to top up their
school-leaving credits – they are not the only students to do this of course –
in order to acquire the basic qualifications which would allow them to
move onwards and upwards educationally. Indeed, no less than half of
Singh's respondents were enrolled full-time at FE Colleges. Singh himself
sounds a note of caution about the eventual value of such activities, for, as
he puts it:

A relatively high proportion of the South Asian sample were taking a two
year 'O' level course at the age of sixteen-plus, and will presumably be

eighteen-plus by the time their courses are completed . . . the reaction of a prospective employer to a young person coming to him with one or more 'O' levels or a college certificate at eighteen-plus is highly debatable.[8]

Some students may well fall by the wayside, but the strength of their determination to succeed cannot be gainsaid. Their aspirations are clearly much higher than those of most English boys and girls from inner urban neighbourhoods, but it would be rash to assume that their expectations are always unrealistic, as teachers and careers officers not infrequently do. In this context Taylor's work provides a valuable perspective, for he shows how South Asians in similar circumstances in Newcastle used the FE system with considerable success. Nine of his eighteen respondents who continued in full-time education (out of an original group of 53) succeeded in gaining places on university or polytechnic degree-level courses. Only one of his English respondents got that far.

There is as yet no reliable information available on the numbers of South Asian students emerging from universities and colleges with advanced academic and professional qualifications. It is our impression, however, on the basis of casual observation that their numbers are obvious and growing as a proportion of the total student population.[9] Certainly at least some South Asian students are achieving the ambitious educational goals which they have set themselves, despite the many obstacles in their path. We may therefore conclude that South Asian students are making extensive use of the educational facilities available at the tertiary as well as the secondary level. A better understanding of the precise way in which they are doing this, and the extent of their success, must await further research.

Conclusion

Our central concern here is with the secondary school pupils about whom we have presented detailed statistics. The schools on which we have concentrated served largely inner-city areas. We are fully aware both of the disparity of resources between such schools and those located elsewhere, and the implications they may hold for the aspirations and expectations of many of the pupils found within them. Yet the figures presented here indicate that South Asian pupils show much less sign of being socialized to failure than seems to be the case with their English peers. South Asians, in common with members of other minorities, do not reproduce the norms of educational performance characteristic of the social class context in which they live by virtue of their inner city residence. Far from being a handicap or disadvantage, as is so often supposed, minority ethnic affiliation must surely be regarded as a positive resource.

Yet to achieve their aspirations, South Asian pupils may have a good deal of ground to make up. Though successful in the schools they attend, their performance may look less handsome when compared with that of pupils in other areas. The work of Taylor and Singh indicates that, while some of their South Asian subjects were able to move on straightforwardly to more advanced study in the sixth form, many found themselves held back by an insufficiency in their achievements in the sixteen-plus examinations. As a result, a considerable number of their respondents found themselves utilizing a critical period in their career development to acquire the necessary threshold qualifications for further study. The results of the present investigation indicate that, although there may still be considerable numbers of South Asian pupils with 'topping up' problems, their number is probably diminishing, although difficulties do still remain in the crucial area of English Language.

A further striking aspect of the figures presented here is afforded by the differences in performance between South Asian boys and girls. The girls obtained higher mean results in all subjects except physics, and the girls had a markedly better record for school persistence than the boys. While the girls' persistence quite probably largely reflects parental constraints, their examination results nevertheless indicate that they were exploiting the opportunities available to them with some success. The school records suggest that South Asian girls are by no means so cowed and downtrodden as is often supposed: in fact the reported levels of achievement for English girls are far more consonant with such a view of the feminine role.

The only way in which explanation of such data can be carried forward is, we believe, by a much closer examination of the content and quality of the transactions that take place between teachers and pupils in the educational process. Every effort must be made to understand what transpires in the course of these interactions, and especially the way in which teachers and pupils of different sorts negotiate with one another, ordering their behaviour on terms which have evolved in specific, but differentiated, cultural and social contexts. We believe that the adoption of such a perspective is crucial to the understanding of differences in outcomes amongst pupil categories of various kinds.

At the level of explanation, the kernel of our argument is that there is a need for more ethnography, particularly within the context of the school.

The figures presented here have allowed us to do nothing more than set up some crude signposts, which indicate that pupils' ethnic affiliations are related in a complex way to patterns of school achievement. 'South Asian' and 'English', the categorical labels which we have used, are of course extremely crude, and more sensitive analysis would need to be ordered in terms of much smaller operational groupings such as Ramgarhia Sikhs or Gujarati Muslims. Such investigations would probably need to be much more ethnographic than statistical in their foundations. They would examine the interaction of the particular styles, skills, perceptions and goals which ethnic communities are continuously evolving, and which pupils and teachers of different ethnic backgrounds bring to their schools. With such information to hand, policy-makers and practitioners would be in a much better position to make a more realistic evaluation of educational processes and problems.

Notes and references

1. J. H. Taylor, *The Half-Way Generation: A Study of Asian Youths in Newcastle upon Tyne*, NFER Publishing Company, Windsor, 1976.
2. Dennis Brooks and Karamjit Singh, *Aspirations Versus Opportunities: Asian and White School Leavers in the Midlands*, Walsall CRC and Leicester CRC in conjunction with the Commission for Racial Equality, 1978.
3. Ibid., p. 15.
4. Taylor, p. 154.
5. G. Driver, *Sex Differences in Secondary School Performance*, (report submitted to the Commission for Racial Equality, 1979); this was subsequently published as *Beyond Underachievement: case studies of English, West Indian and Asian school-leavers at 16-plus* (London: Commission for Racial Equality, 1980).
6. Ibid.
7. Rutter, M., et al., *Fifteen Thousand Hours*, London, Open Books, 1979.
8. Brooks and Singh, op. cit., p. 68.
9. Figures obtained for one university show that the number of UK resident South Asian students embarking on undergaduate degree courses was three times larger for the 1978 entry than it was in 1970.

Table 1 Mean overall school achievement scores for all pupils (scores in sixteen-plus units)

School age grade	A 1	A 2	A 3	D 1	D 2	D 3	E 1	E 2
South Asian boys	6·8	7·5	7·8	8·3	7·8	8·6	8·6	8·2
South Asian girls	8·5	8·3	7·7	6·1	8·5	11·0	9·7	5·3
English boys	5·1	7·6	7·6	7·9	6·2	7·5	7·8	3·7
English girls	5·8	3·7	4·9	5·7	6·9	6·2	6·6	4·5

Table 2 Rank order of pupil categories for overall school achievement

School age grade	A 1	A 2	A 3	D 1	D 2	D 3	E 1	E 2	Position points aggregate
South Asian boys	3	2½	3	4	3	3	3	4	25½
South Asian girls	4	4	3	2	4	4	4	3	28
English boys	1	2½	3	3	1	2	2	1	15½
English girls	2	1	1	1	2	1	1	2	11

In Tables 2–5 and 7–10, the rank order positions in each generation of school-leavers have been represented by a points-system. This allocates four points to the pupil-category in the top position, and ranges down to one point for the pupil-category with the lowest score.

Table 3 Rank order of pupil categories for persistence in school work

School age grade	A 1	A 2	A 3	D 1	D 2	D 3	E 1	E 2	Position points aggregate
South Asian boys	4	1½	3	2	3	3	2	4	22½
South Asian girls	3	1½	4	4	4	4	4	3	27½
English boys	2	3	2	3	1	2	3	2	18
English girls	1	4	1	1	2	1	1	1	12

Table 4 Rank order of pupil categories for results obtained at sixteen-plus per examinee

School age grade	A 1	A 2	A 3	D 1	D 2	D 3	E 1	E 2	Position points aggregate
South Asian boys	2	3	3	4	2	3	3	4	24
South Asian girls	4	4	1½	1	3	4	2	2	21½
English boys	1	2	4	3	4	2	1	1	18
English girls	3	1	1½	2	1	1	4	3	16½

Table 5 Rank order of pupil categories for overall achievement in English language

School age grade	A 1	A 2	A 3	D 1	D 2	D 3	E 1	E 2	Position points aggregate
South Asian boys	2	2	1	4	3	2½	1	3½	19
South Asian girls	1	3½	2	2	1½	4	4	2	20
English boys	3	3½	3	2	1½	1	3	1	18
English girls	4	1	4	2	4	2½	2	3½	23

Table 6 Mean reading ages at thirteen-plus for four pupil categories in the 1977 school-leaving age-grade at school A

	Mean RA	Rank order position points
South Asian boys	9·22	1
South Asian girls	9·73	2
English boys	10·25	3
English girls	10·66	4

Table 7 Rank order of pupil categories for overall achievement in mathematics

School age grade	A 1	A 2	A 3	D 1	D 2	D 3	E 1	E 2	Position points aggregate
South Asian boys	3½	2	3	3	4	4	1	4	24½
South Asian girls	3½	4	4	2	3	3	4	2½	26
English boys	2	3	2	4	2	2	3	1	19
English girls	1	1	1	1	1	1	2	2½	10½

Table 8 Rank order of pupil categories for overall achievement in physics

School age grade	A 1	A 2	A 3	E 1	E 2	Position points aggregate
South Asian boys	3	4	3	4	4	18
South Asian girls	1½	2	2	3	2	10½
English boys	4	3	4	2	3	16
English girls	1½	1	1	1	1	5½

Table 9 Rank order of pupil categories for overall achievement in biology

School age grade	A 1	A 2	A 3	E 1	E 2	Position points aggregate
South Asian boys	3	3	2	3	4	15
South Asian girls	4	4	3	4	2½	17½
English boys	2	1	1	2	1	7
English girls	1	2	4	1	2½	10½

Table 10 Rank order of pupil categories for overall achievement in integrated science

School age grade	D 1	D 2	D 3	Position points aggregate
South Asian boys	4	4	4	12
South Asian girls	3	3	2	8
English boys	2	2	3	7
English girls	1	1	1	3

SECTION 4

CURRICULUM

BIAS IN SCHOOL BOOKS: MESSAGES FROM THE ETHNOCENTRIC CURRICULUM*
DAVID HICKS

Images of the world

A recent survey of British attitudes to overseas aid described its findings as revealing a form of parochialism or 'national introversion'. Attitudes were generally ethnocentric and often racist (Bowles, 1978). The findings of this survey should not really be surprising because people's mental images of the world arise partly out of childhood socialization, partly from the way in which the media portrays other cultures and world events, and partly from the nature of the school curriculum and from teaching materials themselves. In turn these influences can only be understood in a historical context, i.e. the way in which they have been shaped by Britain's historical relationship with the rest of the world.

Thus, whilst many cultures may be ethnocentric to a lesser or greater degree and so take their own values as the norm against which to judge others, not all are racist. Hodge (1975) has defined racism as 'the belief in, and practice of, the domination of one social group, identified as a "race", over another social group, identified as another "race"'. On this basis racism can be seen to involve (i) the belief that people can be grouped according to discrete races; (ii) the belief that some such races are superior to others; and (iii) the belief that self-proclaimed superior races should control allegedly inferior ones.

Western notions of superiority, as the survey referred to above indicates, are still very much with us. They do not have to be conscious

---

* Commissioned article, previously unpublished. The Appendix is taken from pp. 144/5 of *The Slant of the Pen: Racism in Children's Books*, ed R. Preiswerk, World Council of Churches, Geneva, 1980.

but are part of the cultural baggage inherited from recent, and current, colonial relationships with so-called 'third world' countries. Since schooling is a reflection of culture the curriculum itself will essentially be ethnocentric. That is to say, it will be mono-cultural rather than multi-cultural and will accordingly overlook, or misunderstand, the needs of children from minority groups and misinterpret events which require the ability to understand other cultural viewpoints. Thus inequality will be perpetuated in the classroom, racist attitudes often unwittingly held, and since ethnocentrism provides its own defence mechanism, any criticisms to these ends probably ignored.

Other contributions to this book have illustrated some of the effects of the ethnocentric curriculum. The particular focus here is on school textbooks which, it has been argued, one can expect to be outdated by 50 years in their thinking about social affairs. After briefly referring to the role of school books in the classroom this chapter looks at the state of textbook analysis in North America, Europe and the UK, the portrayal of the 'third world' in geography textbooks and guidelines for use both in publishing and education to heighten awareness of the need for unbiased books.

Despite educational cutbacks and the trend towards non-book teaching resources the school textbook remains an integral part of most children's learning experiences. Whilst such books will be only one of the influences at work on a child's imagination they are nevertheless a significant influence. Research on the interaction between the reader and the printed word has been usefully reviewed by Zimet (1976) and, more recently, by Campbell and Wirtenberg (1980). A recurring theme is that children's attitudes differ depending on whether books portray other cultures favourably or unfavourably. The greater attitude and behaviour changes seem to occur when non-racist books are used and opportunity is provided for children to discuss their reading experiences. The printed word may also have an effect on reading achievement in that if a child cannot easily identify with characters or events then their interest and motivation is less. This may in particular affect minority group children when they find themselves negatively, or seldom, portrayed in books.

Textbook analysis

Textbook analysis has a long history both in North America and Europe stretching back to at least the First World War and it is against this background that recent developments in the field need to be seen.

North America

Between 1937 and 1944 several studies were made of the treatment of foreign relations in American textbooks. These studies revealed 'important factual inaccuracies and omissions, uneven selection of data, anachronisms, and excessive stress on conflict and on the exotic and the picturesque' as well as 'an American hegemony reminiscent of Great Britain's days of imperialism' (McDiarmid & Pratt, 1971). Such images were not to change quickly. Another important early study looked at the portrayal of five American minority groups and found them either largely ignored or stereotyped in textbooks.

It was during the 1960s, with the growth of the civil rights movement, that attention became increasingly focused on the education system as a potential lever for social change. Many policies were attacked as discriminatory and this included the presence of widespread bias in teaching materials. Much of the 1960s was thus devoted to analyzing what was wrong with textbooks and putting pressure on publishers for change. Later studies of the portrayal of minority groups began to show some small changes: the position of black Americans in contemporary society was no longer ignored, but native Americans were still seldom referred to except in a historical context.

With the 1970s came more specific studies, often by minority group organizations, which not only identified distortions and omissions but also set out what the missing perspectives were. Amongst these, for example, was an analysis of the presentation of native Americans (Costo, 1970) and one on the portrayal of minorities in history textbooks. During this period interesting studies were also made of the treatment of the Middle East, of Asia and Africa (Hall, 1976) in school textbooks. All were extremely useful in identifying, in detail, the common ethnocentric and racist images.

One of the most detailed studies was Canadian and looked not only at minority groups but also the treatment of various contemporary issues (McDiarmid & Pratt, 1971). The authors noted that in ignoring so many critical social issues 'many texts mistake a middle-of-the-road position for objectivity, as though immorality inhered in the controversy and not in the subject of discussion'. The other unique feature of this study was the development of a simple statistical technique for measuring bias in textbooks.

Gradually therefore changes in textbooks began to take place and some publishing houses produced their own guidelines on avoiding racism in books. Others have argued, however, that the changes are more apparent than real and some evidence indicates that there may now be a backlash against concern for non-racist books. However, taken overall, the North American research on bias in textbooks is relatively comprehensive and forms an important source of inspiration both for research and practical work on bias in books.

Europe

Until recently this certainly cannot be said of textbook research emanating from Europe (the UK is treated separately below) which traditionally has had more of an inward-looking focus. Concern dates from the period immediately after the First World War and related to the portrayal of Germany in the textbooks of other countries, particularly France, where one could learn, for example, that 'the savages on the other side of the Rhine have always menaced us . . .'

In 1925 the League of Nations passed the Casares Resolution which recommended interchange and consultation between countries about the way in which their books described each other. After the Second World War UNESCO sponsored a series of conferences on writing and revision of textbooks and in 1951 the Georg Eckert Institute for International Textbook Research was set up at Brunswick in West Germany. In the 1950s and 60s the Council of Europe was active in promoting the revision of history and geography textbooks.

Much of this research, however, failed to tackle the real issues of racism and cultural imperialism and consequently resulted in changes that were only cosmetic. One of the most recent projects was called *Promoting International Understanding Through School Textbooks* (Boden 1977) and looked at some 70 textbooks published in seven countries (of which four were European). The report does make some useful points but stands in contrast to two more recent studies which link up much more firmly with the North American tradition.

Preiswerk and Perrot's *Ethnocentrism and History* (1978) is a stimulating in-depth study of Western ethnocentrism in history textbooks, illustrating the way in which the Western value-system continually attempts to negate all other non-European cultures. Most recently of all Preiswerk (1980) has . edited papers from the World Council of Churches workshop on racism and children's books. Called *The Slant of the Pen*, this book gathers together some of the most critical writing from both European and non-European writers. In that these more recent studies have looked outward to the world, rather than inwards towards Europe, they have much more in common with the North American research.

The United Kingdom

Much of the concern over bias in teaching materials in the UK has come from those involved in multi-cultural education. Whilst occasional articles about bias in books appeared in the 1960s it was not until the 70s, with race a growing issue in education, that much serious thought was given to the subject. There is now, however, a serious concern both over racism in children's books and racism in school textbooks. The focus has traditionally been somewhat more on the former than the latter, although this is now changing.

The North American research is generally not easy to obtain in Britain but nevertheless has influenced much of the work in this field. David Milner in *Children and Race* (1975) and Sarah Zimet, with Mary Hoffman, in *Print and Prejudice* (1976) were, until recently, the two main sources of information in the UK. However they were soon followed by Bob Dixon's two excellent volumes called *Catching Them Young* (1977) which looked at race, class, sex and political ideas in children's fiction.

Various organizations have also done important work and are helping to (a) keep up the pressure on educational publishers, and (b) keep the issue in the public eye as far as possible for what, to the general public, seems an obscure and esoteric issue. Amongst the important initiatives here four are particularly worth mentioning. The National Association for Multiracial Education in London has put together several comprehensive travelling exhibitions, which are extremely useful at conferences, on in-service courses and at workshops. The National Committee on Racism in Children's Books produces a bulletin called *Dragon's Teeth* which contains reviews, short articles, news and reports on particular campaigns. The Centre for Urban Educational Studies also monitors new publications and reviews them in the educational press.

Finally one of the most impressive organizations must be the Children's Rights Workshop whose *Children's Book Bulletin* carries excellent reviews of a wide range of teaching materials. This bulletin should certainly be taken by all school and public libraries, be studied carefully and then acted upon.

Apart from a re-edited collection of largely dated papers little has recently been published in the book line although the debate continues at seminars, such as those held by the Educational Publishers Council, and in periodicals such as the *New Statesman* (see Nov–Dec. issues 1980).

Concern over racism in textbooks, as against children's books, has tended to be somewhat less emphasized. Not, one hastens to add, because they are felt to be less biased, but perhaps because they are seen as more specialist books. Occasional articles and pamphlets, as well as the work of the Children's Rights Workshop, the National Committee on Racism in Children's Books and the National Association for Multiracial Education, have however ensured that the concern is always there.

One suspects that textbooks will only really begin to change when subject specialists themselves take responsibility for ethnocentric and racist bias in their particular field. Historians have, of course, long recognized that history involves the biases of the recorder, but until the late 1960s the idea that school history was properly national history was for many a long-held conviction. The growth of world history courses was, in part, an attempt to correct assumptions such as the unimportance of Africa until 'discovered' by Europeans:

> The ease and rapidity with which European empires spread across the world seemed only to confirm the validity of this viewpoint. Europe, it seemed, was the seat of progress, the rest of mankind had been left behind, but through the efforts of missionaries, merchants, administrators and soldiers would soon be privileged to share in the benefits of modern progressive civilization (McNeill, 1970).

Historians have thus explored both the relationship between teaching history and prejudice (Hannam, 1978) and they have also begun to analyze their own textbooks in some depth.

Geography: a case study

Of all subjects geography is particularly concerned with conveying and clarifying images of the world. Until recently, however, very little interest has been shown by most geographers about what *sorts* of images their teaching and textbooks might be conveying.

One of the main trends in geography over the last decade has been an increasing concern that geography should be 'relevant', that notwithstanding the statistical trends of the 60s it should focus on real people in real situations. Thus has developed what one might call a 'geography of concern', in which attention is increasingly being paid to issues of global inequality, world resources, urban problems, the environment and so on.

In particular one might expect this change in emphasis to include exploration of (a) differing cultural perspectives, and (b) differing value positions; so far, however, this has seldom been the case. An important distinction must be made here between changes in geography teaching at higher education level, where some airing of these concerns does take place, and changes in school geography where the shift is much slower.

As far as schools are concerned there has been little published comment, although one should mention Storm's brief paper on multi-ethnic geography (1978) which raises vital issues for geography teaching in the eighties. David Wright, in looking at changing images of Africa in textbooks, suggested that 'there seems to be a communication gap between geographers on the one hand, and those concerned with race relations on the other' (1978).

What is clear, however, is that school geography does now see the 'third world' as a legitimate focus of interest and the number of textbooks dealing specifically with this theme has increased rapidly over the last decade. There has not been a commensurate interest in the nature of multi-cultural Britain. A recent survey therefore, the first of its kind, attempted to analyze the nature of ethnocentric and racist bias in geography textbooks commonly used at secondary schools with fourth and fifth year pupils (Hicks, 1980).

Having identified twenty of the most popular textbooks on 'third world' themes and fourteen on the British Isles an attempt was made to analyze overall the various 'images' of the world that they contained. Specific common and/or pertinent themes were identified for analysis and four of these are explored below.

Development and underdevelopment

The most important question that one might expect geography textbooks to answer is 'Why are poor countries poor?' That is not, however, a question that many of the textbooks actually answer although they may describe the *symptoms* of 'third world' poverty.

A third of the textbooks failed to discuss underdevelopment at all and about another third only touched on it in a vague way. In the latter cases poverty either just 'seems to be there' or is somehow to do with chance factors. In the remaining books overpopulation is sometimes suggested as the cause. Whilst detailed indices for measuring underdevelopment may be used, possible underlying causes are not explored. Only seldom is the impact of colonialism on 'third world' economies referred to. When development is discussed it is always in terms of the need to 'catch up' with other more developed countries.

These images of development/underdevelopment beg many questions and it is interesting to note that these questions *have* been aired within geography, as mentioned above, but at the level of higher education. Thus 'third world' poverty has complex causes which are historical and economic rather than being environmental or due to chance. Under-development, far from being a condition that people just happen to find themselves in, is better seen as an historical process arising out of the unequal relationships between rich and poor countries. Various models of development exist, the most recent of which concentrate on the satisfaction of basic-needs rather than trying to emulate Western consumerism.

Food and farming

Whilst many textbooks contain accurate case studies of 'third world' farming there is still a tendency to judge systems by European standards. Shifting cultivators and nomadic herdsmen are thus still often viewed with suspicion and their response to hazardous environments seen as 'primitive' rather than ecological.

Plantation farming is also a popular theme, but it is seldom stated that plantation farming was a colonial innovation which often supplanted the growth of food crops for local consumption. Equally popular is the subject of world food supplies, the dilemmas of which are generally seen to be to do with overpopulation and the need to educate peasant farmers in the 'third world'. The myths of world hunger have, however, been critically analyzed by Lappé and Collins (1980) who start with the fact that only the *poor* go hungry.

Geographers thus need to pay more attention to the role of multi-national agribusiness corporations in controlling and dictating patterns of food supply; the importance of land reform in allowing people to grow their own food; the historical origins of cash crop economies; and the fact that most countries in the world do, in fact, have adequate physical resources to feed their own population.

Colonialism

At school level colonialism is often seen as being to do with history rather than geography. Two important questions to ask, nevertheless, would be (a) whether the profound impact of colonialism on the present day geography of 'third world' countries is considered, and (b) whether the drawbacks of colonial rule are mentioned as well as the possible benefits? Less than a third of the twenty textbooks referred to colonialism in any way and some are very clear about the benefits:

> The first contacts with the 'outside world' have, of course, sometimes been unpleasant. Even the harshest of conquerors have usually brought some benefits, however, in the long run. Even the most greedy exploitation of colonial territories has normally left the 'victims' somewhat better-off than before it began. Despite much propaganda to the contrary, most ex-colonial people agree that their former 'masters' brought them far along the road to modern development (*World Problems*, Ferris & Toyne, Hulton, 1970).

Such an assertion is not only ethnocentric and racist but also justification for most forms of repression! Only three of the books attempted in any way to give a 'third world' perspective on colonialism.

Multicultural Britain

Images of the 'third world' and multi-cultural Britain can be seen as two sides of the same coin, for ethnocentric portrayal of 'third world' people may affect both black self-image and white prejudice in the UK. Similarly it is important to consider how minority groups within the UK are portrayed. To do this fourteen commonly used textbooks on the British Isles were analyzed for reference to race.

Within geography such references could come about in the discussion of migration, employment, urban issues or the rise of ports such as Bristol and Liverpool. In fact four books made no reference to these matters at all and a further eight did so in less than a dozen lines. Only two books, Marsden's *The Changing Geography of Britain* (Oliver & Boyd) 1978 and Turner's *Spotlight on the UK* (Macmillan) 1978, made a serious attempt to look at the minority experience in Britain.

Taken overall the sample of textbooks analyzed tend to convey both ethnocentric and sometimes racist images of the world. Bias arises both from omission and commission and much needs to be changed. Thankfully, however, pupils in school do not gain their images of the world from all these textbooks, but rather from one or two. The importance then lies in making distinctions *between* the textbooks under consideration. As far as multicultural matters in Britain are concerned the only two useful textbooks on the British Isles have already been referred to above.

The 'third world' textbooks can, in fact, be broadly categorized according to the extent of their bias. They can thus be clustered on a spectrum which ranges from racist to anti-racist: In a *racist* book the text implies inferiority and the right to control; an *ethnocentric* book does not do this but fails to take into account other cultural perspectives; a book is *non-racist* if it cannot be criticized on either of the two former counts; whilst an *anti-racist* book takes a positive stand over 'third world' cultures and perspectives and against oppression. About six of the twenty textbooks fell in the latter two categories, amongst the better being Clare's *The Third World* (Macdonald Educational) 1974 and Reed's *The Developing World* (Bell & Hyman) 1979. Whilst both are variable in the consistency of their approach they are amongst the best of the geography books currently available. However:

> The task is essentially one that geographers themselves must carry out: in the name of geography, in schools, colleges, and universities, reactionary and prejudiced attitudes, and a biased – or even wrong – selection of facts, are still being presented. A major task facing British geographers must be to replace the textbooks responsible, which having been found wanting, can only be re-written by geographers. These books came from within the discipline, and should be rejected by its practitioners themselves . . . (Leach, 1973).

Educational publishing

Given the need for widespread changes in many school books – and this is not to demean the work of those who have already helped changes to take place – it is useful to consider briefly the nature of educational publishing. What sort of people write children's books and school textbooks? What sort of books do publishers accept? What notice of criticism do they take? How are books revised?

Long established geography textbooks often continue to sell well and may be in as much as their nineteenth edition. One such textbook was first published in 1929. Of course it has been updated, but revisions generally only refer to statistics, photographs and economic changes. In an interesting study of the politics of educational publishing, Macdonald (1976) suggests that although the quality of learning materials may be improving 'they will give you any information except what is vitally necessary'. The teacher-publisher census, he argues, screens out all 'non-educational' matters such as politics, values, controversy. The overall effect is to create:

Both a positive and negative control of knowledge in textbooks. In the positive aspect, knowledge is selected to emphasize certain values or a certain view of the world. Usually this is a view formed by wider and unexamined social demands – those, for example, of imperialism, industrialism, technocracy or bureaucracy. The negative aspect refers to the range of knowledge left out of texts, or out of the wider school curriculum. School children, as a result, are cut off not only from wide areas of knowledge, but also from many of the terms and ideas which could extend political dialogue.

The hidden agenda of school textbooks is thus seen to be 'the politics of stasis'. The existing order, whether natural or social, is presented as . . . an 'exterior fatality'.

Classroom implications

Understanding the nature of bias in school books is of little use unless it leads to action on the part of those involved in education. Thus in the classroom the first priority must be for the teacher to sensitize herself or himself to the issues of ethnocentrism and racist bias in teaching materials and to learn to detect them. Secondly it is useful to obtain or develop guidelines and checklists to help in analyzing materials. Thirdly one might, as a result, want (a) to rely more on developing one's own teaching resources and/or (b) produce new books in whatever field one works in.

The most useful way of starting is by looking at guidelines for the evaluation of racism in books. Pioneered by the Council on Interracial Books for Children in New York this has also been taken up by ILEA's Centre for Urban Educational Studies and some examples of such checklists are to be found in *Minorities: A Teacher's Resource Book for the Multi-ethnic Curriculum* (Hicks, 1981). One of the best examples came out of a workshop held by the World Council of Churches and some of their evaluative criteria are set out in the appendix to this chapter.

For the classroom teacher there are many possible courses of action and the following suggestions are based on ideas developed by the National Association for Multiracial Education:

1. *Letters of appreciation* – Write letters of appreciation to editors, publishers and authors about those books which you find useful in your work.
2. *Letters of criticism* – Write letters of criticism to editors, publishers and authors saying why you would not buy a book or would give it a poor review.

3. *Publishers' representatives* – Discuss available books with all publishers' representatives who come into school and ask for multi-ethnic book lists.
4. *Check the libraries* – Visit local libraries to check availability of multi-ethnic books and make suggestions if necessary.
5. *Set up an exhibition* – Get appropriate bookshops and libraries to set up exhibitions at school and/or in the local teachers centre.
6. *School working party* – Set up a working party in school so that avoiding racist books becomes a matter of policy not an individual battle.
7. *Sensitize the children* – Teach the children themselves to be aware of bias and stereotyping in books so that they can distinguish for themselves.
8. *Distribution guidelines* – Bring guidelines and book reviews to the attention of colleagues in the staffroom to stimulate a more widely informed debate.
9. *Buy new books* – Check through existing stock to remove that which is inappropriate and replace with new books that meet your criteria.

Only if such courses of action are seriously engaged in by all concerned (pupils, teachers, curriculum developers, publishers, librarians, lecturers and students) will the messages from the ethnocentric curriculum begin to change.

Appendix

Guidelines to be used in the production of anti-racist and non-racist books

What makes a good book?

1. Strong role models with whom third world children can identify positively are presented.
2. Third world people are shown as being able to make decisions concerning the important issues that affect their lives.
3. The customs, life-styles, and traditions of third world people are presented in a manner which explains the value, meaning, and role of these customs in the life of the people.
4. Those people considered heroes by the people of the third world are presented as such and the way they influence the lives of the people are clearly defined.

5. Family relationships are portrayed in a warm and supportive manner.
6. Efforts of third world people to secure their own liberation are acknowledged as valid rather than described as illegal activities which should be suppressed.
7. The material is presented in such a manner as to enhance the self-image of the third world child.
8. The material is presented in such a manner as to eliminate damaging feelings of superiority – based on race – in the European child.
9. The illustrations provided are non-stereotypes and portray third world people in active and dominant roles.
10. The illustrations reflect the distinctive features of third world groups rather than presenting them as 'coloured Caucasians'.
11. The role of women in the development of third world societies and their impact on history is adequately presented.
12. The history of third world people and their role in developing their own society and institutions are accurately presented from their own perspectives.
13. The role of third world people in shaping historical events in their own country and in the world is accurately portrayed.
14. The content is free of terms deemed insulting and degrading by third world people.
15. The language of the people is treated with respect and presented in the proper rhythm and cadence.
16. The material has been developed by an author of recognized scholarship, valid experience, skill and sensitivity.

References

Boden, P. K., *Promoting International Understanding Through Textbooks*, Georg Eckert Institute for International Textbooks Research, Brunswick, West Germany, 1977.

Bowles, T. S., *Survey of Attitudes Towards Overseas Development*, HMSO, 1978.

Campbell, B. & Wirtenberg, J., 'How Books Influence Children: What the Research Shows,' *Interracial Books for Children Bulletin*, 11(6). 1980 (see address below).

Costo, R. (ed), *Textbooks and the American Indian*, Indian Historian Press, San Francisco, 1970.

Dixon, B., *Catching them Young 1: Sex, Race and Class in Children's Fiction; 2: Political Ideas in Children's Fiction*, Pluto Press, London, 1977.

Hall, S. J., *Africa in U.S. Educational Materials*, African-American Institute, New York, 1976.

Hannam, C., 'History and prejudice', in *Teaching History*, no. 22, October 1978.

Hicks, D. W., *Textbook Imperialism: a Study of Ethnocentric Bias in Textbooks with Particular Reference to Geography*, unpublished Ph.D. thesis, Lancaster University, 1980.

Hicks, D. W., *Minorities: A Teacher's Resource Book for the Multi-ethnic Curriculum*, Heinemann Educational, 1981.

Hodge, J. L., *et al. Cultural Bases of Racism and Group Oppression*, Two Riders Press, Berkeley, Calif., 1975.

Lappé, F. M. & Collins J., *Food First: Beyond the Myth of Scarcity*, Souvenir Press Ltd., London, 1980.

Leach, B., 'The Social Geographer and Black People: Can Geography Contribute to Race Relations?' *Race*, 15(2), 1973.

Macdonald, G. The Politics of Educational Publishing, in *Explorations in the Politics of School Knowledge*, Whitty G. & Young, M. (eds), Nafferton Books, 1976.

McDiarmid, G. & Pratt, D., *Teaching Prejudice*, Ontario Institute for Studies in Education, Toronto, 1971.

McNeill, W., World History in Schools, in *New Movements in the Study and Teaching of History*, Ballard, M. (ed), Temple Smith, 1970.

Milner, D., *Children and Race*, Penguin, 1975.

Preiswerk, R. (ed), *The Slant of the Pen: Racism in Children's Books*, World Council of Churches, Geneva, 1980.

Preiswerk, R. & Perrot, D., *Ethnocentrism and History: Africa, Asia and Indian America in Western Textbooks*, NOK Publishers International Ltd., London, 1978.

Storm, M. J., 'Multi-Ethnic Education and Geography', *Schooling and Culture*, Issue 3, Autumn 1978.

Wright, D., *Tropical Africa in the Geography Curriculum*, unpub. M.A. thesis, University of London Institute of Education, 1978.

Zimet, S. G., *Print and Prejudice*, Hodder & Stoughton, 1976.

Addresses

African-American Institute, School Services Division, 833 UN Plaza, New York, NY 10017

Centre for Urban Educational Studies (CUES), 34 Aberdeen Park, London, N5 2BL (publish own guidelines).

Children's Rights Workshop, 4 Aldebert Terrace, London SW8 1BH (publishes *Children's Book Bulletin*, which reviews non-racist books).

Council on Interracial Books for Children (CIBC), 1841 Broadway, New York, NY 10023 (publishes the Bulletin, see Campbell, B., above).

National Association for Multiracial Education (NAME), General Secretary, 23 Doles Lane, Findern, Derby, DE6 6AX (publishes *Multiracial Education*).

National Committee on Racism in Children's Books (NCRCB), The Methodist Church, 240 Lancaster Road, London W11 (publishes *Dragon's Teeth*).

CHAPTER 4.2

MULTIRACIAL BRITAIN AND THE THIRD WORLD: TENSIONS AND APPROACHES IN THE CLASSROOM*
MARY WORRALL

Introduction

Those of us who are working towards a more just and harmonious multiracial society, and those concerned with education for world development are ultimately trying to move in the same direction. At the level of practical classroom innovation, however, it sometimes seems as though these two pressure groups are riding horses going in opposite directions: the first emphasizing the achievements of other cultures and ethnic groups, the second stressing the poverty and disadvantage of the third world poor. Yet like the six blind men in the fable we are all perhaps encountering the same elephant – we are feeling different aspects of the one complex truth.

A multiracial society is one that is plural and diverse; and educating children to enjoy and accept its potential implies educating them to respect customs and values of cultural groups that are different from their own. Cultural values survive migration, and minorities the world over have to meet the challenge of accommodating to a new environment while retaining what matters most to them of their own culture. By culture is meant here not only Beethoven and the Taj Mahal but 'the means by which people identify themselves. The clothes they wear; the language they speak; the ways they walk; the songs they sing; their myths'[1].

Respect for others and a reasonable pride and grounding in one's own family cultures are the twin complementary attributes of people who can feel happy within diversity. It applies to working class children and to the

* *The New Era*, 1978, vol 59/2.

Welsh and Irish within Britain as well as to the more obvious and recent immigrants.

President Nyerere has defined development as: 'the building of a society in which all members have equal rights and equal opportunities: in which all can live at peace with their neighbours without suffering or imposing injustice, being exploited or exploiting; in which all have gradually increasing basic levels of material welfare before any individual lives in luxury'[2].

Development education involves educating children for change in a desirable direction, and to understand and empathize with people, mainly in the third world, who are handicapped from achieving their full potential by poverty, lack of resources, and an economic and political organization that limits their growth.

The objectives of multiracial education and development education would therefore seem to be complementary. Yet in practice choice of curriculum content has been very different.

Contrasts

Aware of the derogatory references in school materials and in the media towards Africans and Asians, teachers working for a just and harmonious multiracial British society have stressed the more positive features of those cultures. The education department of the Community Relations Council (unhappily declined in strength since the merger into the Commission for Racial Equality in 1977) tended to concentrate on 'high culture' – on myth and history, architecture, music, literature and religion. In a handful of London schools, Black Studies has focused on the historical roots of the black British, looking beyond the Caribbean of their parents to the societies of West Africa and to the analogous histories of North American blacks. Projects on India have very often supported an idealized view of traditional family life, embedded in an aura of myth and legend and fine fabrics.

The development educational lobby has offered a sharply contrasting selection of material on third world countries. Led by the aid agencies, whose proper concern is with the poorest of the world's poor, many teachers have chosen to focus on malnutrition, disease, drought, flood, famine and homelessness. Within this grim picture of endless deprivation the concept of development, as introduced in many secondary school curricula, has become equated with concrete inputs: housing, wells, sanitation, factories, hospitals, road networks, seeds and fertilizers. And more often than not, in textbooks and aid agency materials, Asians and Africans are seen almost solely as victims and recipients, rarely as creative people, coping in their own way with the problems of their environment and evolving their own varied contribution to mankind's styles of living.

Of the two sets of interpretations, the second has had by far the greater influence, and it provides the dominant imagery affecting the expectations which white children have of black and Asian people. Both camps, by emphasizing such partial features of infinitely varied and complex continents, have produced curricula which are biased and partisan. Only too often work in schools has confirmed children in the prejudices and half truths they pick up from the media and from old films (Tarzan has a lot to answer for), comics and popular fiction.[3]

Basic attitudes

Before introducing material on any third world country to children, it is wise to discover what notions are already lodged in their minds about cultures outside Europe, and what their concepts are about 'civilization', 'progress', 'development', 'primitive', etc.

There is plenty of evidence from research and from everyday observation to show that children pick up attitudes towards other races and ethnic groups from the age of five or six or even earlier.[4] By six or seven, children in North America, Australia and Europe are likely to have developed a strong set of preferences for their own groups, and distrust and dislike of other groups, especially people from distant and alien cultures of the third world. So a pattern of preferences and dislikes develops before schools actively teach about third world countries.

For example, when children of nine to ten years in different parts of England were recently given a free choice to fantasize on where they would like to go, given a magic carpet or gas-filled balloon, Europe, America and the 'white' Commonwealth were overwhelmingly preferred. And when invited to write about somewhere they did not want to get landed in by mistake, they produced a narrow range of stereotyped descriptions of jungles, 'primitive' natives brandishing spears, and dirty thin people. Africans, Indians and even Brazilian Indians were jumbled up in one confused notion of primitive, poor, uncivilized people.[5]

For many children, the concept of civilization is surrounded by a rather bizarre set of associations. In a village school in the rural West of England a group of nine year olds were talking about India and the images they had gained from television programmes such as *The Disappearing World*, an anthropological series.

Boy 1:   They're not very civilized. They have different food and customs.

Teacher: What do you mean by civilized?

Boy 1:   They haven't got any guns or weapons.

Boy 2:   And tractors and ploughs and machinery.[6]

This equation of civilization with machinery and technology emerges in a lot of children's writing. After seeing a film about West Africa one ten year old wrote: 'At first I didn't know whether they were civilized or not. Then I saw a woman with a sewing machine and so I knew they were civilized.'[6] Some evidence collected by a questionnaire to older students showed that even seventeen year old students have acquired very little knowledge about third world countries. In response to the question 'What things do you tend to think of when the word Africa is mentioned?' virtually all answers could be summed up in the one word: disasters.[7]

It seems clear that the image of the primitive, disaster-prone native is related to anti-black feeling in Britain. A fifteen year old writing about a 'modern problem' repeats the familiar beliefs about immigrants taking over the country and living on social security, and finishes his piece thus:

> And another thing when the war was on where were they then, they were all hiding in their mud huts. So I think the government should listen to Enoch Powell and get the immigrants out.[8]

For British born children of Asian and West Indian parents the mud hut, starvation image can be deeply disturbing. A couple of years ago a class of secondary school pupils in Ealing strongly objected to a course based on Oxfam educational materials published in the 1960s, materials which bore no relation to the farms of their relations in the Punjab, but which were assumed by white classmates to reflect their background. Young children have few mental resources and no store of images to set alongside the pictures of emaciated slum dwellers; older students are often angry at the simplistic, limited stereotypes, and want more attention given to land ownership, unfair trading patterns, and exploitation of labour.

Devaluation of culture

Neglect or pervasive devaluation of the history and culture of Afro-Caribbean and Asian people can damage the sense of identity and self-esteem of children from the British minority groups. Indians and Pakistanis seem in the main confident enough to stand up for themselves, at least as they grow older and learn something of their own religious beliefs and culture in the Mosque or Gurdwara Saturday schools. Even so 'Mucky Packy' is not an easy term of abuse to withstand. Sikh children in Ealing were recently so taunted in predominantly white schools on the outskirts of the borough that they asked to move back into the securer environment of Southall; and in outer ring Birmingham schools, Asian children who had been doing well in the inner city became so distressed by the reception they were getting from white students that their standard of work declined.

All the evidence shows that it is black children of Afro-Caribbean descent who suffer most from cultural devaluation, partly because their own parents, educated in colonial West Indian schools before Afro-Caribbean history and literature were widely introduced, and before the revolution in black consciousness in the United States, were ambivalent about their own African roots. The depth and time scale of cultural repression explains the strength and power of the Rastafarian movement among young blacks. Meanwhile in schools the devaluation of black experience continues, though more by default than intention, and it seems to be a factor behind the under-achievement of black British children.

Yet over-zealous attempts to set the record straight, and to teach more about the achievements than the problems or deficiencies of third world countries, can be just as counter-productive of good relations between groups. The reaction of white middle school children in a London borough with a high proportion of Punjab Sikhs to a project weighted in favour of successful modern developments in India was 'So, if it's marvellous, why don't they go back?'

Propaganda and honesty

Propaganda, whether on behalf of the poor in the third world or of minority groups in Britain, can be self-defeating. The only intellectually honest way to communicate the reality of other cultures to children is to abandon any blinkered, partisan selection of materials and face up to the contrasts and contradictions – both the achievements and strengths and also the problems and tragedies. It is only thus that we begin to eliminate the dichotomy between 'them' and 'us', and see what education for development in a multiracial world really implies. The clue to a synthesis lies quite simply in listening to what people are saying about themselves rather than selecting from the experiences of whole nations only what fits into a pre-determined set of objectives and themes.

Writers and thinkers in the field of development studies and multiracial studies are beginning to say the same thing and to accept a position which any trained historian, anthropologist or literature specialist takes as an essential element in his or her trade: approach sources with an open, questioning mind and try to get inside the skin of people with unfamiliar experiences, whether the context is in the past, in fiction, or in an alien culture.

An acceptance of the significance of culture is returning to development studies: 'if people are to be regarded as the subjects rather than the objects of development processes, any proposals for their future must be adequately related to what they perceive of their past'.[9] 'The terms and characteristics and boundaries of people's identity must be determined by those people themselves. People are not free if there is a more powerful group of people who insist on defining them and keeping them within that definition'.[10] Even geographers are emerging from their self-generated patterns and systems to say: 'The key problem of trying to give a world perspective in geography depends on getting children to stand outside their cultural norms and assumptions, however momentarily. The growing interest in appropriate technology is perhaps more than anything else the result of a real effort to see other people's needs as they see them'.[11]

Attitudes amongst teachers

Since no one should expect pupils to do what their teacher cannot attempt, the first task is to reconsider the concepts of development and change that have been current and influential during the time we have been teachers and students. What is particularly difficult and painful to grasp is the realization that both development theories of the 1960s and the assimilationist position of committees for racial integration were based on an assumption that European civilization and the technologically sophisticated western world were models towards which the third world and minority groups in Britain should 'develop', or into which they should 'integrate'.

Cultural imperialism has underlain huge areas of the school curriculum. The task of shifting this weight needs the concerted efforts of everyone working for the right of all people to be in control of their lives, the essence of development and of multiracial ideologies.

A clue to procedure can be gained from a Bolivian educator, the late Robert Carvajal.

Carvajal perceived the issues that faced him in devising a curriculum for illiterate girls in a knitting and weaving co–operative in the high mountain plains of the Andes.

He was both linguist and anthropologist and had spent years tramping round the villages and outlying farms of the Quechua Indians, studying their folklore and ways of perceiving reality.

Equally he was aware of the forces that had pushed the Quechua to the margins of an economy dominated by the descendants of Spanish settlers and organized for the benefit of white and mestizo (mixed races) townspeople.

The effects of the domination of a culture that saw itself as superior and more 'advanced' than the indigenous Indians had resulted in the Quechua devaluing their own language and traditions much as the Caribbean Africans had done.

Carvajal, himself a Quechua, was concerned with the value of their traditions but also with development within a wider society and he mapped out a curriculum for the Indian girls of Cochabamba which fused the two.

The basic objective was to enable the girls to see that it is not a shameful thing to be a peasant.

'We try and make them proud of being an Indian, proud of their dress and culture, and I've seen over the years that they are happier now.

'They are becoming more sure of themselves. Before, they would hang their head down when they talked to a stranger.

'Now, you can see a girl from the centre and she will hold up her head and talk out.'[12]

Running through the whole education process there needs to be the theme that there are many cultures in the world but that all men and women have the same basic needs – work, food, shelter, clothing, health, language, friendship, education, love, religion, family, society, law and order and 'distraciones' (fiestas). Human groups are different but not superior or inferior.

This is the crux of the matter: this is the attitude that needs to inform the choice from the immense range of possibilities open to teachers who want to educate in the direction of inter-cultural understanding and for a more just distribution of the earth's resources.

Roberto Carvajal's method was to enable his students to define their own needs, appreciate their own strengths, and work out solutions to their own problems – not to start with the problems of people on the far side of the world.

Rather than introducing children in Western countries to the supposed deficiencies and needs of people of whose culture they as yet know nothing, we too could start with a questioning and analyzing process near home:

– What are the effects of the cutback in country bus services?
– Why vandalism?
– Why have motorways been built so close to homes?
– Why do we need special institutions for the old?
– Why do we have so much waste stuff to dispose of?
– Should they build a rubbish crusher in South Oxford?
– What changes have happened in the neighbourhood, village, town, for the better, or for the worse?
– Why are so many Europeans so fat?
– Are all our household objects necessary, beautiful, useful?

A great deal of work needs to be done on the stages at which children may learn to apply a questioning process to problems that are beyond their immediate environment and experienced by people whom they do not know and understand.

But certainly appreciation of the quality and validity of other lifestyles needs to go alongside a growth of critical awareness in one's own immediate situation.

Approaches to curriculum planning

According to the folk psychology of the Sikhs, the first seven or so years of a child's life are given over to imitative play – play at home, being mother, copying father.

From the coming of the second teeth to puberty imagination reigns; children from seven to eleven or so love drama, stories, fantasy, the colour and sounds of a wedding or a festival.

And they enjoy creating pictures, patterns, pots and woven and wooden things. This is the time to learn that common themes run through the myths and legends of mankind; that there are infinitely various ways of expressing human emotions in poetry, music, dance; that the crafts of pottery, weaving, carving, metal work, have reached a high degree of skill and artistry in different cultures at different times.

There is no need to introduce a new subject area in junior schools for third world or minority cultures.

The themes and projects already current – food, clothing, homes, craftwork – may be enriched with extra materials so that children receive a constantly reinforcing message that the artefacts and stories of people from cultures that are strange to them are worth their attention and may give pleasure.

The bulk of the curriculum will remain rooted in British and European culture and history.

There is no cause to squeeze out or devalue what is good and admirable in our own local and national traditions and development.

When children are ready to engage in abstract thinking, they may begin to grapple with the difficult issues of world development, not, however, on a simplistic rich West/poor rest basis but by studying and discussing:

– land ownership patterns – why relatively few have control over so much;
– why large areas of Latin America and the Caribbean are used to grow crops for export while local people are malnourished;
– the rapid technological development of Europe and North America in the past 200 years and its effect on the more normal pace of change in the rest of the world;
– colonization and its effect on indigenous industries – the Indian cotton trade for example;
– the advance of medicines and its effect on population growth;
– the strength of cultural identity and its power to survive transplanting and to adapt to new conditions;
– genuine difficulties of adapting to change in the environment and to new ways of working;
– plural societies – the tensions of living alongside people with different customs and values;
– the advantages of tried and tested ways of behaving;
– choices about priorities in development – large-scale industrial developments on the western model, or small-scale, intermediate-technological change in villages and rural areas.

In Britain it might be wise to introduce these concepts and problems through material on regions that are less hackneyed in schools: Latin America, China, the Middle East, South East Asia and Indonesia.

Children's expectations and prejudgements are less formed about these areas of the world. Whatever the choice of place, however, there is a huge job to be done in re-thinking our underlying assumptions.

Without wishing to jump to the extreme of belittling the real contributions that Europeans have made to the world, perhaps the first question to pose is: 'Why should we ever have thought that other people would want to be more like us?'

References

1. Heath, Roy, *The Function of Myth* in *Caribbean Essays*, Salkey, A. (ed) 1972.
2. Nyerere, Julius, *Socialism and Rural Development*, Dar es Salaam 1967.
3. Dummett, Ann, *A Portrait of English Racism*, Part 4, Pelican 1973.
4. Milner, David, *Children and Race*, chapters 2 and 3 and bibliographies, Penguin 1975.
5. This work took place as part of the Schools Council/NFER project: Education for a Multiracial Society, and is reported in *Children's Racial Ideas and Feelings* by Jeffcoate, Rob, in *English in Education*, Vol 11, No 1, published by the National Association for the Teaching of English.
6. Quotations from Schools Council/NFER project report: *Multiracial Education, Curriculum and Context*, in preparation.
7. Wright, David and others, *Development Studies Handbook*, School of African and Oriental Studies, London 1977.
8. Jeffcoate, Rob, *Schools and Racism* in *Multiracial School*, Winter 1977.
9. Peel, J. D. Y., *The Significance of Culture for Development Studies* in *Institute of Development Studies Bulletin*, University of Sussex, September 1976.
10. *The New Black Presence in Britain*, British Council of Churches, 1976.
11. Hicks, Dave, *Keeping Up with the Third World*, in *Teaching Geography*, July 1977.
12. This account of Robert Carvajal's work is taken from Oxfam's Latin American section files.

CHAPTER 4.3

WORLD RELIGIONS IN THE MULTI-FAITH SCHOOL*
W. OWEN COLE

It might appear obvious that a number of religions should be taught in schools where there are Muslim and Jewish children as well as pupils from many Christian denominations – in such schools the latter are frequently from East Europe and the Caribbean. However, in such places one very often encounters Bible–based, moralistic teaching or no religious education at all, accompanied by either of two statements, 'If they've come here they need to know about our religion,' or 'We don't want to upset anyone, so we treat them all alike and avoid mentioning differences – like religion.' Both assertions are half-true and should not be ignored, though the real reasons for not teaching about Islam in a school with Muslim pupils in it is much more complicated and worthy of someone's careful analytical research.

A host of multiracial schools are now multi-faith in the real sense that the various religions present are recognized both in the classroom and in assembly. There is a growing literature on the subject but, above all, advisers, often themselves self-taught, have encouraged and supported teachers in these schools to look beyond language to the curriculum in general. Nevertheless, this article must still begin with a brief statement of reasons for including teaching about Islam or Judaism, as well as Christianity, in schools with Muslim or Jewish pupils.

First, there is the need of the child from the minority group to feel accepted. In human terms he is, but culturally it is possible for him to draw the conclusion, as English working-class children have done, that the ways and values of his parents are to be despised. After all, in school the

* Chapter 8 of *World Faiths in Education*, W. Owen Cole (ed), 1978, George Allen and Unwin, pp. 85–91.

language, clothes (e.g. turban), dietary customs and beliefs they have given him are ignored if not regarded (e.g. Jewish holidays) as a nuisance! No wonder many Muslim or Sikh teenagers experience severe crises of identity. Teaching about their cultures can contribute to their development of self-esteem, and reassure them that their heritage is not to be despised – and their parents that the aim of British education is not to eradicate all traces of alien ways in an attempt to produce one cultureless, secular society! Secondly, any teacher who takes the trouble to listen to his 'white' pupils (not only teenaged) will soon discover what distorted, prejudiced and dangerously incorrect ideas they have about Jews and other minorities. If ignorance is his enemy, the teacher is likely to feel that he must attempt to provide his pupils with accurate information, at least. Recently, attention has been drawn to a third reason. Sadly, but not surprisingly, Muslim and Sikh children are still being given false information about one another's faith in the mosques and gurdwaras and their own homes. Prejudices worse, if possible, than English Protestant has ever had for Roman Catholic or Jew are still being fostered, and the communalism of the sub-continent is being nurtured in children born in Britain! Teachers, once they are aware of this, might feel a responsibility for attempting to replace malicious gossip with knowledge.

One of the two major difficulties peculiar to teaching in the multi-faith school immediately emerges – the potential divisiveness of what the teacher is doing. All education as opposed to indoctrination is subject to this danger. A child from a sheltered home will hear swearing and learn dirty jokes, whilst another will be encouraged to value literacy and enjoy poetry, music and art. The son of a humanist will encounter Christianity. That Aurangzeb is to Muslims an example of pious orthodoxy and to Sikhs a tyrant needs to be recognized, and also that Gandhi and Jesus in their different ways are controversial figures. 'Jesus Christ' is a term not acceptable to a Jew, though it is to a Muslim.

The knowledge of the child from a minority faith is the other difficulty. The teacher may be fearful of making a mistake and being corrected by a Sikh or Hindu child. The chances are greatest from Jews or Muslims, though being brought up to respect their teachers they may well remain silent. Argument is more likely to come from a humanist home primed to counter those statements of belief which some Christian teachers still put forward as matters of indisputable fact. Of the solutions offered to teachers apprehensive of a pupil's greater knowledge the most commendable seems to be that of adopting the role of a partner in learning. In no situation should the teacher set himself up as the authoritative fount of knowledge, especially in this one. If he can work with the group of Muslim or Hindu children and help them to tell the class about their prayers, festivals or beliefs, he will have overcome the danger of being shown up and at the same time have adopted a sound teaching method. In support it is hoped that the books and audio-visual aids used will be generally acceptable to the minority group and that their help will be obtained in providing a speaker, arranging a visit to the place of worship or organizing an exhibition.

In terms of methodology it would seem that the main difference between teaching Judaism, for example, in a class which has some Jewish members and one in which only Christianity is represented lies in the use one makes of the potential Jewish contribution. The materials should be very much the same, the best available – best, that is, in terms of presenting the faith as a Jew would have it stated. Whether a Jew is present or not, it should be done as if one were. One should never talk about a faith in a manner that one would not adopt were an adherent of it present – nothing should be said about Judaism behind a Jew's back which would not be said to his face. This essential criterion applies to Jehovah's Witnesses and Mormons too.

Both method and content would differ in another way in the multi-faith school. In a so-called Christian school several factors might influence choice of content, and the method might be to study one faith after another. In a school of Muslims, Jews and humanists as well as Christians the choice of minimum content is to some extent determined. The approach can scarcely be that of Christianity first and then, for two terms at fourteen plus, Judaism followed by Islam with a visit from a humanist a year later when the pupils are old enough! Almost immediately the teacher is obliged to make some response to the composition of the class.

'Why doesn't Yaqub eat pork sausages?'

'Why does Jameda wear "trousers"?'

'Why does Sidney Levy say they don't have Christmas in his house, Miss?'

'What is a Jew, Miss?'

These are questions which are posed by first-school children in a multi-faith school. As they grow older, a Muslim boy is likely to ask, more suspiciously, 'Why do we only learn about Christianity?' and he will conclude that the reason is because the teacher wishes to convert him. Some Christians still see the aim of RE as being that of putting the Gospel in front of children clearly and simply so that they may have a chance to accept it or reject it. Understandably, such teachers are bemused at the inclusion of other faiths in the syllabus. Those pupils who come from countries which have been areas of strong missionary activity are equally bewildered at being told that the purpose of learning about religion in schools is not evangelism or conversion but understanding. Dialogue is a comparatively recent activity, still the preserve of a sophist minority. A disinterested approach to the study of religion has, in the same way, been a rare activity. We should not expect Muslims new to Britain to appreciate this open-endedness without some suspicion, any more than we should expect it of indigenous humanists and Jews – especially when the one corporate activity of the school still is, or should be by law, an act of Christian worship!

To return to the questions posed above. What replies can be given? Each has its simple answer: 'Yaqub and Jameda are Muslims'; 'Sidney is a Jew'; 'A Jew is. . . .' Perhaps that one isn't so easy, but sometimes with young children a simplistic formula is employed such as 'Jews are people who don't believe in Jesus' (which must include the majority of Britons nowadays). All these responses pre-suppose considerable existing knowledge of what a Muslim or a Jew is, yet in the young child only folk-knowledge exists, frequently anti-Paki or anti-Semitic. This the child, by implication, is invited to attach to Jameda, Yaqub or Sidney. Far better with younger pupils would seem to be answers couched in positive, affective terms rather than cognitive and theological. A topic 'Things People Eat' could cover similarities and differences, acquaint children with cultural peculiarities, our dependence on farmers in other lands, and perhaps introduce them to new foods such as chapattis, burfi, or Hamantaschen. They might learn that some societies eat fish as their only meat; that others will not eat meat at all; some will eat the flesh of some animals; all apparently have some restrictions – dogs and snails don't seem to go down very well with most Britons!

'The Clothes People Wear' is a topic which fascinates most first-school pupils, especially if they can make clothes for their own dolls or manufacture and dress pipe-cleaner figures for an Indian village or a costume parade. Drapers' shops will often give teachers oddments and leftovers, and some of those obtained from Asian stores have silver and gold threads, wonderful colours and sometimes a bit of mirror-work. Children may have costume dolls at home which they can bring to create further stimulus. Similarly 'Our Homes' might look at festivals, family life, names and customs, but again in very down-to-earth terms, assembling Eid, Diwali, Jewish New Year and Christmas cards and concentrating on what happens rather than why. Through such topics one hopes that differences will come to be accepted positively as interesting and important, providing variety long before their particular significance can be understood.

Nothing has yet been said of religious stories. They are, of course, the stuff of every faith and the means by which moral and doctrinal tenets are transmitted. However, the teacher needs to ask a number of questions before using them.

Is her aim the transmission of religious beliefs or moral ideas or cultural folk-lore? If it is the first, are these really being conveyed and can they be understood by the pupils? Telling the story of Noah must include the Covenant, the Nativity of Jesus must include the virginal conception, if theological requirements are to be met – if they are to be religious stories, that is. Emasculated of their theology they become cultural folk-lore, important in the child's education but not part of religious education. In a multi-faith or pluralist society one might mention the wisdom of providing hostages to fortune. If some of the indigenous population find stories about the infant Nanak or Krishna far-fetched, may not Muslims find Judeo-Christian narratives equally peculiar? Furthermore, those children who come from homes where there is no religious belief of any kind and no respect for religion might regard them as amusing or ridiculous. Religious stories, places and objects, as well as sacred songs, pandits, rabbis or vicars, owe their respected status to the beliefs of either individuals or society at large. Britain is no longer such a society.

The use of stories to transmit moral ideas might be more acceptable, to show that moral courage, forgiveness, caring are virtues world-wide, but two comments must be made. First, it is not through knowledge that people become moral. Jesus said, 'Love your enemies,' but Christians have been known to be vindictive. The cliché is true; morality is caught not taught. Neither mottoes nor sermonizing produce schools in which human virtues are to be found. Secondly, children have been known to say, 'OK. God said, "Thou shalt not steal"; but I don't believe in God, so I can pinch things if I like!'

Religious stories in the first school should, it seems, play a supporting role in RE, be used sparingly, and each one should be used only after considerable thought. Their use now needs to be justified where once it was taken for granted.

In the middle years 'Where We Worship' might provide a first introduction to religious practices other than the domestic and social celebrations which accompany festivals, births and weddings. Visits to places of worship often stimulate nine-, ten-, or eleven-year olds not only to make models or draw pictures, but also to talk and write about their experiences. The visit to any empty synagogue or gurdwara proves interesting because it is different; the value is enhanced if good guides are available (i.e., those who can talk to children), and of course film-strips or slides, accompanied by such sounds as the Muslim call to prayer or the singing of bhajans in a Hindu temple, go far towards providing the authenticity which can only be obtained fully by attending an act of worship. One must remember that for many Hindus or Sikhs a visit to a Christian church is also novel and interesting, and that for the child from a traditional English home it is perhaps no less strange.

From the places of worship, besides moving towards ways of worshipping, it is also natural to progress towards books used in worship (hymn-books as well as sacred texts) and to the people through whom the particular faith was revealed. The last of the middle-school years, in many ways, provides an appropriate time for gathering together the fragmentary knowledge of various kinds, geographical and historical as well as religious, which has been acquired since the age of five.

The upper years, from thirteen to sixteen, are those when the teacher might try to probe as far as possible in assisting the student to understand what it means in terms of practices, belief or commitment to be a Jew, a Muslim or a Christian. This might be done, as the Birmingham Syllabus (1975) suggests, through courses on individual religions chosen in such a way that the pupil would study the dominant religion of the culture, Christianity, another religion (probably his own if his background were not Christian) and perhaps an interpretation of life which was not religious. Two snags are obvious. The first is the staffing of courses once any element of choice is introduced in a department with only one or two members of staff. The second is the objection of parents to their children being allowed to choose a course on humanism or Marxism, options which many Asians and Christians, especially from Eastern Europe (and these form considerable minorities in our larger cities), view with astonishment and dismay.

A preferable approach might be a continuation of the thematic one. Where and when people worship and how they worship is incomplete without answering why Muslims, Christian denominations, or Sikhs worship in their various ways and why do people worship at all, recognizing that forms of worship vary and that humanists and others do not engage in this activity. Here the emphasis is shifting from the practices in themselves to the beliefs which lie behind them, an essential progression if depth is to be achieved and justice done to the various faiths and to the pupils' education. Too often traditional Christian RE has spent its time and energy arguing the historicity of the Resurrection, whilst neglecting to explain any of the meanings which Christians attach to it. This defect must not be repeated and multiplied in the multi-faith school.

Dialogue

The high school should not necessarily be regarded as an opportunity for dialogue, but even if this is not the intention it might well become a reality. After all, it has often happened in the past between the student who would not accept the moral or religious position being stated and the teacher-apologist. Often this was rather like bear-baiting. If the teacher can now act as an organizer and resource guide, helping the Muslim or humanist students to obtain and assemble their material, there is no reason why such topics as prayer, life after death, or the concept of God should not be explored and serious questions asked about the purpose of religion and the meaning of life itself. There can be little that is more fascinating than hearing a group of Jewish pupils explaining why they cannot accept the messiahship of Jesus, or a Christian student explaining to a Muslim what Jesus means to him. Of course, such a topic as suffering may be beyond the abilities of most teenagers, even sixth-formers, and so might mysticism. They may lack both the knowledge and the personal awareness of the issues. Nevertheless, there are many points at which the uncertainties and perplexities of existence impinge upon the teenager, and one does not have to be a theologian to be concerned about them or highly intelligent to discuss them. Through concern and the need to convey ideas to others as well as the interest which can be aroused through encountering unfamiliar practices and beliefs, theological education and coherent articulation of ideas can be developed.

The multi-faith school, at every age, is potentially a place for growth and enrichment of a kind never before experienced in Britain. Through it the study of world religions can become more than an armchair intellectual exercise. All high schools in Britain are multi-faith in the sense of being pluralist in belief and values. Though this is not the same as having a variety of religions, it presents similar potential for dialogue, the same need to present Christianity coherently and fully in its many dimensions. It makes the same demands upon the teacher to help the pupils understand and articulate their beliefs or disbeliefs. It requires from all, teachers and students alike, a respectful spirit of inquiry in place of the childish curiosity of earlier years. For various reasons some of them, both teachers and pupils, may not wish to share in exchanges which they feel might put their faith at risk or subject it to questioning. Dialogue cannot be forced and, rather than subject a whole class to it, there is a case for organizing a lunch-time or after-school discussion group.

CHAPTER 4.4

SOCIAL STUDIES FOR A MULTIRACIAL SOCIETY★
MARGARET NANDY

There is a sense in which every school in Britain is multiracial. Whether or not our multiracialism is reflected in the school population, every child in every school is going to be an adult in a multiracial society. Although most schools and teachers are not faced with the urgency to create a curriculum which will have some impact on their pupils' thinking on race relations, the reason for doing this applies in every school. Changes are long overdue, particularly in the teaching of colonial history, and the development of courses broadly in the social-studies field, which will enable pupils to acquire tolerant attitudes to people of different races and nationalities, whether they are living in Britain or throughout the rest of the world. In fact it is only because there are now coloured children in our classes, that teachers have had their eyes focused on an area of study which has been in need of change for many years. Suddenly, we have been made aware that the most readily available materials on, for example, the Age of Exploration, on slavery, on colonialism, are embarrassingly ethnocentric, and aware too that the teacher's traditional attitude of studied impartiality when 'hot' issues come under discussion is inadequate, and in fact potentially damaging when race relations is the issue.

Race relations is, of course, only one of many 'crisis issues' which teachers are beginning to see as their legitimate concern. One reason for their increasing interest is because for the first time society's 'problem members' do not all leave school at fifteen; nor do they all congregate at the lower end of the most neglected secondary modern. Most urban schools have coloured pupils and the inadequacy of education in race relations is plain; but most secondary schools too have amongst their

★ *The Multiracial School*, eds J. McNeal and M. Rogers, Penguin Books, 1971 pp. 122–33. Reprinted by permission of Penguin Books Ltd.

pupils drug takers, the sexually experienced, members of skinhead gangs, despite the fact that teachers often convince themselves that these all attend the school down the road. Their presence has contributed to an unprecedented growth in social science teaching. In my view the whole of social science or social studies teaching presents problems to teachers in the same way in which the exaggerated case of race relations does. The central problem seems to me to be this: we want to impart knowledge not for its own sake, but to contribute to the formation of a rational viewpoint in our pupils; but our objective is thwarted by the personal involvement of the pupils, and their tenacious predisposition to a viewpoint they have already acquired by non-rational means. It is in the general context of social science teaching that I see education for a multiracial society, and race-relations goals formed only part of the project which we devised.

The two Leicestershire schools in which I have been working are an eleven to fourteen and an eleven to eighteen comprehensive. In both schools there is a wide range of ability, and the social-class composition is predominantly skilled working class. In both schools, the basic organization is not streamed, and in neither is there any attempt to grade children academically in their social science work. In common with most multi-racial schools (schools who have some minority group pupils) they are overwhelmingly English schools – their character has not really been altered by the presence of children from the Commonwealth. They have not felt the pressures which have inspired some schools to change their curriculum in order to take more account of different nationalities and cultures.

We began by examining existing types of social science courses, to see if, in isolating the reasons for their inadequacy, we could begin to specify the essentials of a course that would achieve something really worthwhile. There has been a tremendous growth of social science courses in schools recently, bearing all the marks of a panic response to an unexpected demand. The vogue for exposing social problems in the mass media has intensified the sense of urgency and the result has been a mushrooming of *ad hoc* courses to fill the gap. There seem to be two main types of stop-gap courses, neither of which appears to be capable of enlarging children's perception of the social environment, but both of which certainly cause the frustration which many teachers feel at beating their heads against the impenetrable apathy and insensitivity of their pupils. The first type of course I call *cataloguing institutions*. We are now all too familiar with textbooks available for schools whose chapter headings go something like this: the individual, the family, the home, the school, industry, government, justice, religion.

The implicit justification for such a course is that pupils will 'bank' the information provided and will emerge with a total picture of their society. In our view this seemed optimistic and unproven: it was just as likely that pupils would look on this knowledge as bits of information unrelated to their real concerns or interests. It might well end up, that is, not as a bank from which they draw, but as a rubbish dump! Courses of this kind fail in two ways. First, they fail to provide the analytical tools which are essential if pupils are to build up a coherent picture of society as a whole, in which the relationships between the institutions, culture and individuals make some kind of pattern. Secondly, it provides no way in which pupils can evaluate the institutions they are learning about – in other words, no comparative perspective. The second type of course I call 'social problem spotting'. The chapter headings are familiar too: war, race, drugs, poverty, strikes. . . . The rationale of this kind of course is that by giving the child the opportunity to discuss these topics he is enabled to form his own viewpoint. In fact, the typical response is quite different. The pupil starts with a hazy knowledge of the subject, but is unwilling to accept the fact that his knowledge is incomplete, because the subjects are so familiar to him – he is likely to have heard them discussed on television, for example. He expresses his viewpoint, rejects any information that does not fit into that viewpoint, and leaves the class with his views probably reinforced because he has had to articulate them in public.

Once a public stance of this sort is taken up, no amount of information or evidence will transform what is essentially a prejudiced viewpoint into a rational one. What is wrong in both types of courses is that they provide no training in the logic of forming a point of view after looking at the facts and of altering a point of view in the light of new evidence. The whole process of forming conclusions in the light of factual evidence is missing. Teaching this process must be the first priority of social studies courses.

I think it is important to remind ourselves frequently that to most children there is nothing self-evident about the moves between evidence and conclusions. There is no intrinsic reason why facts should be more convincing to him than, say, loyalty to parents or friends, in fact very much the opposite is often the case. We need to be aware that unreasoned action is not the same as irrational action. Loyalty is often, for adults as well as children, a much more important social attribute than the ability to stand apart and reason. In a strike, a gang fight, an election campaign, in love relationships, loyalty is vital. We cannot, should not try to, supplant it. But we can make pupils more rationally aware of it, and try to provide some understanding of the occasions when it is inappropriate or harmful, when personal integrity should come first. We can only hope to succeed in this when our pupils have learned to have confidence in their own powers of analysis and reasoning, their own judgement. As teachers we are, of course, committed to rational decision-making, but so often we forget how artificial it is for most school children.

I am emphasizing this point because it is obviously very important for teachers attempting to improve race relations. We know from studies like the PEP Report[1] that appeals to group loyalty are frequently made to try and justify racial discrimination ('what would the neighbours/employees think?'); in the ugliest incidents of race hatred and violence, group loyalty becomes the loyalty to pack, or lynch mob; the issue of how far anyone can differ from his peer group also arises in multiracial classrooms when minority pupils are baited, or more often ostracized, by the majority. What I would argue is that the individual teacher cannot hope to do much about this kind of situation by providing more *knowledge* unless the general curriculum of the school is geared to building up open-minded and reasoning attitudes in pupils, and giving them confidence in their own reasoning powers.

I think it fair to say that the two models of social studies courses dominate social science teaching in secondary schools today. Their objectives – to facilitate a comprehension of society, its problems, its direction, its potentiality for change and the leeway of the individual in it – are indeed honourable. The trouble is that their approach is self-defeating. This is because the material used in such courses – material drawn from the children's own society and time – is too emotionally charged to be examined with detachment, too complex to exhibit patterns readily, too familiar to ask fundamental questions about. We cannot automatically expect children to find the structure and function of sundry assorted institutions interesting if they take them as given, as fixed landmarks. It is only when they have acquired an awareness that things could be differently ordered that they can be led to ask why things are ordered in this particular way, and whether that way is efficient, desirable, humane and so on. The final defect of the typical social studies courses is that they usually begin so late. Any serious attempt at education in this field must start early enough to teach methods of approach and to build up understanding of the essential concepts which pupils will need to examine the society in which they live.

At least three points emerge from this examination of the inadequacies of our present typical courses. First, the value of starting social science teaching with a younger age group than is normally the case – in fact, the younger, the better. Ideally I think this should start in primary school. Already a great deal of unconscious social education goes on there, through drama-play in wendy houses, and so on. But it is usually unconscious because there is no follow-up discussion and writing about social relationships deliberately fostered by the teacher. So the effect of such play and drama is only to make more explicit the existing knowledge which children have of their world, and it is not used to open up the possibility of considering other structures. I am not suggesting that primary-school teachers should labour this, but simply that they should give these essentially useful play activities the same serious thought which is given to 'work' which begins, e.g. at playing shops, and is used to create a learning situation about money and number. At the secondary stage, it is sometimes thought that sociological material will be dull at the age when children's natural enthusiasm is the teacher's main source of success. In fact, I used anthropological material and found that here was a wealth of material which fascinated the eleven- and twelve-year olds I was teaching. It was ideal for use as a base from which the children could begin to make tentative hypotheses about the nature of human social relationships. There is a vast collection of traditional history and geography material, already familiar to teachers, which only needs rearranging to emphasize the human behaviour content in order to become immediately useful.

Secondly, there has to be a leisurely rate of progress. There needs to be time for the child to ponder sufficiently over the whole subject, so that he can possess the results of his study inwardly and can draw on it as working capital in the future. Experimental research has shown us that knowledge of 'facts', however interestingly they may be presented, is usually short-lived and rarely enables children to make generalizations within a subject. One reason is surely that we have been trying to teach too much in social science. The current trend away from traditional GCE courses and towards an increasing element of individual project work is an attempt to teach less, but to make an individual impact on the pupils' own thinking. In our approach, we were concerned to test not how much information the children had remembered, but the kind of thinking they learned from the materials we and they provided. But an approach of this kind, where children are not under pressure to rote-learn, but are pursuing a theme for its own intrinsic interest to them, needs time.

Thirdly, an effective teaching approach requires a huge bank of materials. Fortunately there is more and more suitable printed material coming on to the market, and more collections of documents and project kits are being produced commercially. However, there is certainly never enough material available from these sources either to stock a whole course completely, or to satisfy the individual requirements of each school's courses. We found that there had to be a personal commitment on the part of all the staff involved in our social studies course: we had to be prepared and able to make slides, make film, record programmes, write texts, annotate standard texts, and so on. The work involved seemed overwhelming sometimes, and could not have been done if it had not been planned by a team of teachers. This kind of effort highlights the critical lack of technical assistance in most schools.

We realized from the start that how children acquired sociological material would be of crucial importance – because on this would depend to a large extent how they handled the material, and how they used it to arrive at a point of view. It was obviously necessary to establish a pattern of inquiry, followed by discussion and conclusions, and to encourage constant criticism of statements which could not be substantiated. The process of inquiry throws a great burden on teachers and there is a great deal of intrinsic value in children being left to find out information themselves, because there will come a time when this is the only method available to them. But there are drawbacks. As you watch children in the lower secondary school doing this you cannot fail to note that it is in many ways an inefficient way of proceeding and provides too many potential digressions from the real objective of the exercise. Children can go into the library to find out something quite specific and return with something related but different; or they can find a problem too hard and scale it down; or they can spend hours collecting data for its own sake and retain very little of it. Of course library resources must be made available, but I do not think anything is lost educationally if teachers sometimes provide children with the essential and relevant information directly.

In two years of teaching some anthropology to first-year pupils I was able to compare the results of the two methods of acquiring information. In the first year the children were largely dependent on library books for information about a hunting society. The results of their researches looked good, but they retained only a small proportion of the information they had gathered. It was therefore difficult to proceed to the original objective of the course – a discussion of the rationale of such societies. In the second year, the introduction to the course was provided for them – it was, in fact, a brilliant anthropological film on the Kalahari Bushmen. It led to first-class discussion and further inquiry, and was still vividly remembered after six months. There are clearly many ways in which teachers can vary their methods at the inquiry stage.

But whatever method of information collection, it is only a preliminary to the essential work of evaluation. We had to find ways in which children could begin to find answers to questions like 'what does this tell me about Man?' In another class where the basic theme concerned ancient history, the children used materials about Roman society to investigate the concept of 'civilization'. They started with formulations like 'cleaner', 'better houses', and so on. But because some of the children emphasized aspects of Roman society like slavery, while others were concerned with mosaics and baths, their initial formulations evolved into a discussion of the question 'better for whom?'. They produced quite a sophisticated debate on whether Roman society had on the whole done anything for anyone who was not a freeman. They had started with a hazy and undifferentiated notion of 'civilization' as in general an approved thing, and had come to appreciate the much more complicated notion that a state of affairs (like 'civilization') which produced welfare for some could also produce dis-welfare for others.

At the very beginning of our social studies course, however, the most important objective was to enable the children to grasp some of the basic aspects of human life – its social character, the abilities which are unique to man, the fact that there is a logic to all patterns of human social development. We found the necessary materials to provide a comparative perspective initially in studies of animal organization, and later in anthropology. The eleven-year olds spend six to eight weeks right at the start of their secondary schooling with materials about animal social organization, birds, insects, fish, primates. Of course at this stage there are incidental objectives: the complex business of getting used to a library, training to use the printed word as rather more than a copy book, training to use tape-recorders and slide projectors, experience in organizing groups for discussion. So perhaps the two main academic achievements of this stage of the project are an assorted accumulation of facts about animal behaviour, and a vague realization that there is something different about 'our cat claws the door to say that she wants to go out' and human communication. The notion that 'they're just like humans' takes a knock. It is at this stage, when it can be assumed that most of the children will feel some confidence in our 'peculiar' methods of work, that we turn to anthropology, on which they spend about ten weeks using much more structured material. My own fascination is in the Bushmen of the Kalahari because their organization is on a small enough scale for children to make their first attempts to grasp some of the fundamental prerequisites of human organization. But material about Eskimos, Australian Aborigines or any other hunting-gathering group would be equally suitable. Towards the end of the period of work the pupils are encouraged to make cross-cultural comparisons, and to re-examine their ideas of Stone Age man in Europe in the light of their new knowledge.

At the end of this part of the course, the majority of children are no longer satisfied with simplistic (and derisory) answers such as 'they build houses like this because they are stupid'. We looked, for example, at the question of what a Bushman would do if rehoused in a new council house, and the pupils were able to argue that such a house would be an encumbrance if one's way of life involved constant travel, and would be abandoned. Detailed testing of the effect of such work on children's thinking is not easy. It is clear from discussions, from recorded work and from their writing that they learn a great deal about the *fact* of Bushman society – but this is not the point of the course. I devised two kinds of test to attempt to find out about the development of the children's thoughts about that society. One test involved children making choices between pairs of statements, for example, between 'Bushmen don't write because they don't need to' and 'Bushmen don't write because they are unintelligent'. To my surprise, when I used this as a pre-test the children scored incredibly highly. I could only explain this as a reflection of their views of me, that I was unlikely to spend my time being interested in a group of people who were unintelligent, greedy, selfish, etc. The second type of test, an open-ended one, I found more helpful. The same questions, e.g. 'Bushmen do not write because . . .' is left for the children to complete. It is then scored on a positive, negative and neutral scale, and administered before and after the unit of work. In general I found that when asked particular questions to test the degree to which they had internalized the logic of the totally different society, they produced startlingly sophisticated reasoning. What is more, they had implicitly accepted the notion that no human culture can be regarded as a curio or as a demonstration of the right or wrong way to do things, but they had seen that another society, quite different from their own, could work for its members, provide physical and emotional security and provide a code of right and wrong. This provided an invaluable basis from which to begin future work which involved material drawn from Indian and West Indian cultures, and some of the common preconceptions and prejudices had already been countered.

In the complete five-year course as now planned, contemporary British society and race relations in Britain are not included explicitly until the fourth and fifth years. Of course, comparative work leads children to use material from their own society, and in discussion these fields are not avoided, but the lead-up to more intensive study of them continues in the second and third years. In both years, the children will make a thorough-going study of another society's culture. In year two, we have chosen the Indian subcontinent, and in year three, America. But although better race relations is only one of the aims of the whole course, we have, even in the lead-up period, quite clear objectives. For example, in the study of other cultures we are quite clear about attempting to build up a sympathetic appreciation of them, to delay hostile judgements, and make it harder for pupils to come to oversimplified conclusions. In the study of India and America, the materials are designed to immerse the pupils as fully as possible in the total culture, not only its geography and history. I believe this is essential if we are to avoid the possible worsening of the pupils' attitudes to the peoples they encounter. (In standard geography texts the student learns that the Indian peasant uses very out-of-date methods of farming, and learns little else. He cannot be blamed for concluding that the Indians he meets are likely to be simple-minded. From his studies of Indian history, or more rightly, the history of the British in India, he is likely to feel that the Indians had no culture, and that the arrival of British colonialism was an unmixed benefit.) If we are to do anything to improve race relations through social studies work, the pupils must be given enough varied material to begin to understand the complexities of Indian society, to contemplate its cultural and historical achievements and to understand its contemporary problems. This kind of appreciation, understanding, of the society from which one of Britain's minorities has come, can be triggered to some use in future discussion of race relations as such. It is also an attempt to show the English pupil the Indian pupil in a new light – not as an immigrant, but as a person with a cultural identity.

The materials which we use as background to immigration from the West Indies are in two parts: a unit in the second year which focuses largely on developments in Africa before European exploration and up to the period of liberation; and a unit in the third year on America. Again, pupils' usual encounters with Africa at school are confined to the slave trade and the Boer Wars. The usual teaching methods encourage the view (often shared by West Indian pupils) that Africans were indeed lucky to be rescued from savagery! One of the problems faced by black youngsters is that their formal education here and in the West Indies and America has done nothing so far to challenge this view, and is one cause of the phenomenon of self-hate. The reaction away from this has produced a growing demand for so-called Black Studies, a demand which urgently needs to be met. Reviewing the materials available, one finds that the best is very much orientated towards the British view, and this is not good enough. At best, they might engender pity for the slave, who is seen through the eyes of the nineteenth-century liberal reformers. Our problem was to get beyond pity, to respect for the person. We tried to do this by virtually rewriting all the material to stress the culture of Africa, the reasons within African society which allowed enslavement to take place, its effects in Africa, and we have put much more stress on African liberation movements and the slave rebellions than is usually the case. We attempt to give both black and white pupils some idea of Negro history to develop respect for self or respect for others which is the crucial missing factor in contemporary race relations.

The whole course is meant to serve a two-fold purpose. It is intended to provide the comparative material which is the essential perspective giving information necessary to a study of contemporary society. And it is also intended to provide the essential background to an intelligent study of race, in a way which does not call forth the pupils' prejudices and fears, effectively stopping all learning. Research indicates that provision of knowledge to counteract prejudice has little impact; I would describe our approach to social studies as an attempt to *forestall* prejudice. It, too, may be a failure, but it is certainly worth attempting. It is, in fact, a way of providing black, brown and white studies for all children, black, brown and white; to try to cultivate conscious knowledge and respect of people who are different, something which we felt was dangerously lacking in race relations in many schools.

Note

1. See Daniel, W. W., *Racial Discrimination in England*, Penguin, 1966.

CHAPTER 4.5

TEACHING RACE NEUTRALLY★
J. P. PARKINSON AND B. MACDONALD

Philip Parkinson was one of fifteen teachers who took part in the Schools Council/Nuffield Humanities Curriculum Project pilot experiment in the teaching of race in the autumn of 1970. Barry MacDonald, as a non-participant observer, visited Mr. Parkinson's school to study the experiment in action and interview those involved. The results of a psychometric evaluation of the pilot experiment are reported elsewhere.[1] The intention of the present article is to describe and comment upon Philip Parkinson's experience, in order to expose some of the phenomena and dynamics which may be encountered in the classroom when race is the subject of discussion. Whereas statistical generalizations can aid policy-making, they offer little guidance to the individual teacher who is contemplating action in his school. We hope that this account, which emphasizes typical rather than idiosyncratic events, will help teachers to anticipate some of the problems that they may have to cope with if they decide to take up this particular challenge. That many will do so seems likely. The systematic study of race as a curriculum element in the education of adolescents has been brought one step nearer with the decision of the Humanities project, following the pilot study, to go ahead with the production and dissemination of a collection of teaching materials

★ *Race*, 1972, vol XIII/3, pp. 299–307, published by the Institute of Race Relations, London. In January 1972 the Schools Council decided not to publish the pack of 'race' materials which were the subject of the research described in this article – a decision which led to considerable national controversy. Lawrence Stenhouse and his colleagues, who were responsible for the research, subsequently developed their ideas on teaching about race relations in a further project funded by the Social Science Research Council and the Gulbenkian Foundation between 1972 and 1975. For more information see the articles listed under the first two notes after Robert Jeffcoate's paper which completes this section.

on this theme, on the same lines as already published collections dealing with war, education, the family, poverty, relations between the sexes, and people and work, which are now in use in more than 800 British schools.

A brief résumé of the project's approach to the teaching of these themes will help those readers who are not familiar with its work.[2] The themes are all controversial, that is to say they involve problems about which people in our society advocate different courses of action. The collections of material, which include printed prose, poetry, drama, photographs, and songs, aspire to represent views and perspectives on the controversies in a balanced way, and the project's teaching strategy is designed to give pupils access to the problems in a reflective educational climate. Schools which adopt the project's recommendations organize their pupils into discussion groups which are chaired by teachers. The teachers take responsibility for the conduct of the discussion, which includes tasks ranging from the feeding-in of documentary evidence to the protection of individual pupils against group social pressures. The teacher's overall task may be described as the development of open, coherent, and rigorous enquiry.

A significant aspect of the teacher's role is that which concerns his own personal values. If he adopts the project's strategy then he does his best not to express or endorse any point of view on the issues under discussion. This 'procedural neutrality' is in practice very difficult to achieve, but was seen by the project team as the only tenable teaching strategy in dealing with controversial issues. Two alternative positions were considered:

1. A school might attempt to lay down a line to be followed by all teachers. This does not seem practicable. It would be impossible to achieve consensus on all the issues involved, and to adopt a majority decision would be to involve those teachers in the overruled minority in a systematic hypocrisy. Nor is it clear how the position of the school could be justified to parents who disagreed with the majority line.

2. Each teacher might be held free to give his own sincerely held point of view. At first, this appears a much more attractive and acceptable principle, but our own observations and other research findings suggest that the inescapable authority position of the teacher in the classroom is such that his view will be given an undue emphasis and regard which will seriously limit the readiness of the students to consider other views. It is difficult to absolve the teacher from the charge that he is attempting to use his position of authority and privilege as a platform from which to propagate his own views.

Moreover, the profession, if this view were taken, would necessarily have to commit itself to defending any teacher who urged any view on his students so long as that view were sincerely held. For example, the teacher who advocated total sexual licence or war as a means of developing masculine qualities would have to be supported by his colleagues. This position seems untenable in practice.[3]

The strategy adopted by the project is not value-free. On the contrary, it embodies educational values: 'education is committed to a preference for rationality rather than irrationality, imaginativeness rather than unimaginativeness, sensitivity rather than insensitivity. It must stand for respect for persons and readiness to listen to the views of others.'[4]

Compared with previous collections, 'race' was approached. with unusual caution by the project team who decided to carry out a small feasibility study in six schools with a mini-pack of materials before proceeding further. Three of these schools had no previous association with the project. One of these three was Sandilands Boys' School (not its real name), whose staff included Philip Parkinson. Barry MacDonald was assigned the task of evaluating the experiment in Sandilands, his report to be based on two one-day visits to the school, the first in the early stage of the study and the second when the study was completed. During these visits he tape-recorded unstructured interviews with the headmaster, members of staff, and pupils involved in the experiment. He also studied tape-recordings of group discussion made by Philip Parkinson.

Sandilands is located in one of the central, urban areas (we shall call it Deeside) of a large city in the Midlands. During the last century Deeside was the home of the city's aristocracy and self-made men who had made the city wealthy. Their houses were large, often three storeys with attic and basement, and were situated in tree-lined avenues – the remains of which may still be seen on a walk through the neighbourhood. As suburban development grew, so Deeside's population slowly drifted to the new housing areas, leaving its larger houses to a new generation of incomers. In time, these larger properties were bought up and converted into flats for subletting. With the influx of coloured immigrants to the city during the sixties, most converged on Deeside. Deeside is now a multiracial community, with its children, West Indian, English, Scottish, Irish, Pakistani, Indian, Kenyan, German, Italian, French, Polish, Estonian, Latvian, Greek, and Iraqi, growing up in an entirely new situation with its own problems and its own challenges.

The school itself, a tall building erected in the 1890s, is flanked on three sides by streets of terraced housing which wind their way up the hill to the local park. Its apex roofs, tall brick chimney, and formal architecture blend convincingly with the Polish church which stands alongside. Inside, the lay-out is built around two central halls, one above the other. The classrooms lead straight off these busy thoroughfares and with narrow stairways at each end of the building, movement is difficult and noise always a problem. The classrooms are typical of their kind – square in shape with high ceilings and windows which begin just above eye-level. Much of the school is used extensively in the evenings and during the holidays and this contributes to the general pressure on accommodation. The building imposes many restrictions on the school, on the staff, and on the pupils.

The history of Sandilands is one of shifting categories in response to changing policies of secondary organization within the authority. It is now a secondary modern all-boys 'neighbourhood' school with a five-form entry, a pupil roll of 600 and a staff complement of 32. All the staff are white. The breakdown of the pupil roll into ethnic groups was, at the time of the project, as shown in Table 1.

The school has a strong academic ethos with many of the pupils following a fairly traditional form of curriculum. Considerable stress is placed upon examination achievement although the number of pupils who 'succeed' in such terms is small. There is also a well-developed craft department and in recent years a remedial department has been built up, almost exclusively dealing with linguistically handicapped children from the Asian subcontinent and East Africa. The patterns of control and

Table 1

English	(White or 'coloured' children whose parent(s) had lived in England for more than 10 years)		211	36%
Kenyan	106	18%		
Other Commonwealth Africa	32	5%		
Indian	151	25%	319	53%
Pakistani	24	4%		
Other Asians	6	1%		
West Indians			62	11%
Other European			2	—
Total			594	

discipline within the school are traditional and the cane is still used whenever it is felt to be necessary. Despite the very adverse physical conditions, the school had had quite a remarkably low turn-over rate of staff in the past three or four years, seldom more than two or three leaving each session.

The position of Philip Parkinson in relation both to the school and the project was somewhat unusual. Although a member of the school staff his primary responsibility was as a youth worker of the Deeside area. It was as a result of a contact he developed with a member of the Humanities team that the project came to the school. When it was initially broached there was some reluctance on the part of the headmaster to participate due to the overwhelming view within the school that the best approach to race relations was to play it down. It was decided to go ahead, however, and the head of English in the school was approached to help conduct the project in the school.

Largely because Sandilands was a late replacement in the pilot study there was very little time for the two members of staff to familiarize themselves with the project strategy and the materials to be used. They decided that the nature of the materials would demand at least a reasonable degree of proficiency in English, and so they chose to work with the top form in the fourth year. There were 32 pupils in the class and these were divided into two discussion groups, each with an almost equal number of English and Asian boys. As there were only two West Indians in the class it was felt more desirable to put them in one group. Philip Parkinson's group had no West Indians in it.

Three double periods a week were set aside for the six weeks' study. Schools had been asked to tape-record the discussions but the Sandilands classrooms proved to be acoustically unsuitable for this purpose. After a couple of weeks a decision was made to move out of the school completely into a local church hall where the two groups were able to meet in far more amenable and pleasant surroundings. This not only gave better conditions for tape-recording but also produced a more relaxed and informal relationship within the group.

The two groups came together for the initial introduction to the experiment, for a lecturette on genetics given by the biology master, and thereafter for the showing of films. Otherwise, they functioned autonomously. A list of books was provided with the materials, and many of these were made available to the pupils by means of a special arrangement with the local public library. There were two kinds of book borrowing

– compulsory, in connection with a project, or voluntary. Each boy in Philip Parkinson's group undertook a project, either on his own or with another pupil, concerned with cross-cultural aspects of music, art, religion, sport, or games. In the course of this project pupils were assigned a particular book from the recommended list. Additional reading was voluntary, and not systematically documented. Pupil comment indicated a general preference for non-fiction books, while their evaluative response suggested that their reading tended on the whole to reinforce previously held views.

Philip Parkinson came to his group of young people with no experience of having taught them before and with no 'formal' contact with them either. Much of the time in the initial discussion was wasted in the group settling down and getting used to the mode of approach and to the idea of having discussions tape-recorded. In the first week two films – *The Brotherhood of Man* and *The Colour of Man* – were shown and followed by discussion in the group. In these early discussions the chairman, Mr. Parkinson, took up a very recessive role, being more concerned with participation than with quality and standards. This extreme recessiveness was short-lived. The incoherent and irrelevant character of many of the comments made it necessary for the chairman to intervene in the interests of continuity and relevance.

A number of problems quickly emerged. The first concerned language, or more precisely, ethnic terminology. Some of the boys, especially the Asians, found difficulty in talking about 'black people' and in differentiating between 'blacks'. In order to distinguish between themselves and the West Indians they resorted initially to terms such as 'wog' and 'coon', which provoked titters of nervous laughter in the group. This kind of difficulty and embarrassment, which did not continue, is not unique to the theme of race. The project has encountered similar difficulties in discussions of sexual behaviour and of social class.

The second problem to surface placed a great strain on the chairman's *ad hoc* commitment to the neutral role. Whilst the two ethnic groups present maintained a degree of politeness towards each other, they happily indulged in a character 'assassination' of the West Indian community, which was not represented in this particular group. This did not occur in the parallel group which included two West Indians. Pupils from Philip Parkinson's group, interviewed about this, thought that this was likely to happen to any ethnic group which was part of the community but not represented in the discussion. If this is true, then it may be important for multiracial schools to consider very carefully the composition of pupil groups in relation to the composition of the school. The chairman in this instance was unable to restrain his opposition to the views being expressed. He felt compelled, not for the last time, to breach his neutrality by hostile questioning. As the discussions went on, he managed to control his speech and intonation although his achievements continued to fall short of his aspirations. (Experienced project teachers involved in the pilot study claimed afterwards that race had posed no special difficulties for them in terms of maintaining procedural neutrality.) One pupil commented tellingly at the end of the study: 'If he had agreed with you, he'd start nodding his head.'

Apart from the films, discussion relied heavily on the pack of material provided by the project, supplemented by local press cuttings, photographs, and tape-recordings of radio and television broadcasts. One sample of materials selected from the pack afforded a detailed look at apartheid using several items: a report of a speech to the UN General Assembly by the South African Secretary of Foreign Affairs putting the case for apartheid, an extract from *Naught for your Comfort,* a book by Father Trevor Huddleston looking at the pass laws, and a series of illustrative slides.

Another session took a verbatim report of Enoch Powell's first two major speeches on immigration and repatriation, and it was in this discussion that one had the first opportunity to test whether the introduction of controversial material did have any special effects. The atmosphere within the group changed immediately; at times the pupils were very difficult to control and it was hard to get one boy to speak at a time. Constant interventions on the part of the chairman were required in order to restore an atmosphere in which discussion could continue. The discussion of the Enoch Powell items was dominated by two factions within the group – one white and one Asian. They adopted opposing views and their arguments reflected many of the attitudes and opinions expressed in typical discussions about race and immigration. Both factions were intent on portraying their own ethnic case and for the first time the group became visibly split. One significant effect of this was that 'moderates' of both ethnic groups were put under pressure to take sides and had to align themselves with their own race. To the observer, the acrimony which characterized this discussion could only harm relationships between those concerned. The pupils, on the other hand, dismissed such fears. 'I don't feel any different about the immigrants in this school who are me friends.' 'I don't feel any different about it through being in the discussion. You know, it's like outside discussion you are still friends,' 'You may argue your head off in the actual discussion, but it doesn't matter when you get outside. I still feel the same way.' The implicit assertion of such remarks seemed to be that their personal relationships were not so precariously based that they could be injured by mere argument, however heated. (Sociometric test data for this group indicated slight shifts, on the part of both native and Asian pupils, in favour of interethnic preferences.) It should be kept in mind that the pupils had known each other for many years.

The pilot study continued with some films and discussions about the Ku-Klux-Klan and some tape-recorded speeches by Dr. Martin Luther King. Several sessions were devoted to general issues such as employment, housing, mixed marriages. There was not a great deal of set work, but on a number of occasions the group was encouraged to write creatively in response to seeing a photograph, listening to a piece of music, or a tape-recording.

The six-week study was, for the pupils, a fairly intense and demanding experience and by the time it ended, most of them had had enough. Interest throughout had been uneven, a matter of peaks and troughs, the greatest being shown in concrete issues which directly concerned them, such as immigration into Britain, the least in concrete issues which they saw as remote, such as the situation of the American Negro. This is hardly surprising, and indeed is reminiscent of pupil response to other humanities themes, but it is fair to say that in the case of race, this motivational pattern was more marked. It could be argued that this variation is desirable, even necessary. Philip Parkinson found it useful on several occasions, when the discussion became very heated, to switch the group focus to an analogous, but more distant situation. This tactic, although usually resisted, had the effect of 'cooling' the climate.

One distinctive feature of the discussion on race was the almost total absence of personal anecdotes from the pupils. Whereas with other themes such as family or education, where the pupil also has a great deal of relevant personal experience to offer, teachers face the problem of restricting anecdotal contributions in an attempt to wean pupils from an over-reliance on their individual life experience, it was noticeable that in discussions on prejudice or discrimination, Philip Parkinson's pupils rarely supported their arguments with accounts from their own lives. We interpret this as evidence, if any is needed, of the sensitivity of individual feelings in this area and of the difficulty of establishing an emotional climate in which pupils will not feel personally at risk. Should such difficulty prove to be common among adolescent groups brought together for the discussion of race problems, then this would appear to support teaching approaches akin to the project's, whereby the materials themselves embody experiences and points of view sufficiently representative to permit pupils to develop their 'self' and 'other' understanding in a depersonalized situation.

Looking at the project in retrospect, and taking into account the reactions expressed by the pupils in interview, a number of factors emerge. Of obvious importance is the question of effects. The psychometric measures referred to earlier showed no statistically significant changes in this group, but consistent shifts, within the margin of error, in the direction of interethnic tolerance. These results are compatible with views expressed by the pupils, who generally maintained that their attitudes had not been modified as a result of the study, although many added that their understanding had been enhanced. Thus some of the boys commented that they, 'probably know more about how they feel about race now' than before the project started. One Asian boy felt that he had learned a lot more about race relations and that he was 'better equipped' than his parents. 'They are only talking from their own sort of Indian wisdom and I'm talking about the whole future of coloured people, whites, blacks, because I know what their attitudes are, their feelings.' Perhaps though the overall impression may be summed up by the Asian boy who said: 'I learned a little bit more about race relations, a little bit, but I wouldn't say my views had changed.'

What seems clear is that there were no marked difficulties in terms of personal relationships between the pupils involved. An Asian boy, asked if discussions made them (whites) colour prejudiced replied: 'I think they were just trying to defend their colour, the whites. When we get into an argument about the whites being responsible, you know, they just come in and defend themselves.' Again, several boys said that they did not feel that their relationships with their peers were in any way threatened. Throughout the six weeks of the study there were no reports of conflicts between pupils outside the classroom, although the teachers concerned were very attentive to this possibility. One of the English boys in the group expressed the view that the study had helped 'the welding together of the school community'.

There were certainly aspects of the pilot study which produced difficulties. Some of these have already been referred to. Additionally, in Philip Parkinson's group, there was a significant minority in each ethnic group who made very little contribution to the discussions. Because everything was condensed into so short a period of time these particular youngsters may not have had enough time to get used to the discussion and gain confidence. The more articulate and self-confident revelled in the experience, but this made it even more difficult for the diffident members to speak. Sometimes, when they did make a contribution, their comments were ridiculed or quickly passed over by the more volatile members of the group. (There was no formal follow-up evaluation of the experiment but it may be worth mentioning that Philip Parkinson had a chance meeting with two of these non-participants a year after the study took place. They discussed the experiment, and both boys said they had enjoyed it and profited from it.) The explanation for the non-participation of some of the 'silent minority' may be rooted in political prudence. One boy, who was interviewed after the project ended, recalled the early days when he was discussing it with his father. He was warned 'to be careful what he said'. He thought his parents were afraid he might say something which 'the Government might take notice of and chuck them out.' This could be just one pessimistic view by a Kenyan Asian 'chucked out' once before, or it could reflect a feeling of insecurity within the Asian community.

In retrospect one might question that the parents of the boys concerned were not approached prior to the project taking place. The Humanities project advocates the desirability of informing parents about the nature and aims of this particular curriculum. Perhaps, in the area of race, informing parents should be regarded as an essential prerequisite.

Finally, it may be worth reporting Philip Parkinson's personal response to the experiment, recorded by Barry MacDonald at the end of the study.

> Within the discussion my principal difficulty was not to get very angry with the boys who expressed out-and-out racialist feelings. Perhaps not anger at them; anger at the absurdity of what they were saying.

Question: Did you tend to get more angry with the whites than with the Asians?

> I certainly get more angry with the whites, and have sympathy for what lies behind some of the views of the Asians, because I feel basically that the Asians never said anything that wasn't true, whereas the white person in the group was trying to prove the Asian wrong all the time . . . it was the Asian boy who was on the defensive, the white boy didn't have any need to defend.

Question: Is neutrality of chairmanship worth striving for?

> I think it depends on whether you're setting yourself up to teach race relations or whether you are in fact encouraging young people to learn to

broaden their experience at their own hands. In the latter case, I think there is value in a neutral chairman. Otherwise, for many young people, the mere fact that the teacher declares his hand may in effect write off everything he has to say as attributable, say, to the stereotype of the white liberal.

Question: Is it a good thing to let young people's emotions and attitudes surface in this setting?

I just don't think at this point of time we know, and I would be prepared to say that more experiments of this nature are needed so that we get a wider knowledge of what is involved. One is always faced with a dilemma; do you let young people go through an education system pretending that the real facts outside the school don't exist, and in effect chalking up a success tag on the basis that there's been no trouble, or do you grasp the issues and give them an airing? I'm inclined to think that a school situation is perhaps a 'safe' one in which to encourage this kind of discussion.

References

1. Verma, G. K. and Barry MacDonald, 'Teaching Race in Schools: Some Effects on the Attitudinal and Sociometric Patterns of Adolescents', *Race*, vol. XIII, No. 2, 1971.
2. The Schools Council/Nuffield Humanities Project, *The Humanities Project: An Introduction*, London, Heinemann Educational Books, 1970.
3. Ibid., p. 7.
4. Ibid., p. 9.

CHAPTER 4.6

CLASSROOM INTERACTION IN THE MULTIRACIAL SCHOOL*
JOAN GOODY

The pupils we teach come from so many cultural traditions and family backgrounds, standpoints and outlooks, from so many different stages of experience of coping with life over here, whether or not they were born here. They are groping towards making sense of it all. When they come to school, particularly secondary school, they are all too often subjected to learning situations where they are not properly in the picture, have not got their bearings, and cannot see how the parcels of knowledge they are being given fit into any real life framework. In this article I want to talk about the challenge of this situation for the English teacher, the part that talk and classroom interaction can play in helping all of our pupils to make sense of the world, about the contribution they make from themselves as they grope towards an understanding, and about the way that particular books assist in this process, in helping the children to stand back and look more objectively at the situation they find themselves in.

A group of children, then, from many different backgrounds, and an adult, have been put together, and out of this arises the opportunity to establish a way of working together, learning together. These human beings are the main raw material, resources and feedback rolled into one. Of course there are extra difficulties in a multi-racial classroom, where there is no common background to draw on, but sometimes it is useful that attitudes cannot be taken for granted, and there is consequently a fresher questioning, a deeper probing. All that can be taken for granted is a common humanity, a common curiosity about life.

* *English in Education,* vol 11/1, Spring 1977.

How is one going to encourage, and bring about the situation where working together, talk, listening and understanding are all going on in the classroom, where one has the sort of interaction between pupils and between teacher and pupils which creates a demand for more precision, more complexity and subtlety in the use of language, which in turn brings about a closer, more productive and more satisfying interaction? It is a long term business, and we have to look on it as such. We have to give priority to the need for children to get on together, to understand each other, which means making the most of every opportunity, socially and through work. It means taking the trouble to see that children are having the chance to work with people they feel all right with – and that is not necessarily the same thing as working in friendship groups. Indeed sometimes it is useful to manipulate the groups, to find reasons for trying out different combinations of pupils, who, if the combination is productive, will want to go on working together.

Children need practice in working together, and the teacher has to set up situations where discussion is needed to get things done; then it is a question of watching for opportunities for development, for creative collaboration. But things do not work out straight away; it takes time, obviously, for productive interaction to take place. One has to have faith that it will eventually come about. There seems to be a need for utterances, which are more satisfying if they can be joint ones. Children want to make their own contributions but within a group context, and it is important at this stage that the lack of genuine interaction is not made apparent, and therefore suggestive of failure – in other words that one finds ways of helping them to succeed.

Jimmy, an English boy in a class of so-called backward and difficult children (although it was unstreamed) was considered by many teachers to be the most backward. He was very conscious of his failings and had bouts of very difficult behaviour. Robert Kennedy had been assassinated during a half-term holiday and when he came back to school he talked to me about it. He seemed to want to *do* something, but had only been able to think of cutting out pictures from papers. Besides talking to him, and asking him to write about a dream he had, which seemed to be on his mind, all I could suggest – tentatively – was that he join Fred and Elias (of whom more later), who were thinking of making a tape. What in fact happened was that Jimmy worked the tape-recorder, made, with great dignity, all the announcements, and listened actively to what Fred and Elias were contributing. They were making, declaiming perhaps, their own utterances, which were a mixture of what they themselves felt and what they had heard on television. Jimmy had worked seriously and wholeheartedly with the other boys – both more confident and articulate than he was – had shared in the feeling of achievement and had at the same time connected himself to a major event in the world outside himself. This may seem a small example, but such instances of 'connecting up' are important.

All the time one is trying to be aware of what needs to be talked about in the more ordered and calm way that a group in a classroom can achieve – as opposed to the playground. And at the same time one is extending the range of their talking experience. I remember, in this same form, who were by now in their second year, there was consternation after one of the major Powell speeches, and a demand to talk about it. A group of five or six children, West Indian and English, wanted a discussion with the tape-recorder, and wanted me to take part too. I was glad of the tape-recorder because I knew it would impose its own order; *they* wanted it because they felt that what they had to say was worth recording. It was an outpouring about Powell's policies and figures, about the kind of damage he was doing. But although they were all clamouring to speak they *listened* to each other; they concurred, supported, and sometimes took up each other's points. I think they listened to each other because of the feeling of solidarity the speech had created in them. So here they had an opportunity for excited, passionate, often fluent speaking, with the warmth of feeling on the same side against a common problem. I hardly needed to intervene to make sure everyone had a hearing, and acted as a focus rather than a chairman. That was all that was needed from me on this occasion. Later they would be able to do without me as a responsive audience and be able to direct their remarks to each other. But we have to take discussion in stages, and there are times when an interested adult is needed to ask genuine questions. A group of third year West Indian boys, all born over here, were talking recently with quiet understanding about their parents' attitudes, which were different from their own, and about aspects of their West Indian background that they thought would live on, and might even affect society here. Some of these glimmerings of ideas might never have developed into conscious thought if a space had not been cleared round them, if they had not had an interested adult to make explicit their thoughts to. As Connie and Harold Rosen say, in *The Language of Primary School Children*, '. . . there are kinds of talk that are fanned into life and sustained by the teacher . . . and the teacher in this role urges into articulation what was only half formed, and moves children towards new verbal ambitions. Such attempts might never occur in their own group talk, or at best be fleeting. Yet by virtue of the fact that a teacher has made such things possible she has also added important new items to the children's repertoire so that they can in fact use them when the teacher is no longer present.'

Pupils sometimes choose a topic that they can use as a starting point to explore what is perplexing them in their own lives. It turns into an occasion for them to bring out, to put into some sort of setting, thoughts that have been in their minds – perhaps just idly turned over, perhaps nagging at them. One such discussion took place between four fourth year boys, all of whom were considered by some members of staff to be failures. There was Jimmy, the English boy already mentioned, Carlton and Raymond, both born in this country but with parents from Jamaica, and Franklin who came from Montserrat when he was nine or ten. They are exploring the immediate world around them, and trying to see it in its wider setting. They have decided to talk about Black Power, but it is really difficulties between whites and blacks they are discussing. In the world outside they stand on opposite sides, but here they are in the no-man's land of adolescence, of idealism.

Carlton holds the conversation together: he provides the framework and takes the main part. Raymond speaks a lot, and quite freely. Some teachers would laugh cynically to hear him because they would feel his behaviour does not bear out his ideas; but his ideas are an important part of himself, even if his behaviour for one reason or another cannot match up to them. Jimmy and Franklin only speak a little. Jimmy's *function* seems to be a listener, a stabilizing listener, keeping things down to earth, asking them questions that have been nagging at him, and that genuinely make him curious. The black boys feel free with him but his presence makes them think more carefully; they are never tempted to lapse into a one-side moan; they have to enlarge their view to include his. Franklin is always very quiet in class except when he is creating a disturbance of some sort, largely by clowning. He finds it difficult to communicate directly with people. Carlton and Raymond both have to draw him out.

They start by talking about Black Power meetings. They wonder whether 'these people' simply wanted to be treated equally, to 'get their own back' as they put it, or actually to take over power. This leads them, as so often happens, back to Africa, and they try to piece together what happened . They are confused and groping, genuinely searching. (History teachers please note.)

They discuss what could be done to ease the present situation, and mention mixed relationships, TV plays and documentaries they have seen, and move on to race riots and question how they come about. Inevitably they get on to the police, and all four boys are together on this.

They come back to Black Power and Franklin is brought in and voices his private fears. He sees it very simply: if the black people bring it to a fight they will die because they are outnumbered. He is genuinely afraid of this. They then speculate about what would happen if there were to be an uprising in South Africa. Would the world think 'Right, if the black people won't stand for second rights we've got to give them equal rights'? And back they come to their own lives and living conditions and how their parents manage; and onto living conditions and work conditions for white people in black countries. Then Franklin is brought in again, eased in, and gives a dramatic presentation of what happened when the place he lived in started to disintegrate – speaking of this vivid experience so rhythmically that I found myself arranging it in lines when I tried to transcribe it. He had held the floor and spoken, and after this he came in more readily.

They talk about apparent unfairness, about problems at the labour exchange; and Jimmy brings into the open something his uncle has talked about: that he had seen some West Indians getting more money than he himself got. They discuss this, come to a possible explanation, and realize you cannot jump to hasty conclusions about what you see. They talk about their parents, the difficulties they have in filling in forms for family allowances, free dinners, etc. They seem to understand, be sensitive to, their parents' problems and to see the confusion some of them are in. Finally Jimmy wants to know what exactly happens in Black Power meetings; and they end up by talking about why people are called black and white, and the actual physical properties of the skin. They have stood back and taken a quiet look together at their daily lives, at all the pressures and uncertainties that surround them.

Children can get a great deal from reflection on their own experience and observations but they also need the help of books (and other literature); they need to be able to take a more objective look. They want to sort out human values for themselves, to look at and make sense of issues, but they cannot always see clearly in the rushed overcrowded lives they lead. They are, besides, too affected by loyalties they may feel to the family and friends that they do not want disturbed, and these blind patches prevent clear objective looking. They need a peephole through which to look calmly at a limited circle of life, which is outside themselves and yet related to them in deeper ways – in the characters and in the issues. I want now to say something about two books, and the way children have reacted to them.

The Eagle of the Ninth by Rosemary Sutcliff is an excellent book for all children in a multiracial classroom, and particularly for West Indian children. It presents to the children the living situations and problems they are faced with themselves. These relate implicitly to their own experiences, and the children can have an objective and untroubled look at them, and a chance to realize that their experiences are universal. There is no feeling of giving the children ideas and issues to cope with before they are ready for them.

Nothing corresponds exactly to the children's own experience; it is another variation of a familiar theme. Marcus, the hero, a young Roman centurion, is the homesick unhappy person finding himself in a hostile world; but the difference is that he is in charge, part of the occupying force in Britain. He is meeting not open rebelliousness, but reservation, withdrawal, and quiet resentment. He is missing too the hot sun and clear blue skies of Rome, and having to adjust to the English weather; and Rosemary Sutcliffe sympathizes, but delicately shows West Indians, Cypriots, Asians and English alike that variety and changeability are compensations. Esca is the most badly done by, you might say, for he is a slave, and therefore has most in common with the heritage of the West Indian children; but he is British. And this in itself is, of course, a new idea for most of the pupils in a multiracial classroom. Cottia, again British, suffers from her family wanting her to forget her loyalty to her roots, and conform to the new and socially superior way of living. For the children there is a validation of their own experiences, and some are able to move from the implicit to the explicit, although they do not always make the connection explicit in their talking and writing. However, they may carry the relation a stage further as did the Jamaican boy who wrote a play about a British family feeling resentful about the Romans trying to change their way of life (in spite of the material advantages), and with, as the inevitable climax, the daughter 'going out' with a Roman soldier. Many of his problems are being examined. All is contained in the 'secondary world' and on the whole the spectators stay with it; there is no too disturbing exact relevance, no open confrontation, no disturbance of loyalties to families, or even directly to previous thinking.

What is made explicit through the characters is a recognition of the importance of cultural differences, a realization that people cannot develop freely under an imposed culture, whatever the advantages may seem to be, but that once that is accepted there can be a completely close understanding between individuals.

There is of course an added advantage in reading this book with a multiracial class, for it makes available something of our English past to those who are probably going to settle here permanently and would like a share in it. A not-at-all anglicized West Indian girl was so caught up at one point that she asked me when *we* got rid of the Romans; momentarily she was able to make something of our past her own.

I ought to mention that *The Eagle of the Ninth* is not an easy book to read to a class; the language is at times difficult and some chapters are heavy going, and it is no good taking it on unless one has faith that it is going to work. I like using it best with a third year mixed ability group; younger pupils can enjoy it as a story, but cannot get so much out of it.

In passing I want to mention *Animal Farm* which I find invaluable at the beginning of the fourth year when children are still full of idealism about making the world a better place, and some of them full of confidence that the world can be changed, and yet at the same time becoming very much aware of all the injustices and hardships that exist. They are feeling their way towards understanding social grouping and political maxims and tactics; but it is all too much for them to be able to sort out for themselves. They need a relaxed look at some of the possibilities, and *Animal Farm* provides that same peepshow, recognizably reflecting something of what they see in the world, and yet apart, self-contained, able to be seen as a whole.

Finally I want to look in some detail at a tape made by three fourth year boys after they had read the book *Tell Freedom* by Peter Abrahams. The book is the autobiography of a coloured South African, up to the age of twenty. The details of his early childhood are very movingly told, and the separation from members of his family and his unsettled life echo the experiences of many of our children. You hear of his struggle to get himself educated, and the consequent difficulties this brought him, the way it affected his relationship with his family, and changed his whole outlook on life. And finally his reflections on Christianity, in particular in relation to the white missionaries; and on Marxism as a possible solution.

The great thing about the book is that it is set in South Africa, not in London, not in the Caribbean, For all the children it is removed geographically and in a way psychologically: they are in a sense on neutral ground. They get imaginatively involved; they are able to understand the issues that are raised within the limits of the book and are therefore in a position to discuss them, to link them up with what they already know and what their increased awareness is leading them to find out. It seems to me that for black children in particular this sort of thing is an essential stage before meeting political writing about situations nearer to home, which they cannot yet look at clearly.

But first something about the boys themselves. Elias came from Dominica when he was about nine, and his first language is French Creole, which he keeps up. He had been rather aggressively debating in previous discussions, but this time his attitude is different. With this book he feels on his own ground, because he has the experience of being black both personally and publicly. Often the two are in conflict and he is confused. In a discussion he once turned to Fred and said: 'You and I are friends. But if I was to come to your house would your mother let me in? No, I'm black.' And with exasperation Fred replied, 'But Elias, you've been to my house.' He wants his personal life to be evidence of his public viewpoints, and the public viewpoints of other people; but it is not as simple as he wants it to be. Here he is given the chance to see a whole structure. He can identify with Peter Abrahams and he can understand the outside forces. He is not this time coming in with debating questions but can explore the novel with the assurance that he has both the experience and factual knowledge. It is near to his special interest, the African heritage. He is at the centre of it; and he can see it as a whole and stand back and look at it with the others. With his own life he cannot.

Fred is a white boy, half Spanish and half American. He is bilingual. You can sense the effect it has on him to have the positive experience of Peter Abrahams; he has taken it into his own world view and is thus able to, entitled to, talk with the two black boys in a way which he might not have been able to before. Set in London he could not have talked to them in the same way. He makes positive contributions himself, but he is very responsive and is weaving what the others have to say into his own understanding. He is in an acute learning situation, having a secure standpoint, and being alert and open to all he can take in and add to his understanding.

Tony came from St. Lucia when he was six. He is perhaps the one who has the greatest insights into the book but he needs this type of discussion to bring out what is in him; he needs the friendly support of the others to help him to formulate his ideas.

The opening of the discussion is strikingly different from one they had had on *Animal Farm*. There they were eager to try out their theories on each other, to explore, and they cut in sharply and excitedly. Here the opening speeches are longer, more fluent, and altogether there is a relaxed way of speaking. At the end of Elias's second speech, which is competent and fluent, he turns to Tony and asks him to carry on:

Elias: . . . But I think he himself was, he was an educated starved youth who was unable to pay for his education, who was intelligent enough to read and yet unable to further his education. Fortunately he was discovered by some educated coloured men who introduced him to Dabula. Well, what do you – could you carry on where I started, Tony?

But Tony is not ready. He is waiting quietly, thinking, and then the third time he is prompted he is able to explain what kind of a book it is:

Tony: You know what I like about the book, too – it's an autobiography, a political autobiography. Because he – er – he tells of his early days, and how life was then you know – because it was a very rough life, wasn't it . . . and then he goes on to his political life, and it doesn't sort of overdo the political, does it? The political side's not overdone.

Fred: Oh, no. Yes.

Elias: I think the older you are the more understanding, the more you understand the book.

Fred: Because although the book could be quite easy to read maybe, in the beginning, but later on it gets more difficult. You know when it starts to introduce politics – that is Trotskyism and everything.

Throughout the discussion they are loosely anchored to the common experience, the book. They start by describing it to themselves, thus increasing their familiarity and understanding of it. They move on to the whole business of apartheid and discuss calmly how it all came about, fitting together what they know with what they can conjecture; they discuss the exploitation (they do not know the word but they manage without it); and they examine whether or not it is actually hatred that is involved. From here they go back more closely to *Tell Freedom* and take up Christianity:

Fred: Long ago the black South Africans thought that the solution to, you know, equality was Christianity, or so it says in *Tell Freedom*. And then they found out it didn't work.

Elias: Well, that's it. That's where Lee (Peter Abrahams) couldn't solve the unmathematical equation because . . .

Fred: Who said it was mathematical?

Elias: *Un* – I said *un*mathematical. You see, Fred, he thought that these whites, they introduced us to the bible and all the good things God done, and how equal men are, yes . . .

Fred: And all how one must love thy neighbour like thyself – what, you know, and in the end it so happens that the blacks stay (inaudible) and the whites are looking down, like Tony said, spitting in their faces.

They get on to the subject of education and here too they keep very close to the experience of the book. They speculate as to exactly why it is that the whites keep the blacks uneducated.

Elias later mentions information he has written to the South African Embassy for. This is an occasion for sharing it, for talking it over. It leads them on to consider why full information was not made available.

Fred: Why do you think, you know, they do this?

Elias: Why do they do this?

Fred: They don't want this to er – er – these things to leak out. You see they want to be secretive. They know they're doing wrong. They don't want this to – er – know the world.

Tony: It's not that they know what they're doing is wrong.

Fred: (inaudible) the world knows.

Tony: It's not so much that what they're doing is wrong as just that they, they just don't want the, you know – I mean they want to get on with what they're doing – you know what I mean? They don't want any interference.

Elias: Well, they haven't been disturbed. They haven't been disturbed.

Tony: They have been disturbed. They're under great pressure right now.

Fred: They're under pressure but they're not disturbed. I mean they're not really disturbed.

Tony: Oh, they're, they're . . .

Fred: How 'bout when countries . . .

Elias: Like the outer world itself . . .

Fred: How 'bout when you know, sometimes er countries you know – I'm sure that's how they were kicked out of the United Nations. Maybe countries have been complaining. Maybe – did they go out themselves or were they kicked out?

Elias: They went out themselves.

Fred: Why? Because countries were complaining. They didn't want – you know – if they were part of the United Nations they knew they couldn't be like that.

Elias: They were kicked out without being kicked out.

Fred: ⎫
Tony: ⎬ Yeah.

Tony: Because look, you see, it's not that they're getting them – um – they're getting at them for little things you see, now. The other countries are getting at South Africa for little things like sport.

Here they are groping to piece things together and their speech shows this. Most of the time that they are thinking things out as they are speaking there are pauses, changes of direction in the sentence. They can understand each other easily because they all *want* to understand each other as well as to be understood.

They go on to discuss Hitler, the Americans in Vietnam, and Enoch Powell, until they decide to bring themselves back. 'We've been circling round' says Elias. Now they slot in a coloured South African who had come to talk to the class and had made a strong impression on them. This leads naturally to the position, or fate, of the educated South African, and to whether it stems from being a political threat, or resentment, or jealousy. Finally they decide again to get back to *Tell Freedom*, to sum up:

Fred: Let's see if we can assemble all this, and you know . . .

Elias: That's a good idea.

Tony: Make something out – make something – yeah, all right.

Elias: And construct.

Assemble, make, construct. And so they go back to Lee's (Peter Abraham's) childhood.

Tony: . . . so Lee, he has a very mixed childhood, very rough childhood, where he's been passed from one hand to another – doesn't he? So he grows up with a mixture of feeling inside of him, doesn't he.

Fred: Yeah, Lee . . .

Tony: You know what I mean – because he sees things from so many views. You know, so – er –

Elias: That's what makes the book so interesting.

And these boys have been able to share that 'mixture of feeling', to 'see things from so many views'.

They take this on until they get to Lee's disenchantment with the Stalinists and Trotskyists when vital discussion springs up again. Finally they remind one that they are boisterous fourteen- and fifteen-year olds by making a funny noise into the microphone to bring the discussion to an end.

I have outlined the whole of the discussion because I think there is such a satisfying shape to it. These boys fit together, with the book as the centrepiece, much that they have done, and come up against, in connection with South Africa. Talk is consolidating what they have experienced, is ordering it, helping to make sense of it, and to put the whole thing into perspective.

I am aware that what I have been considering is not important only in the multiracial school, but the need is highlighted there. We have to recognize the cultural diversity and the variety of family backgrounds and outlooks and out of them create something positive. There are many ways of doing this: through the visual surroundings, through the books and other materials we are making available and drawing on, through developing a more genuinely multi-ethnic approach to the curriculum, and through our attitudes to language. But I have been concerned here with something more basic: with the need to create, in the fragmented life of the secondary school, the kind of working environment that the child can feel part of and can positively contribute to; an environment where his experience is taken into account, where in fact he can be helped to get his bearings. It is true that this sort of thing takes time to bring about, but if one measures it against all the time that is wasted in underachievement, then it may seem worthwhile.

CHAPTER 4.7

EVALUATING THE MULTICULTURAL CURRICULUM: PUPILS' PERSPECTIVES*
ROBERT JEFFCOATE

'I think we are learning about India because there are so many in schools now that we have *got* to learn what they are like.'

Twelve-year old white girl

The last decade has witnessed the emergence of a powerful rhetoric on multicultural education which has been strong on prescriptions and proscriptions for school and teacher practice but notably deficient in substantiations from the classroom. Detailed evaluations of multicultural innovations in the curriculum have been few and far between. The only significant corpus of research is that of Lawrence Stenhouse and his colleagues into the effectiveness of different strategies for teaching race relations to adolescents; most of which is in the form of quantifications of measured racial attitude change as a result of the teaching across a number of schools,[1] although case studies of individual classrooms describing process as well as outcome have also been published.[2]

Whilst the rhetoric acknowledges the role to be played by teaching older pupils about race as a major political and social issue, it has directed its attention by and large to the development of an across the curriculum policy to ensure that a diversity of cultural sources are drawn on in the everyday learning experiences of younger children. The Schools Council project, Education for a Multiracial Society (1973–76), attempted both to elaborate a theory to underpin such a policy and to illustrate and illuminate the theory through practical exemplars. By building up a bank of descriptions of innovation in action we hoped not only that we might inject a sense of reality into the debate, but also to extract from

* *Journal of Curriculum Studies*, 1981, vol 13/1.

the exemplars principles of good practice which could serve as guidelines for others.

During this period on the project my own main interest lay in evaluating multicultural innovations in the humanities area of the middle school curriculum – with particular reference to what is often called 'teaching about other cultures'. Given the nature of the project the objects for this kind of teaching were invariably the cultures of the countries of immigrant origin in Africa, the Caribbean and the Indian sub-continent. The aim of the evaluation was to ascertain the impact of the teaching on the children's knowledge, sensitivities, opinions and attitudes; the assessment instrument for this purpose usually comprised knowledge tests, classroom observation, scrutiny of written and art work, and taped interviews with teachers and pupils. At the time I was conscious of working within a style of educational evaluation which was already being designated 'illuminative' and whose defining characteristics can now be seen to include: a preference for case study; a commitment to non-technical language in writing up; a weighting in favour of qualitative rather that quantitative material; an attention to unintended as well as intended effects; a concern for processes as well as intentions and outcomes; a regard for the views and interpretations of the different groups involved.[3]

In none of my evaluations, however, did I renounce the evaluator's traditional role of external critic and judge. One type of illuminative evaluation, which is normally associated with Barry MacDonald's adumbration of a 'democratic' model for the evaluator's work, aspires to recognize 'value pluralism' by confining itself to 'the collection of definitions of, and reactions to, the programme' and withdrawing from the business of conclusions and recommendations.[4] Recently this model has been translated to the field of multicultural education in an insightful article by MacDonald and colleagues, several of whom were co-workers in the Stenhouse research.[5] My own evaluations fit into their model to the extent that they tried to take account of the 'many-sided reality' and 'developing dynamics of innovations in *situ*', but in no case did I refrain from communicating the judgements and conclusions I had formed regarding particular initiatives. I can appreciate why the advocates of 'democratic' evaluation should attach such importance to 'value-free' or 'pluralistic' descriptions of innovations in the multicultural field, not least because of the risk of what they call 'ideological contamination', but it was not within my discretion during the project years to opt for descriptions, had I even conceded the cogency of the case. I was required to form and communicate opinions on two counts. First, the schools and teachers involved, regarding me as in some sense an expert in view of my status as a Schools Council researcher and my experience of working in multicultural classrooms, expected me to fulfil the function of friendly critic; secondly, my project function was to contribute to the bank of descriptions of innovation in action with a view to helping formulate principles of good practice. So, although I certainly incorporated the opinions and interpretations of pupils and teachers wherever possible, I always saw myself as ultimate arbiter of an innovation's success or failure – which is not to say that I was unaware of the influence on my judgements of my value position, nor that I never phrased some conclusions tentatively or subsequently revised some opinions.

Case study: a topic on India

One conclusion, one embryonic principle for good practice, already formulated in the early summer of 1976 was that the most obvious kind of multicultural innovation for eight to thirteen-year olds – overt teaching about countries of immigrant origin – might not necessarily be the best, indeed might actually be harmful especially in schools with poor race relations and without comprehensive multicultural curriculum policies. We monitored a number of innovations of this kind which appeared to suffer counterproductive effects – antagonizing white children and embarrassing or upsetting the minority children whose culture was suddenly experiencing such public exposure – and felt, therefore, disposed to argue that it might be sounder curriculum tactics to draw on minority cultures in a more subtle and oblique manner, not just to prevent counter-productive effects, but also to ensure they made more regular appearances in everyday classwork.

At about this time the humanities adviser in an outer London borough drew my attention to a topic on India being undertaken by a top middle school class of eleven- and twelve-year-olds. Ten of the class were Indian (nine of them Sikhs), seven were English, and one was Jamaican. The teacher (Mrs. S), who was responsible for teaching the class all their humanities subjects (roughly half the timetable), was a home economics specialist and strongly committed to the idea of multicultural education. Her intentions in embarking on the topic were generally to increase knowledge and appreciation of Indian culture and, in addition, in the case of the Indian children to furnish them with the opportunity for enhancing self-esteem. The topic had begun with the BBC television series *Near and Far* which had programmes covering different aspects of life in India – physical geography, crops, a village in the Himalayas, industrial development, Diwali, and so on – to which the teacher had added lessons of her own on recent Indian history – the Mutiny, the Independence movement, partition in 1947 and the war over what was to become Bangladesh in 1971. Finally, the children did individual or group study on things as various as ancient India, the history of New Delhi, Guru Nanak, hockey and cookery.

It was at this point that I arrived. I quickly fell into conversation with a Sikh boy who had clearly both benefited from the classwork and thoroughly enjoyed his own private research. During our conversation a white girl sitting nearby leaned over and whispered behind the back of her hand, 'Sir, some of us don't think we should be doing this work.' 'Why not?' I asked. She seemed inhibited from replying by the approach of the teacher. At the end of the lesson I asked the white girl and the Sikh boy to choose three friends each for separate taped discussions on the India topic the following week. I guessed (correctly) the white girl would choose three white girls and the Sikh boy three Sikh boys.

Essentially my evaluation of this topic on India consisted of conclusions based on these two taped discussions – involving eight children in all, just under half the class. I had not been able to observe lessons because news of the topic had only reached me when it was virtually complete, and constraints imposed by the Schools Council project schedule did not allow me to explore in detail the reactions of the rest of the class, the teacher or the staff as a whole. It is, therefore, best seen as a *partial* evaluation whose conclusions, such as they are, should be approached with caution.[6] However, the data have always struck me as sufficiently remarkable to merit a fuller examination than the two pages accorded to them in the as yet unpublished project report. They focus attention on that most interesting of areas for curriculum evaluation – what I call here 'pupils' perspectives'.

Until quite recently pupils have figured in curriculum evaluation as objects. They have been tested and investigated, on a diversity of measures, to establish how far changes in knowledge, perception, sensitivity and attitude have been in the direction of the curriculum's prespecified objectives. Some of my own evaluation falls into this category. For example, one of the reasons for a taped discussion is to see how substantial and accurate the increase in pupils' knowledge has been. But integral to the concept of 'illuminative' evaluation is the conviction that participants, even school children, are autonomous actors entitled to their own interpretations and opinions. In sampling 'pupils' perspectives' I seek both to learn what a particular innovation has done for their knowledge, thoughts and feelings, and also what their own view of its success or failure, strengths and weaknesses, might be.

Pupils' perspectives 1: four Sikh boys

The main difficulty involved in assessing the quality and quantity of the knowledge the Sikh boys had acquired from the topic was disentangling school learning from parental instruction and childhood or holiday memories. For instance, three of the four could recall village life in some detail:

SB 1: I can remember my village, how it looks.
SB 2: I can't.
SB 1: There was a river about a hundred yards away from our house and a road going right over a bridge. I remember every few days I used to go to the river and splash in the water with my friends.
SB 3: We used to have a sort of sugar field.
SB 1: We had loads of sugar-cane fields at the back of our house.
SB 4: And rice fields.
RJ: Your parents were farmers?
Boys: Yes.
SB 2: All the Indians are nearly farmers.
SB 3: I remember what my grandfather's house looks like.
SB 4: Some of our relations, they are carpenters.
SB 1: Nearly every person in the village knows their next door neighbour and all the people in the village because it is so small.
SB 4: In small villages everybody knows everybody.

Similarly all four claimed to have been told something of the history of India, particularly the independence movement, by their parents. I was most aware of parental influence, to say nothing of Sikh bias, in the boys' graphic anecdotes about partition in 1947 and war with Pakistan in 1965 and 1971:

RJ: Do you think it has turned out for the best that there was partition?
Boys: Yes.
SB 3: If it weren't, there would be murder right now all over the country.

SB 4:   And we wouldn't be here.

RJ: You wouldn't be here? Why not?

SB 4:   They kidnapped the young children and killed them.

RJ: Who did?

Boys: The Muslims.

SB 4:   They used to put them in little boxes and, once they had crippled or blinded them, make them beg.

★ ★ ★ ★ ★ ★

SB 3:   The Sikhs find the cow so holy because when they had a war with Pakistan the Pakistanis got a cow and they cut it up and put it in the river which was running through between them and the Indians never crossed it because there was cow blood in it.

RJ: I see.

SB 3:   The Sikhs cut pigs into little bits and threw it across as far as they could possibly throw it.

I tried to distinguish the contributions of home and school by asking the boys directly:

RJ: Did you know this before you started the work with Mrs. S?

SB 1:   My mum told me about it.

Boys: Some of it yes.

SB 3:   How we got independence, about our religion and about the Muslim religion.

SB 4:   My dad told me all these, you know, stories and histories of India.

SB 2:   My dad told me as well.

RJ: What was new to you in what you learned at school?

SB 1:   We didn't know *how* they got independence. We knew about Gandhi. We didn't know about how they split and how they got, exactly how they got . . . my mum had told me a few bits but not exactly how.

Whatever the provenance of the boys' information, and considerable as much of it was, it was often also garbled, patchy and uncertain. They confused the Mutiny with the Amritsar Massacre, were vague over dates and unsure who killed Gandhi and why. For example:

SB 3:   Some of us didn't know who killed Gandhi.

SB 4:   It was a Muslim, I think.

SB 1:   It was a Hindu.

SB 3.   It was Nehruran★.

* It was, in fact, Nathuran Godse, a Hindu fanatic.

SB 1: He was on the British side – er, on the Hindu side.

The quality and quantity of their knowledge are perhaps best exemplified by their discussion of partition, the concluding section of which has already been quoted. It began as follows:

RJ: Why do you think the British decided to divide India in 1947?

SB 1: Because there was a lot of rioting and murder in the country against the Muslims and the Hindus.

RJ: Why did that happen, do you think?

SB 1: Because the Muslims have their own community and the Hindus have their own.

SB 4: No, wait. The Hindus, they had their place in parliament, a post, but the Muslims didn't, so they made up their own party.

RJ: But why couldn't they get on together? Why did they have to. . . ?

SB 2: Because they had different castes.

RJ: Who had different castes?

SB 2: The Muslims.

SB 3: The Muslims thought a pig was unclean and the Hindus thought that a cow was sacred to them.

SB 4: They sort of had a quarrel about it.

SB 1: Eventually there was murdering all over the country.

The most striking feature of the boys' discussion – a feature tape transcript can scarcely convey – was its enthusiasm. They were never more enthusiastic than when talking about Gandhi on whose death, they reminded me, Nehru had said 'the most important saying in all India, "the light has come out of us and the dark has come into us"':

RJ: Do you think Gandhi was a great man?

Boys: Yes.

RJ: What made him great? What were his qualities?

SB 2: He was one of the leaders of India.

SB 4: He made India independent. He freed India and even now people follow him, you know, believe in him. But Gandhi didn't believe in castes and he didn't believe in low caste people.

SB 3: Yes, and he went and ate with the untouchables . . .

SB 4: And slept . . .

SB 3: Who were the lowest caste.

SB 4: And he helped the untouchables and all the high castes followed Gandhi and went and ate with the low castes, you know, sleep with the low castes.

But their enthusiasm was more broadly directed than simple reverence for the heroes of the independence struggle; it was for the whole idea and experience of having their culture and country of origin accorded recognition and status in the regular school curriculum. After an interruption to the discussion one boy continued:

SB 4: I was saying about things which we didn't know and we learned at school; to an Indian child this is very important because things they don't know they suddenly pick up at school during their lessons and all that.

SB 3: Some people have come from India when they were small and they don't know all that much about India and they haven't got all that much money to go to India, so they learn about it here.

SB 2: Like me, because I was born here and I don't know as much. I had to pick it up from my parents and from school.

RJ: Do you think it is important that you should know?

Boys: Yes

SB 3: Very important.

RJ: Why?

SB 3: Because we came from that country.

SB 4: Because you learn about the religion and we need to know about the country and how we live and . . . different parts of it.

On the other hand, the boys were only too aware that their own enthusiasm for the topic had to be set against its unpopularity with some of their white classmates:

SB 3: They got very annoyed. They didn't know that much.

SB 1: They didn't like it when we saw a television programme and they were turning the rice with their feet; they complained about it.

SB 3: They were conferring all the time.

SB 2: They were saying that the rice got dirty but the rice was still inside the outer case; they were only drying it when it is wet.

SB 3: But with the feet.

RJ: What about learning about the history? How did they react to that?

SB 4: They were all fussy.

SB 1: Some of the people were interested but one or two were really fussy and they didn't do good work.

SB 3: Some people said they wanted to learn British.

RJ: Why don't they want to learn about India?

SB 3: Because they are not . . .

SB 4: We have that in geography as well.

SB 2: They wanted to do something else.

The full intensity, if not extent, of disgruntlement was revealed in my discussion with the four white girls a few days later.

Pupils' perspectives 2: four white girls

Considering that they probably started off with little or no knowledge, and their overall reluctance to study India at all, it was remarkable how much these four white girls knew, especially about Indian history. Here they are, for example, near the beginning of the discussion talking about Gandhi:

WG 1: And when we did about Gandhi, we were learning about his autobiography and things like that.

RJ: What can you remember about Gandhi?

WG 1: He wanted to be a lawyer when he was young and he went – he had to lose his caste to come over to England to train as a lawyer.

WG 3: Then he came back to India and he started to help the low castes.

RJ: What were they called?

Girls: Untouchables.

WG 3: And they had a salt march and he was put in prison because of that. They all went down to the sea to collect salt water.

WG 4: He was sent to prison.

RJ: Why was he put in prison?

WG 1: Because . . .

WG 2: It was against the law to get salt from the salt lakes.

WG 3: He stayed in prison and went on a hunger strike.

WG 1: And the British were afraid that he would kill himself, that he would die, because there would be riots or something like that, so they let him out.

Much of what they had to say, however, in the early part of the discussion was vague and inaccurate. Moreover they were quite unapologetic about their ignorance. They made it amply plain that they could not have cared less, for example, why Gandhi went to South Africa, who the first Indian prime minister was or whether Pakistan was a Hindu or Muslim state. The extent of their knowledge, and their attitude towards it, are best illustrated by their discussion of the Mutiny:

RJ: Now somebody mentioned the Mutiny. What was that?

WG 2: That was a war.

WG 4: That was sort of army.

WG 1: Yes.

RJ: What happened in it?

WG 1: I think it was us trying to get India – or they're trying to get India for themselves.

WG 4: They sort of had a fight, you know, that you had to grease the gun and they didn't like that.

WG 2: With pig's or cow's fat.

WG 3: And you had to do it because of the bullets.

WG 1: One night they killed some of the generals.

WG 3: What, when there were the big riots?

WG 1: While they were asleep in this place. I don't know where it was, but the Indians killed some of the generals.

WG 2: And when the Indians were all going out of this great big fort, I think it was.

WG 1: Hospital.

WG 2: Yes, the English killed every man that was standing.

WG 1 & 3: I thought it was the Indians killed the English!

WG 2: Was it?

WG 1 & 3: Yes, it was the Indians shot all the English.

Whenever the British entered the discussion, the apathy, real or feigned, evaporated. Not that it was replaced by crude jingoism. When I asked the girls to say where their sympathies lay in regard to the independence movement, a childlike sense of justice vied with paternalistic condescension in their response:

RJ: When you were learning about the independence movement, where did your sympathies lie? Who did you feel sympathetic towards?

WG 1: The Indians, I think, because if it is their own country, their native country, I don't think . . .

WG 4: Yes, they should rule it themselves.

WG 3: They should have a president or King.

WG 1: I think we were right at first, not to let them have it, because they might fight, you know, the Hindus and Muslims, I thought we were right then. But when we kept on saying 'We'll give it to you' and then not, I thought that was wrong. We should have kept our promises.

WG 2: But I am glad they're sort of independent – they made Pakistan and India separate.

RJ: Why?

WG 2: Well because there would be a war together if they didn't. West Pakistan and the other Pakistan, they are separate, and I think that is a bit stupid. They should be both together.

Shortly afterwards one girl (WG 1), the most loquacious in the group, changed not only the course of the discussion but its whole tenor and ethos. From being languid and desultory it became animated and impassioned:

WG 1: I watched this film the other day and you know when we gave the Indians independence they said that we will still keep with the British, they said that, well, there was this programme on the other day and you know all the Indians are coming over into our country, well this man on the TV (it was quite some time ago actually), this Indian man goes, 'We stayed with Britain and they are the only country that will take us in. They must take us into the country, because we kept with them in independence.' 'Cause none of the other countries wanted them to come in and so they said, 'Britain must take us in.' Now, I'd like to know why they are coming into here, instead of staying over in their country.

This remarkable speech bequeathed the discussion two lines of development – one, the causes of migration from India, short-term; the other, the transformation of the town as a result of Indian settlement, long-term – which threatened my chosen role as detached enquirer. On the first the girls' preoccupation was with poverty:

WG 3: It is because they are poor, or what? They aren't really poor, are they?

RJ: Well, what picture did you get from the work that you did? Did you get the impression that India was a poor country?

WG 4: From the television programmes it is.

WG 1: But it isn't, not in the big cities. I mean, they could do a lot for their country. There are so many people in there; there is quite a bit.

RJ: Oh yes.

WG 1: It's the third biggest population country in the world, isn't it?

RJ: I don't know about that, but it's pretty big anyway.

WG 1: Well there is a lot of people in there and they could do wonders for the world. I mean, you watch Russia, they built their country up well except that they come up communist.

RJ: So why do you think it is that India has still this tremendous problem of poverty, even though there are, as you say, big cities?

WG 1: I think it is because they are . . .

WG 2: They're lazy

WG 1: Well, most of them when you see the films they are all thin. They're not very fat and they aren't very strong.

WG 4: There isn't enough food then.

WG 2: They're lazy.

WG 4: I think it is because of the children.

★ ★ ★ ★ ★

WG 2: If you see these things like droughts, all they do is sit round. They're sort of not trying to get more crops in.

WG 3: They're just sitting round trying to save the ones that are dying. Why don't they plant some more and try and keep those?

RJ: How can you if there is a drought? You've got no rain.

The other line of development, the transformation of the town following Indian settlement, began from the same white girl's description of 'debates' between white and Sikh children which took place in their teacher's absence:

WG 1: You know the other boys you had the other day (i.e. the Sikh boys), well while Mrs. S is out of the room we have debates, you know, all moaning at each other, and they keep on going, 'Oh, India is a great country. It's the richest country.' They're going, 'It's got lots of money' and that. I go, 'Why don't you go there? Why are you all coming over here?' And they don't take no notice of you. And there's P and he goes, 'India's the best country', and I said 'Why don't you go over and live there? You only come over here to take our money,' you know, out of the shops and everything like that. Why don't you go to India?' And they just don't answer.

WG 3: Then we say, 'Well you've taken B (the borough in which they lived) off of us.'

WG 1: Well, they're trying to.

RJ: What do you mean?

WG 2: They said they're going to try and name it another name.

★ ★ ★ ★ ★

WG 2: Look at all the film shows there used to be here. There used to be a really good film show but look at it. It's all Indian. Like 'Karahara', something like that (laughter). There's not one good film show.

WG 1: My sister works in a travel agents in town and she heard Indians standing on boxes like Hyde Park Corner and they were saying, 'We're going to take over B and they are really, because everyone in B is moving out. Then they are going to buy the houses and then it is going to be all Indian.

WG 3: My mum said, 'Even if we are all shot down dead, we are not going to move from this house.'

This white girl (WG 3) was later to provide a further verbatim account of a 'debate' with a Sikh girl:

WG 3: I goes, 'Why don't you go back to your own country?'
  She goes, 'I'm not going back to my own country.'
  I goes, 'Why don't you?'
  She goes, 'Because I like this country.'
  I goes, 'Do you like this country better than India?'
  She goes, 'No.'
  I goes, 'Why don't you go back then?'
  She goes, 'Because I was born here and I am English.'
  I goes, 'Well, your mum and dad are Indian, why don't they take you to India to see what it is like?'
  She goes, 'I don't want to'.

The strongest indication of real hostility between Sikh and white children came towards the end of the discussion:

WG 2: They swear at us in Indian too.

WG 4: Yeah.

WG 1: In this school they are not allowed to speak in Indian but they do. They just swear at you in Indian. They go . . . (imitation of Punjabi) . . . and laugh their heads off. They stick their tongues out.

WG 3: So we speak in back slang back to them.

RJ: Aren't there any Indian children you count amongst your friends?

Girls: Well.

RJ: Any that you would take home for tea or go to a party with?

Girls: No (laughter).

This is not to suggest that the impression left by the girls' discussion was of blanket hostility towards the topic and their Asian classmates, nor that they simply reinforced one another's opinions in an irresistible thrust towards a racist consensus. For instance, one girl's assertion that there were no white-owned shops left in a particular street was challenged by another – 'Oh yes there is, don't talk rubbish' – and there were, by the end, several dents in the group's repatriationism – 'I suppose she can't go to India really because she doesn't know much Indian' – and in the overall antagonism:

WG 1: There used to be one girl, Nilah, she was nice. She's gone to India.

WG 2: And Nirmala.

Girls: Yes.

WG 3: She was quiet though.

WG 2: She was a good drawer, she was. I liked her.

WG 1: She was nice, she was.

WG 4: We've got an Indian lady friend at home.

However, there is no escaping the conclusion that the topic was unpopular with these four white girls, in principle and in execution, and that it had exacerbated rather than assuaged the resentments which they already harboured.

RJ: But let's go back to the work you did on India. What you have been talking about now (i.e. the transformation of the town), how did your feelings about that affect what you thought about the work on India?

WG 1: Nothing, not mine.

WG 2: Not mine either.

WG 3: No.

RJ: Didn't you see the two connected in any way?

WG 1: I don't know. But if we went to that country, the English and it was our country and this was their country, I think it would be a good country, because I think that everyone would work hard enough to make it a good country.

RJ: I think it was you, Y, you were complaining a bit when I spoke to you when I first came, at having to learn about it.

Girls: Yes, everything, history, geography, religion.

WG 2: We don't seem to learn much about England or any other country. We want to learn about England.

★ ★ ★ ★ ★

RJ: Now you've been in school for seven years and are you telling me you have learned nothing about England in seven years?

Girls: Well, we have learned things.

WG 3: We haven't learned much about England and English things in Mrs. S's class.

WG 2: She's going to hear this (laughter).

WG 1: We would like to learn about the people of Britain. There are lots of different kinds of people in Britain. I mean, we'd like to learn about that kind of thing. Or things about America. That's big

enough. We'd like to learn things like that about another country.
You see, I think we are learning about India because there are so
many in schools now that we have *got* to learn what they are like.

RJ: Isn't that a good reason?

WG 1: It is a good reason all right.

WG 3: You can make criticisms of them more now than what you used to.

Aftermath

Both Sikh boys and white girls were sufficiently pleased with their
discussions to suggest to me, independently of one another, that I play
their tape to the rest of the class. In the case of the white girls the
suggestion was made in the spirit of provocative bravado. Having got away
in the taped discussion with comments which would probably have been
inadmissible in the classroom, they seemed keen to see how far they could
push their luck. To both groups I explained that the decision had to be
their teacher's not mine; to the girls I added my view, from which they did
not dissent, that some of our discussion had covered ground too sensitive
for a full class hearing. In any event I did not feel disposed to pass on the
suggestion to the teacher. Either the children should repeat it to her or it
should strike her unprompted as a good idea. Her reactions to the tapes
might have been predicted. She was delighted with the Sikh boys'
discussion – their enthusiasm for the topic, the quality of their English –
and played it to the rest of the staff, who were equally appreciative, one
day after school. On the other hand she was not delighted with the girls'
discussion; nor were her colleagues. Indeed I have to say I found their
response defensive and evasive. They appeared to believe that the girls'
disgruntlement could be explained away simply because one of the group
(WG 1), who dominated certain passages of discussion and was the most
talkative overall, had a parent in the National Front. The staff made their
own copy of the boys' tape but not of the girls'. On the latter I was
summoned by the headteacher. He wanted my assurance that the school's
anonymity would be guaranteed in the project's report and that I would
only make use of the girls' tape, again with the identity of the school
concealed, in removed contexts such as research seminars and in-service
courses for teachers. I was happy to assure him on both counts since what
he was asking was established professional practice, but he made no
attempt to conceal from me the fact that his special reason in this instance
for underlining established professional practice was that the girls'
discussion seriously threatened the school's publicly declared image of

itself as an oasis of interracial harmony. Eventually the tapes were used as evidence in the project report to substantiate our scepticism about overt topics on countries of origin because the success this particular topic could claim for having enhanced the cultural knowledge and pride of the Indian children appeared to have been at the expense of alienating and nourishing the prejudices of some of their white classmates. Even at the time I was uneasy about this simplistic conclusion, and indeed about the exploitation of the tapes for such an end, since I had, after all, participated in two fascinating discussions which had in themselves felt like successes; so I added a qualification to the effect that, whatever the topic may have done to the white girls' attitudes there could be no doubt that they had derived some sort of benefit, of a cathartic nature perhaps, from the opportunity to talk out deep-seated anxieties and resentments with an uncensorious white adult. Over the past three years I have played the tapes to a variety of audiences – students in training, teachers on in-service courses, advisers, educational researchers – inviting them to debate the question of 'success' or 'failure'. Their deliberations have assisted me in the clarification of my thoughts – not least concerning my performance as a curriculum evaluator.

The evaluator's role

I approached this evaluation, like its predecessors, as an outside expert and the two taped discussions as a detached enquirer. To fulfil my twofold function – serving the school and the Schools Council project – I wanted to try and establish what the topic had done for the pupils' knowledge and attitudes and what their opinions of it were; or, to put it another way, whether the teacher's broad aims of increasing knowledge and appreciation of India (and, in the case of the Indian children, self-esteem) had been achieved. The Sikh boys fell in with my expectations readily. The white girls, on the other hand, albeit compliant at the outset, implicitly challenged my chosen role and induced a serious case of role-conflict.

The turning point was WG 1's unsolicited monologue shifting the discussion's attention to Indian immigration. At the end of it she asked me an indirect question ('I'd like to know why they are coming into here') which WG 3 quickly followed with a direct one ('Is it because they are poor, or what?'). I was momentarily at a loss. On no other occasion in an interview had a pupil turned round and asked me a question. Feebly I attempted to retain my role intact ('Well, what picture did you get from the work that you did?'), but, although they immediately responded to that ('From the television programmes it is'), further questions ensued at intervals throughout the rest of the tape. There can be no doubt about their motivation. They asked me questions because they wanted to know the answer. They were treating me, in other words, as a teacher. From that point onwards I was, in effect, *in loco magistri* – but, it must be stressed, this is not to suggest they saw me as a simple substitute for their actual teacher. On the contrary, for they were clearly prepared to say things in front of me which they would not have been prepared to say in front of her. Either, then, they saw me as a 'soft' teacher or they saw me as a confidant – a knowledgeable but uncensorious white adult.

At one or two sessions I have run in connection with the girls' tape I have been criticized by participants for giving them their heads and thereby tacitly supporting their incipient racism. This is one way of looking at it although, I believe, a mistaken one. I simply wanted to get to the roots of their antagonism. Subsequently, adopting their definition of me as a teacher, I began to query and challenge wild assertions and doubtful values. ('How can you if there is a drought?' 'Isn't that a good reason?' 'That's a bit of an exaggeration.' 'Isn't that understandable and right?') All of which led me to conclude that what teachers need to evaluate their curriculum innovations is not outside experts but the time, facilities and skills to do it themselves as an integral part of the teaching and learning process.[7]

Discussion

When set against her own objectives 'success' and 'failure' for the teacher of this topic on India were finely balanced. Obviously she had succeeded in imparting a good deal of knowledge to both Indian and white children, although gaps and confusions persisted, and in enhancing the self-esteem of the Indians, but equally she could be said to have failed to the extent that the topic appeared to have merely alienated at least half her white pupils from herself, their Indian classmates and the curriculum in general. The precise nature of the 'failure' requires more detailed analysis. For the purposes of the Schools Council project's argument we attributed the teacher's failure to her decision to opt for an overt topic on India rather than broader themes into which Indian culture could be incorporated along with others. This, or so we hypothesized, would at least have had the tactical advantage of forestalling any childlike complaints about her being 'unfair'.

Many participants in workshops I have run have criticized the teacher for not observing the hoary maxim – 'start where the children are' – or, rather, for not observing it consistently or completely. Whilst she had made some use of the Indian children's knowledge of their country of origin, she seemed to have taken no account of Indian immigration into Britain, the transformation of the borough into a multicultural community, the new evolving forms of Indian culture, nor, above all, what her white pupils knew and felt about all three. Whether interpreting the old maxim in these senses would have yielded more or fewer counterproductive effects is a moot point. Either way there are some who argue that counterproductive effects of this ilk are no bad thing; first, because for the children of the ethnic majority to undergo a sense of curriculum alienation is a salutary experience (part of unlearning attitudes acquired from the imperialist legacy), and, secondly, because if myths and prejudices are to be countered they must first be exposed.

My own considered view, almost four years after the event, is that if there was a failure it was pedagogic. The teacher had, as far as the class was concerned, publicly committed herself to multicultural education and Britain as a multicultural society. This is right and proper, and all too rare. But her commitment appeared to have expressed itself in such a fashion as to convince half her white pupils that she was on the Indian children's side and not theirs, and to conclude, rightly or wrongly, that statements and views they strongly subscribed to were inadmissible in the classroom. I am not referring here to racial slanging or personal remarks, which quite clearly infringe the basic ground-rules for class discussion any teacher would hope to lay down, but to the white girls' views, for example, on the state of India, immigration into Britain and the transformation of the local borough. Whether Britain and India are or are not 'great' countries seems to me a perfectly legitimate subject for classroom discussion with eleven- and twelve-year olds. The 'debates' which, on the girls' evidence, took place in their teacher's absence ought to have taken place in her presence. Similarly, their conversation with me (and, of course, the boys') ought to have been central to their experience of the topic – an integral discussion with their teacher, not an external discussion afterwards with a stranger. It is indisputably important that teachers should 'come clean' on salient social and moral issues. It is equally important, as a matter of rights as well as tactics, that pupils who have views on these same issues should have some kind of classroom forum for expressing and exploring them.

Notes and references

1. The research falls into two parts. The first part covers the evaluation of the so-called 'race-pack' of the Schools Council Humanities Curriculum Project in 1970, the second the evaluation of the three different strategies for teaching race relations in the SSRC/Gulbenkian Foundation Project between 1972 and 1975. On the first, see, for example, Bagley, C. and Verma, G. K. (1972) 'Some effects of teaching designed to promote understanding of racial issues in adolescence' *Journal of Moral Education* Vol. 1 No. 3; and, on the second, Verma, G. K. and Bagley, C. (1979) 'Measured changes in racial attitudes following the use of three different teaching methods' in *Race, Education and Identity* (eds) Verma and Bagley (Macmillan).

2. Two interesting case studies are, from the first stage of the research, Parkinson, J. P. and Macdonald, B. (1972) 'Teaching race neutrally' *Race* January (reproduced in this Reader as 4.5) and, from the second, Sikes, P. J. and Sheard, D. J. S. 'Teaching for better race relations?' (1978) *Cambridge Journal of Education* Vol. 8 No. 2/3.

3. These characteristics are defined and analyzed in Scrimshaw, P. (1979) 'Illuminative evaluation: some reflections' *Journal of Further and Higher Education*, Summer.

4. MacDonald, B. (1976) 'Evaluation and the control of education' in *Curriculum Evaluation: Trends and Implications* ed. D. Tawney.

5. Jenkins, D., Kemmis, S., MacDonald, B., Verma, G. K. (1979) 'Racism and educational evaluation' *Race, Education and Identity* eds. Verma and Bagley (Macmillan).

6. More comprehensive evaluations are to be found in the unpublished project report. One published example is 'A multi-racial classroom observed', Chapter 3 of my book (1979) *Positive Image: towards a multi-racial curriculum* (Writers and Readers Publishing Cooperative). This book also includes examples of attempts at teacher self-evaluation – a concept basic to the Stenhouse research. Two other teachers who have written valuably about their own innovations in the multicultural classroom are Searle, C. (1977) *The World in a Classroom* (Writers and Readers Publishing Cooperative) and Nandy, M. (1971) 'Social studies for a multi-racial society' in *The Multiracial School* eds. McNeal and Rogers (Penguin), reproduced in this Reader as 4.4.

7. The case for the teacher as his/her own evaluator and researcher has been fully developed by Lawrence Stenhouse (1975) in Chapter 10 of *An Introduction to Curriculum Research and Development* (Heinemann).

SECTION 5

PUPILS AND TEACHERS

CHAPTER 5.1

WHAT THE BRITISH SCHOOL SYSTEM DOES TO THE BLACK CHILD*
BERNARD COARD

The book from which this extract is taken was the first major published statement by a black educationalist in Britain. It made a considerable impact on its appearance in 1971. The author's argument is based on his own teaching experience and the social psychological research evidence available at the time suggesting that black children in the United States and Britain tended to suffer from negative self-image, poor self-concept and an insecure sense of identity. The relevance of this data a decade later has been challenged by more recent research – see, for example, Maureen Stone's piece, Chapter 1.4.

Some time ago a white boy of thirteen in the school for educationally subnormal children, where I teach, asked my permission to draw a picture of me. I had been his class teacher for one year. I had a very good relationship with him, and he was very fond of me. He enjoyed drawing. The picture he did of me was quite good. He had included my spectacles, which he always teased me about, and he also drew my moustache and beard while he made great jokes about them. When he was finished, he passed me the paper with the portrait of myself, looking very pleased with himself at having drawn what he considered a near-likeness. I said to him: 'Haven't you forgotten to do something?'

'What?' he said, looking curious and suspicious.

'You forgot to colour my face. My face and cheeks, etc – they are not white, are they?'

'No, no! I can't do that!' he said, looking worried.

* Chapter 5 of *How the West Indian Child is Made Educationally Sub-Normal in the British School System*, 1971, New Beacon Books, pp. 26–31.

'Well, you said you were painting a picture of me. Presumably you wanted it to look like me. You painted my hair, moustache and beard, and you painted them black – which they are. So you have to paint my face dark brown if it is to look like me at all.'

'No! I can't. I can't do that. No. No,' he said, looking highly embarrassed and disturbed. He then got up and walked away, finding himself a hammer to do woodwork with in the corner of the room far away from me.

This same boy, along with one of his white school friends, had waited outside the school gate for me one afternoon the previous week. When I approached, one of them said: 'People are saying that you are coloured, but you aren't, sir, are you?' This was a rhetorical question on their part. They both looked very worried that 'some people' should be calling me 'coloured', and wanted my reassurance that I was not. They both liked and admired me, and hated thinking that I might be coloured! I explained to them then, as I *had* done many times before in class, that I *was* black, that I was from the West Indies, and that my forefathers came from Africa. They obviously had mental blocks against accepting me as being black.

This white boy, who did not even know who 'coloured people' were, obviously had the most fearful image of what black people were supposed to be like, even though his favourite teacher was black, and one of his closest friends in class was a black child. I happened to know that his house-mother at the children's home where he lives has never discussed race with him, and does not display any open prejudice to black people. In fact she has, over the years, been an excellent foster-mother to two West Indian boys. Yet he picked up from somewhere a sufficiently adverse image of black people, that he couldn't bear to have his favourite teacher be 'coloured', and could not bring himself to draw me as I was – a black man. He had to have my face white!

This experience of mine gave me an idea; if this is how two white boys in the class felt about me, then perhaps they felt the same way about their close friend, Desmond, a black boy of eleven from Jamaica. So I gathered together all the drawings and paintings which the children had done of each other, and sure enough, Desmond got painted white by all the white children! What's worse, Desmond and the other four black children had painted each other white also!

A week later, Desmond, the West Indian boy, asked me to draw a picture of him. I drew the outline, as he watched, making critical comments from time to time. Having completed the outline, I began shading his face black. He immediately said: 'What – what are you doing? You are *spoiling* me!'

I said: 'No, of course not. I am painting you as you are – black; just like *I* am. Black *is* beautiful, you know. You aren't ashamed of that, are you?'

At that he calmed down, and I completed shading his face black. Then I did his hair. His hair was black, short, and very African in texture. I drew it exactly as his hair really was. When he saw it, he jumped out of his chair and shouted: 'You painted me to look like a golliwog! You make me look just like a golliwog!' and he was half about to cry, half about to pounce on me for having done so terrible a thing as to have drawn his hair like it was, instead of making it long, straight and brown, as he had drawn himself in the past!

After I had calmed him down, again by pointing out that my hair was exactly the same as his, and that *I* liked mine, he decided to retaliate by drawing one of me. He drew my hair black and African-like, he drew my moustache and beard, but he, like the white boy before, refused to shade my face dark brown or black even though I had done his that way. When I asked him to draw my face the colour it really was, rather than leaving it white, he said very emotionally: 'You do it yourself', and walked out of the room.

Obviously in an English classroom it is terrible to be black. The white child is concerned lest his best friend be considered black, and the black child is more than concerned that he should be considered black!

And this is what this society, with the aid of the school system, is doing to our black children!

The examples I have given above are not isolated ones. There is the Indian girl in my class who wears Indian clothes to school and whose mother wears her caste-marks and sari when going anywhere, and yet this girl once denied she was Indian when speaking to her English friends in the class. Or there is the case of the Jamaican girl in my class who pretended not to know where Jamaica was, and stated indignantly that she was not from 'there' when speaking to some of the other children one day. Both conversations I overheard by accident. I could give case after case, for they are endless. In fact, none of the West Indian children, whom I taught and ran clubs for over a period of three years, have failed to reveal their feelings of ambiguity, ambivalence, and at times despair, at being black. Many have been made neurotic by their school experience.

How the system works

The black child's true identity is denied daily in the classroom. In so far as he is given an identity, it is a false one. He is made to feel inferior in every way. In addition to being told he is dirty and ugly and 'sexually unreliable', he is told by a variety of means that he is intellectually inferior. When he prepares to leave school, and even before, he is made to realize that he and 'his kind' are only fit for manual, menial jobs.

The West Indian child is told on first entering the school that his language is second rate, to say the least. Namely, the only way he knows how to speak, the way he has always communicated with his parents and family and friends; the language in which he has expressed all his emotions, from joy to sorrow; the language of his innermost thoughts and ideas, is 'the wrong way to speak'.

A man's language is part of him. It is his only vehicle for expressing his thoughts and feelings. To say that his language and that of his entire family and culture is second rate, is to accuse him of *being* second rate. But this is what the West Indian child is told in one manner or another on his first day in an English school.

As the weeks and months progress, the black child discovers that all the great men of history were white – at least, those are the only ones he has been told about. His reading-books show him white children and white adults exclusively. He discovers that white horses, white rocks and white unicorns are beautiful and good; but the word 'black' is reserved for describing the pirates, the thieves, the ugly, the witches, etc. This is the *conditioning effect* of what psychologists call *word association* on people's minds. If every reference on TV, radio, newspapers, reading books and story-books in school shows 'black' as being horrible and ugly, and everything 'white' as being pure, clean and beautiful, then people begin to think this way on racial matters.

Several months ago in my class I was reading one of S. K. McCullagh's story-books for children, *The Country of the Red Birds*. This author is world famous, and she has written numerous story-books and reading series for children, used in schools in many parts of the world. She is actually a lecturer in psychology. In this story, these two white children went out to the 'island of Golden Sands'. They got to the 'white rock', where the very helpful 'white unicorn' lives. When they met the unicorn, 'the first thing that they saw was a black ship, with black sails, sailing towards the white rock'.

'The black pirates! The black pirates!' cried the little unicorn. 'They'll kill us! Oh, what shall we do?'

Finally they escaped from the white rock, which the 'black pirates' had taken over, and went to the island of the 'red birds'. There ' a black pirate stood on the sand, with a red bird in his hand', about to kill it. The white boys and the white unicorn, along with the other red birds, managed to beat off the black pirate, and the red birds in gratitude to the white boys and white unicorn state: 'We will do anything for you, for you have saved a red bird from the black pirates.'

For those who may be sceptical about the influence of word association on people's minds, it is interesting to note that when I said 'black pirates' in the story, several of the white children in the class turned their heads and looked at the black children, who in turn looked acutely embarrassed.

When the pictures, illustrations, music, heroes, great historical and contemporary figures in the classroom are all white, it is difficult for a child to identify with anyone who is not white. When in addition the pictures of blacks are golliwog stereotypes, about whom filthy jokes are made; when most plays show black men doing servant jobs; when the word 'black' in every story-book is synonymous with evil, then it becomes impossible for the child to want to be black. Put another way, it would be unnatural of him not to want to be white. Does this not explain why Desmond and the other black children draw themselves as white? Can you blame them?

But this is not the end of the picture, unfortunately, for the black children know they are black. Whenever they might begin in their fantasy to believe otherwise, they are soon reassured on this score by being told they are 'black bastards' whenever there is a row in the playground – and even when there isn't.

The children are therefore made neurotic about their race and culture. Some show behaviour problems as a result. They become resentful and bitter at being told their language is second-rate, and their history and culture is non-existent; that they hardly exist at all, except by grace of the whites – and then only as platform sweepers on the Underground, manual workers, and domestic helps.

The black child under these influences develops a deep inferiority complex. He soon loses motivation to succeed academically, since, at best, the learning experience in the classroom is an elaborate irrelevance to his personal life situation, and at worst it is a racially humiliating experience. He discovers in an amazingly short space of time the true role of the black man in a white-controlled society, and he abandons all intellectual and career goals. Remember the four-year-old black girl in America, mentioned earlier, who said to Mary Goodman: 'The people that are white, they can go up. The people that are brown, they have to go down.' When two other psychologists in America (Radke and Trager) investigated 'Children's perception of the social roles of negroes and whites' (in the *Journal of Psychology*, 29:1950) the 'poor house' was assigned to negroes and the 'good house' to whites by the great majority of white and negro children aged five to eight years.

Conclusion

The black child acquires two fundamental attitudes or beliefs as a result of his experiencing the British school system: a low self-image, and consequently low self-expectations in life. These are obtained through streaming, banding, bussing, ESN schools, racist news media, and a white middle-class curriculum; by totally ignoring the black child's language, history, culture, identity. Through the choice of teaching materials, the society emphasizes who and what it thinks is important – and by implication, by omission, who and what it thinks is unimportant, infinitesimal, irrelevant. Through the belittling, ignoring or denial of a person's identity, one can destroy perhaps the most important aspect of a person's personality – his sense of identity, of who he is. Without this, he will get nowhere.

CHAPTER 5.2

TEACHING YOUNG BLACKS★
FARRUKH DHONDY

I have been a teacher in London's secondary schools for nearly nine years. When I was at university before that I never considered teaching as a career. A number of my contemporaries at university, some of them my friends, wanted to be teachers. They used to talk about the schools they'd been to, and about the changes they would make, the attitudes they would take with them when they were on the other side of the teacher's desk, the other side of the staffroom door. This was Cambridge University. Coming from Poona, I shared feelings and good times with other students from India, Pakistan and Africa. There were, at that time, only two young men from the West Indies, and they were training to be oil engineers.

Very many of us 'foreign students', when we got comfortable with the ways and workings of the university, made friends amongst the minority of students who came from the British working class and seemed acutely conscious of having come from it. Some of them talked about 'comprehensive' schools. They spoke passionately about the school system and how for too long it had been divided into corridors of privilege; how most students who went to our university came from fee-paying public schools or from grammar schools which took the 'cleverest' pupils from the working class, those who had proved themselves in an examination at the age of eleven called the 'eleven plus'. They gave me the impression that this 'eleven plus' exam was the enemy of everything, that it had to go, that

★ *Race Today*, 1978, May/June, pp. 80–85. This article, which refers to a number of episodes and issues in the race and education debate in London in the 1970s, develops a similar argument to an earlier one by the same author published in the same journal in February 1974 – 'The Black Explosion in Schools'. Farrukh Dhondy's stories, mentioned at the end of the article, have been published as *East End at Your Feet* (Macmillan Topliner) and *Come to Mecca and Other Stories* (Collins).

they were at university because they were hard-working and because the British system of concessions allowed a few from the working class to slip through the net and become doctors, lawyers etc. At the time, very few people talked about blacks in schools. The problem was a class problem, and the articles which I read about it seemed to say that the Labour Party would sort all that out by putting all pupils in school under the same purpose-built roof, ironing out once and for all the schooling system which preserved privilege as surely as a gentleman's club preserves its membership.

I became a teacher because I was poor when I left university, wanted a wage, and it was one of the few areas of employment in which I would be accepted. I went into it with uncertainty and no sense of mission.

In the staffroom of the school at which I first taught, nobody talked about 'class'. It was as though the word didn't exist in the vocabulary. All the teachers talked about was blacks, because something very special was happening to that school. It was called Henry Thornton. It is situated in Clapham in South London, and at the time I started to teach there, it had been formed as a new school through the amalgamation of an old grammar school and two other schools called Aristotle and Tennyson, which had been closed down. It was panic. The schools named after the Greek philosopher and the Victorian poet were mixing very uneasily with the boys of Henry Thornton. A very large proportion of the Aristotelians and the Tennysonians was black. The grammar school was almost all white. What the headmaster and the Inner London Education Authority, which runs the school, had done, was to divide the school into eleven classes for each year. The casses were numbered from one to eleven, or, in some years, from one to ten, and two classes called X and Y were tagged onto the end.

Remember that at the time I read in the newspapers, almost every day, that the Labour Government of Harold Wilson was giving every child in Britain a new opportunity of equality through schooling. I read this on the bus to school, and when I actually went into the classroom to teach, I saw that all the top classes or forms in the school were exclusively white, and all the bottom forms, including the two, X and Y, which were composed of all the trouble-makers who wouldn't take instruction in the other forms, were black.

Black studies

In the staffroom, and in teachers' meetings to which I went, teachers constantly talked about the West Indians. Nobody knew how to deal with them. Very many of them in the lower forms wouldn't allow the teacher to start a lesson. All sixty minutes of the lesson would be spent fighting and arguing and learning to cope with rudeness and resistance to whatever it was you had taken trouble to plan to teach. It was frustrating. It was a baptism of abuse.

In the top classes it was somewhat simpler. The youth in those classes, who were exclusively white, seemed to want to know how to interpret a poem written by Wilfred Owen, or how to read a scene from Shakespeare, or where to put commas when writing a long sentence, or even what Bob Dylan was saying when he said 'A Hard Rain's A-Gonna Fall'. In the black streams of the school, I only managed to achieve peace through threats, entreaties, and by talking to the youths about themselves, getting them to talk about themselves, giving them tape recorders and cameras to record their opinions and images, to tell stories, play with the technology of tape and film and amplifier and represent themselves.

The black power movement had captured attention at the time. It made many demands. Amongst them, it asked for black studies in the schools. It was asking for the history of the Caribbean to be taught, for the truth to be told about slavery and colonialism and for the language of the ghetto to be brought into the language of the classroom. Teachers talked about all these things in their own time and in seminars organized by the state which paid us. What was remarkable was that the teachers' union to which I belong didn't whisper a word about it. At the meetings which I attended it was as though pupils didn't exist. I began to discover that there were 'left-wing' groups operating in the union. They didn't say anything about blacks either. Perhaps they were too busy trying to get teachers to vote in union meetings for the resolutions they were pushing which asked for better pay. They called for strikes, and demonstrations, for which I voted, and on which I and my colleagues went. Whenever it came to a strike, the left-wingers began to issue leaflets to parents about the 'quality of education'. It was a strategy to build public opinion behind teachers' claims. The argument was, and still is, that if you paid the teachers more, hired more teachers, or gave more money from the budget to the schools, so that we could have more equipment, secretarial help and more books or whatever, then the working class would inevitably benefit.

Of course that wasn't new and didn't start when I entered teaching. The Labour Party had been saying that for a long time, and very many teachers still believe that schools are part of the welfare facilities that the

British state offers its population. It follows from this, that they must be improved and must be made to seem fair to everybody.

The black education movement

In the late sixties and early seventies, blacks began to complain that schools weren't fair to them. A group of West Indian parents in Haringey in North London protested and fought the education authority to do away with a system of 'banding' which appeared to them to put blacks in a second class position in the school. The Asian communities began protesting about the 'bussing' of their children to different parts of a borough, because they knew that the few Asian children who came from outside the area into schools miles away from their homes and their communities, were picked on and attacked by other pupils. West Indian groups began to protest about the large numbers of black pupils who were being sent to schools for the educationally sub-normal (ESN). There isn't space here to give it the detailed history it deserves. I simply want to give the impression that there was a lot of activity from the black population of Britain on the educational issue. There was a black movement in education in this country from the time that our children began to be schooled here. Its spokesmen were the parents of the young blacks who were born here or brought here from the West Indies, from India, Pakistan, Bangladesh and Africa, as dependants.

In the classrooms I taught, in the playgrounds of the school, in the neighbourhoods and ghettoes from which the school drew its population, another movement was in progress. To the classroom teacher it was merely a nuisance at first. It grew into something else. It forced recognition for itself.

The first time it took the public stage was in 1974. Three West Indian youths had been arrested by police after an affray at a fair in Brockwell Park in Brixton. One of the youths, Robin Sterling, went to Tulse Hill school round the corner from Brockwell Park. He and his friends said he had nothing to do with the affray. There had undoubtedly been a fight on a Saturday afternoon between hundreds of black youths and hundreds of police. It was the product of a tension that existed and still exists between the police and the youth whom they harass, patrol and attempt to control. The arrest of Robin Sterling several days after the affray had taken place, in June 1973, and the trial of the three nine months later brought the students of Tulse Hill into the open as an organized public force. They formed a committee, the Black Students' Action Collective (Black Sac) and invited participation from four other schools in the area in which they knew they had support and friends. They called a one day strike of pupils from schools. They had very little of a machinery of organization. They knew only that the case and the trial had excited a lot of comment in the school, and felt that teachers at Tulse Hill, and at other schools were, for the first time, clearly on the side of the victimized and not on the side of the police. One or two teachers, considered by the pupils as hardliners, even as racists, actually wrote testimonials for the youths to present in court.

On the day of the strike 100 black youths from my school, joined by 60 white friends, declared their intention to come out on strike. A few teachers went along with them. In fact the headmaster, having learnt of the strike through the leaflets that were circulating in our schools, was in favour of teachers going with them to ensure that they got into as little trouble as possible. The headmaster of Tulse Hill had taken no such stance. He locked the gates of the school. The leaders of the strike demonstration were from his school and they led the 800 strong demonstration past the gates of several schools in Southwark and Brixton. They were joined by a few hundred more. The demonstration reached Tulse Hill. It was break-time and the youth swarmed out into the playground and over the walls to join the demo. Some teachers, who had earlier told me that they supported the youth against the police in the case, didn't show up. They stood in the playground and urged the youth back into the classes. They later referred to the demonstration as 'adventurist', and were angry with those teachers who went on it.

I recall their attitude for a specific reason. I meet the same teachers, and members of the political groups to which they belong nowadays, at all sorts of rallies and conferences of teachers to debate race. On occasion they say to me that the stand I take on black youth is not inspired by the actions of black youth, but by my reading of Marx or something else. It's funny. When there's action they're for theory, when there's theory, they pretend to be for action.

The Brockwell Park demonstration proved that black youth are capable of very fast, quickly organized mass action of an agitational nature. It also seemed to prove, as other demonstrations, walk-outs and pickets of black students have done since, that the black students in schools will more readily concentrate on the interference of police in their lives and educational institutions, than they will on the quality of the curriculum. I know of no committee, no strike, no demonstration from Asian or West

Indian youth which demanded that world geography be taught, that slavery replace Tudor history as part of the syllabus, or any other such tinkering with the subject matter of schooling. That doesn't mean that I find students apathetic or uncaring about curricular changes. It only means that with them it doesn't seem to me to be a political obsession. Work and police and money and the relative strength of black gangs and white gangs, self-defence against whites who attack them, feeling against racist teachers and an opposition to the boredom and routine and discipline of schooling, seem to be the issues which interest them.

These are the concerns they have articulated collectively, but without an organization that I can name, to whose secretary I can write, whose committee can be called upon to meet in a hall to discuss anything with anybody. That is the state of play today. The collective action that they offer as a challenge in the classrooms of schools and further education colleges has led, if nothing else, to a deep concern on the part of the state, to a polarization of teachers on the question of race (though they haven't said what that question is) and, I believe, to a power in the schools which is destined to change them.

Policing schools and colleges

School, as Britain has known it, is falling apart under the impact. Let me point to some of the symptoms. At present I teach in a school in Southwark, in South London. Southwark is one of the ten divisions into which the Inner London Education Authority is divided. It has 25 secondary schools and about a 100 primary schools. In that division alone, there are 500 pupils, many of them black, whom the schools refuse to accept because of their record of behaviour or non-attendance or something or the other with which they have been stigmatized. They are the extreme cases who have refused to live at peace with the school institution. I know a few of them. In the school they repeatedly do what they like. They don't care about succeeding in the exams, about keeping their note-books tidy, or even about keeping them. They get into arguments with teachers at the least excuse and offer a lot of cheek and abuse. They carry other pupils with them in acts of severe indiscipline. Nobody ever taught them anything. When schools have a lot of trouble with a pupil, they call in the parents. Hasn't it always been so? In the Caribbean, in India, in any society where the pupil is a 'kid', which means that he or she has no independent means of living and has to rely on the family for food, clothes, shelter, pocket-money, and therefore has to conform to the discipline that the family imposes? These 'unplaceables' have in a sense gone beyond the point where the family can make promises to the school and ensure that they are carried out. They have become fully-fledged, independent members of the unruly section of the working class at the bottom of the British ladder of labour.

Take another case. In two colleges of further education in South London, the union of public employees (workers who clean and service the building in which the colleges operate) have called for Securicor guards to police the gates and the corridors. The National Union of Public Employees (NUPE) branches have been supported by the unions to which the teachers belong. The Securicor guards are normally employed to see that industrial premises are not vandalized, that banks transfer money from one place to another without it being robbed etc. They are a private police force deployed mainly by capitalist institutions. The colleges in question have taken this decision because they are situated in an area where a lot of black youth refuse to take the employment that is offered to them when they leave school. There's a generation which won't go on the buses, which won't clean up in the hospitals, which won't accept that kind of work at all. They are in my classes at school.

Truancy, 'sin bins' and useless exams

A large part of this generation doesn't get certificates which will qualify them for any sort of skilled labour when they leave school. They hang around colleges because their friends are enrolled in courses there, or because they want something to do during the day. They eat the subsidized food in the canteen, they intrude on classes, they hang around the buildings and are generally considered a threat.

Some colleges have tried to offer them courses in non-exam subjects, or have even dreamt up exams for them. The struggle of the teachers who run these courses has been to find materials for teaching them, subjects and areas of knowledge and discovery which would motivate them to pass their time for a few years and possibly give them some basic qualification and the will to go to work. Other colleges have moved to the Securicor and identity card system.

A month ago in Bradford, in the north of England, the education authority hired a helicopter and some vans to patrol the town and chase truants who have posed a threat of social disorder in the town. I am told that the helicopter, in its zeal, flew too low over the housetops and knocked down the chimney of a house. The bill will come to the taxpayer.

Another bill which the government will settle is the expenditure of millions of pounds on what they have called educational priority areas. Mr Callaghan's government has just announced that it will pay the schools in the inner cities (a million pounds in London alone) to start units for disruptive pupils who can't be accommodated in the normal classroom. The money will pay for sin-bins to siphon off the hard malcontents and leave us teachers with those who can be induced to go through school either as men and women who hope to get 'O' and 'A' levels and ultimately good jobs, or as the vast majority who will do CSEs (Certificates of Secondary Education) which are worthless on the job market, or even as the non-exam groups whom the schools have barely taught to read and write but have child-minded successfully with all manner of projects and curricula cobbled together by teachers.

Britain is not there yet. The symptoms seem to promise a malignant cancer. They seem to point to a future in which the sort of schools in which we work will have to employ armed guards to mediate their multi-ethnicity, as they do in New York.

Teachers resisting racism

And teachers are bothered. They are concerned. Not only because they want a peaceful life, but because most of us don't want to be in the firing line of a battle between the state who wants the schools to put out a graded and disciplined labour force and a pupil population who don't care for the plan. There's another reason too. Like those would-be teachers I met at university, there are thousands in the staffrooms who cling to some ideal of 'education'. Faced with a crisis of identity, which means quite simply that they don't know what role they can play and which side they want to be on, they hate to be described as people who are earning their wage in a labour power or child-minding industry.

At this moment in Britain, crucial for the black population, the concern has emerged in many ways. All over the country teachers are gathering into formations to fight 'racism and fascism'. The programmes which they set themselves are clearly political. The black issue is the first one on which masses of teachers have declared themselves. In London, on March 20, a small committee of teachers called a rally to express this concern. Six months before the rally the National Front, a tiny fascist organization in Britain, which constantly campaigns for the repatriation of black people, had announced its intention to stand at the school gates and distribute leaflets which would spread racial hatred and specifically ask white students to challenge 'red' teachers.

The announcement of this intention caused more furore in the papers and in the staffrooms than it did activity amongst the pupils of schools. Very few of these leaflets appeared at the school gates. I don't think the National Front had the forces to deliver them, and besides, they had learnt from their marches and rallies elsewhere that black youth would not take democratic action against them and complain to the Home Secretary. They would just give them a good thrashing if they turned up with racial leaflets or anti-black talk at the school gates. In the months before the rally, Margaret Thatcher also made her intervention on the race question. Now, racist intentions have been publicized in Britain by all manner of people, including Enoch Powell, some prominent Labour politicians, and parties and groups of the right. They haven't brought forth a commitment from teachers to fight them. This time, however, that peculiar amalgam of facts and pressures which makes history, came together. I can give no analysis of the chemistry of it. I only know that for the last year the race question has become the central one in the school, and when it became the central one in Britain's electoral and extra-parliamentary politics, teachers thought, all over the country, that it was time to make some declaration of where we stood.

The All London Teachers Against Racism and Fascism (ALTARF) committee and rally had been called by teachers who had nothing to do with left wing parties. The 3000 teachers who gathered at Central Hall Westminister, and many more who offered their support in meetings in the staffrooms and the union branches to publicize the rally, knew what they were against but hadn't quite decided what they were for. Some of them had the attitude expressed by one of the founders of ALTARF who said to me 'I want to show the pupils in my classes, black and white, that I am for blacks and I want to publicly oppose anyone who is against them'. Another said, and again I'm sure she expressed the spirit of thousands like her, 'I am for the black kids because I come from a working class background myself and I know what they feel when they are up against a system they can't tolerate'.

ALTARF, the rally they called, had the job of transforming that concern into an organized movement of teachers. The left parties joined the bandwagon. The state climbed on too. Here was a declared movement of teachers, not a mass of opinions gathered in a staffroom, not a vague hunch that a 'question' had to be sociologized and propagandized, but a lot of people coming together in halls all over the country to discuss what to do.

On the platform of the rally (at which I spoke), all sorts of viewpoints were represented. It was as though the organizers had set out to represent the confusion that exists on the race question in the staffrooms. There were the professional headteachers, not clearly aligned with political shades, who put the idea that schools must reflect the multi-culture of their pupils by teaching whites to cook papadoms, and presumably by forcing Indians to eat black pudding. There were the 'left' who said that the race question must be resolved into a fight against the Nazis, and the Labour Party left in the person of Mr Arthur Latham, who was determined to fight the fascists in the trade union and labour movements. I more or less said, much more briefly, from the platform, what I'm trying to say here. I pointed out how the race question forced itself on teachers, how people came from all over the world to work in other parts of the world and that any assessment of the effect on racism in schools must ask blacks for their experience, and any force that begins to counter it must understand what blacks have been doing to fight it. You can't be for blacks without knowing what they are doing.

Against multi-culturalism

I was making a plea for active support from teachers for the independent movement of black people. Before I go any further, I'd better explain what I mean by 'independent'. In this context, I mean independent of the initiatives of the state which employs us, independent of what it wants us to do, and independent of the small parties of the left who want to use blacks, teachers, or anyone they can lay a membership form on, in order to gain the leadership of the labour movement. If teachers support the 'independent' movement of blacks, they will have to do it as an independent movement of teachers. There's no other way.

ALTARF started as an attempt at organization by that independent movement. We must be very clear about that. The teachers who started ALTARF did not see themselves or the people they called upon as part of 'an alliance of the broad left'. They saw themselves as teachers paid to do a job, people for whom the race question is a vital hinge on which the doors to new dimensions in schooling could swing. If they had been asking for multi-cultural direction, they could, instead of attempting to organize a rally and a standing organization of teachers, have gone to the National Association for Multi-Racial Education (NAME); they could have called willing and informed Inspectors from the the Inner London Education Authority to wind them up and set them off. I don't believe that a section of the teachers who organized ALTARF, or the vast mass who responded to their call, saw anti-Nazism as the channel of their needs, the answer to their animus. There are enough anti-Nazi fronts in existence with well-organized badges, posters and marching orders to blot them up, if that's where they want to be.

ALTARF's original committee allowed both multiculturalism and anti-Nazi demonstrative politics to take its platform. It was a measure of the weakness of the independent movement of teachers that it had evolved no forum, before calling a rally, to take into political account the movement of black pupils, of black parents. It had not connected its own material interests with the forces which have been battling the colonial institution in which teachers work. Without such a consideration, without principled political organization in other words, they naturally ended up talking about how to 'stimulate' pupils to fight racism. That's like Noah trying to stimulate the flood.

I want to deal with each of these posed directions in turn. Multiculturalism wasn't dreamt up by the state. For years the National Association for Multi-Racial Education (NAME) has pushed, as a group of teachers, for the presentation of black history, literature and art in schools. Now the state has backed it up. Today there exist several documents put out by the education authorities, by the Select Committee on Race Relations and Immigration of the British Parliament, by the Schools Council and by other bodies who control or suggest shifts in the practice of schooling. All of them are agreed that part of the reason for the 'failure' of blacks in British schools is that the culture of the black communities is not represented in the curriculum. This is a novel idea. For the first time in a hundred years the state has concerned itself with the culture of the people who pass through schools. 'For the curriculum to have the meaning and relevance for all pupils now in our schools, its content, emphasis and the values and assumptions contained must reflect the wide range of cultures, histories and life-styles in our multiracial society', says the Parliamentary Select Committee Report.

What is black culture?

This of course is an absurd view of culture, a nationalist one. It lumps the 'values' and the 'assumptions' of working class culture, the ideas and interests that come out of the life of the working class British, together with those that emerge from Britain's imperial history and high cultural artefacts. If the state, the educational authorities and inspectors of schools are serious about what they say, it will mean that teachers will have to examine what working class values and culture are, and begin to feed into the curriculum the primary fact of working class life – the struggle against the ownership of wealth and distribution of wealth in a capitalist society. If I, as a teacher, want to represent black culture, black values, histories, assumptions, life-styles of the people I am paid to school, I am determined to start from the fact that young blacks fight the police, they refuse dirty jobs; their forms of culture gathering always bring them into conflict with the rulers of this society, their very music, professed philosophies and life-styles, contain in them an antagonism to school and to society as it is. I don't think the multi-ethnic inspectors will like that, buy that, or tell the other teachers with whom they come in contact to adopt it.

Another absurdity plagues me. When I look for the culture of young blacks, it eludes me. I read a lot of Caribbean poets; one of my favourite novelists is V. S. Naipaul; I know something about Indian religions and history. Yet when I think of how these are going to translate into worksheets in my class, my immediate reaction is that they will be no more inspiring as 'culture' than the other stuff on the 'O' and 'A' level exam syllabuses.

When I think of representing the language of the Caribbean in the classroom, I confess myself defeated. I've tried to write some stories about young blacks in Britain, but even my best and most well-wishing friends tell me that there are flaws in my understanding of the dialects of these tribes. Am I going to undertake to be the classroom representative of these dialects? And even if I put myself through months of reading on them, will I further anything that my pupils want out of the clash and change of this society? What finally concerns me about this direction is that it will do little to alter the fact that the examination system will not recognize my new cultural emphasis. School will still produce a small percentage of skilled workers, a larger percentage of semi-skilled ones and a very large percentage of unskilled ones. I will have kept the last categories busy, motivated and believing that I am somehow on their side because I know the facts about slavery.

Student power

As a direction, this multiculturalism certainly tests my dedication as a teacher. So does the anti-Nazi line when it calls me to demonstrate against the National Front using my daytime workplace as a forum for their election meetings in the evenings. I have been to these demonstrations, in spite of knowing that in my own school the staff had a meeting, signed a petition and told the headmaster and governors that they had to see to it that the school was not available for any fascist meetings. Our petition was, I believe, effective. The headmaster told us and everyone else, that the school hall was booked on any and every evening on which the National Front could possibly apply to use it. Nevertheless, where the staff of a school have been too weak to induce their administration to deny the facility of the building to fascists, I have gone along and attempted to ensure that a large force of teachers does on overtime what the school's staff couldn't do on the shift.

And when I'm on these jaunts, an anxiety overcomes me. I go on the demonstration and feel all the time that it doesn't take into account my experience of schooling or the interests of my colleagues who share that experience. I get the feeling that my demonstration has something to do with the buildings or something to do with one set of ideas fighting another in this society, but nothing to do with schooling. When I hear the speeches and the calls on these demonstrations, and know that the politics being perpetrated there don't begin from the concerns and actions of the population that they pretend to champion, I look around me to see who I am with. Put it another way: to be professedly anti-racist and not to be informed by the action and interests of the population, that faces the brunt of racism, is racist.

Besides, it prevents teachers making an alliance with the forces that will change the schools. As a teacher I don't want to contain indiscipline, I want to do away with the system that causes it. In the classroom I don't merely want to wear my anti-Nazi badge to prove that I am on the side of pupils who know that I am paid for processing them. I want instead to work towards developing the power and the alliance that will defeat that processing. I don't want as a teacher to write into my curriculum a chapter about Indian history (if any pupil wants to know about it, I shall put myself and my knowledge completely at his or her disposal, but that's another thing). I would rather represent in my teaching material the strengths of the black population and try and inculcate in the white pupils of my multi-ethnic classroom, a respect of those strengths. Rather than say how we were once strong and once defeated, I would try and say how we are strong today and how we are proceeding today to inflict defeats.

CHAPTER 5.3

BLACK GIRLS IN A LONDON COMPREHENSIVE*
MARY FULLER

In the areas of housing, the law, employment, education and welfare, black people and women continue to be disadvantaged in comparison with men and whites. The facts of racial and sexual disadvantage in Britain mean that, whatever their social class, black women and girls are in a doubly subordinate position within the social formation.

With regard to education, those people in Britain writing about academic aspirations and achievement of pupils have compared black and white pupils, and made similar comparisons between females and males. At the time when I began my research (in 1975) I was unable to find any instance of work which attempted to analyze simultaneously the bearing which pupils' sex and race might have in this area. With the single exception of Driver, writings about the academic achievements of black pupils continue to treat them as a sexually undifferentiated group. Other writers, working in the interactionist and/or deviancy tradition, and concerned to document and analyze the experiential world of the adolescent, inside and outside school, have been equally limited in their focus. Their efforts have been almost exclusively concentrated on white sub-cultures – with Sharpe (1976) being a notable exception – and the balance being heavily towards male (and white) adolescent experiences and cultural expressions. In other words, not only does this tradition in sociology treat the world of adolescence as essentially male, but it also considers adolescents to be racially undifferentiated.

What seemed to be clear was that black pupils were under-achieving academically,[1] and that black youth (and some parents) were increasingly disaffected from schooling (Dhondy, 1974). It seemed equally clear from the studies by Hargreaves and Lacey that similar anti-school and what were termed 'delinquent' sub-cultures among white boys were related to the

* Chapter 4 of *Schooling for Women's Work*, ed. Rosmary Deem, 1980, Routledge & Kegan Paul, pp. 52–65.

pupils' social class. In the cases of both race and social class, disaffection from school and relatively poor scholastic performance were connected.

In the absence of specific work about them it was difficult to know where black girls came into this schema. If one assumed the primacy of social class and/or racial category in developing an anti-school stance, black girls could be straightforwardly accommodated, since there would be little difference between them and their male peers. But the fact of being female might alter this picture – by virtue of their sex girls are in a particular subordinate position. There are no a priori reasons for assuming a greater importance for either sex or race in this respect, and no certain guidelines as to the effect of an interaction between the two. From logic and guesswork only, the fact of being female could have rather different implications for black girls' sub-cultural response to schooling. Given an additive model of subordination, it would seem that black girls would be essentially like their male peers, only more so; i.e., even more disaffected than similar male pupils. On the other hand, and in line with the common view that females as a group are more conformist, less likely to rebel and generally less 'troublesome' in the school context, black girls could be expected to demonstrate similar but less strongly manifested alienation from school. This is not something to be decided by logic; rather it is an empirical question, though not, as already indicated, one which has actually been given prominence by previous writers.

In this chapter I shall describe a small group of black girls (of West Indian parentage, though mostly themselves of British birth) who formed a discernible sub-culture in the comprehensive school in which I carried out research during 1975 and 1976. As part of a much larger study[2] involving male and female pupils from Indo-Pakistani, West Indian and white British family backgrounds I spent two terms in the school in daily participation and observation of pupils' school lives. At that time and subsequently, observational material was supplemented by interviews, questionnaires and the analysis of various school documents. The larger project aimed to examine in what ways pupils and teachers sex-structured their position within the school as well as the ways in which teachers' and pupils' relations with each other were structured by their respective notions of gender (i.e. masculinity/ feminity). Hence the work took place in a mixed school. To confront adequately the question 'How much does sex matter in school?' some additional and equally important referent is required, so that inferences about sexual differentiation may be subject to alternative explanation.[3] For this reason the school selected was multiracial, and the possibility of social class and race as alternative or additional explanations for differentiation among pupils was integrated into the analysis. This point has been laboured because in the ordinary way a study based on only eight people could hardly expect to be taken as a serious contribution to the sociological literature; although in our present state of ignorance concerning black girls and schooling, such considerations might be waived.

As I shall go on to argue, the existence and specific defining features of this sub-culture of black girls call into question some of our present assumptions and thinking, not only about black pupils but also about the development of school-based sub-cultures. I make this argument with greater confidence because what follows, while relating to a small and particular group, is informed by constant comparisons with other same-age peers within the school: male and female, white, Asian and black.

Torville school

The school was a ten-form entry comprehensive in the north London Borough of Brent, and the students, in their final year of compulsory schooling, were aged fifteen to sixteen years. The fifth year was divided into two parallel bands, one containing 128 pupils who followed a mixed curriculum of practical/vocational subjects with some more academic ones, and who would be expected to take some 'O' level or CSE exams; the other band (the one with which I worked) containing 142 pupils following a more thorough-going academic curriculum, with the expectation that they would take a rather larger number of 'O' level and CSE exams than those in the practical band.

The academic band contained significantly fewer girls than boys (with the reverse sex-ratio in the practical band). There were fewer West Indian girls in the academic than the practical band, as was true also of white British and Asian girls. Although there were in general more boys in the academic than the practical band, a greater proportion (and absolute number) of West Indian boys was to be found in the practical band. Relating this to other writers' work (e.g. Coard, 1971; Troyna, 1976), it is clear that the situation with regard to West Indian boys, but not with respect to girls, confirms the view that West Indian pupils are found in disproportionate numbers in the lower streams (or equivalent groupings) within school.

Within the fifth year nearly a quarter of pupils were of West Indian parentage, a further one in four were of Indo-Pakistani parentage, and just over half were white and British-born with only a very few other white Europeans. Within the academic band the majority of West Indian pupils was British-born, whereas the majority of Asian students was immigrant (with by far the majority of these being of East African rather than Indian sub-continental birth).

The girls

Five of the eight girls were British-born, three having migrated to Britain from Jamaica, two when aged three, and one when aged eleven. One of the British-born girls had spent four years in the West Indies as a small child (aged two to six). Six lived in a two-parent family and two in mother-headed families. All had at least one brother or sister living with them, and in most cases considerably more than one. The mothers of six of the girls were permanently employed outside the home in full-time jobs, one girl's mother had a permanent part-time job, and in one case the mother took seasonal jobs according to availability. All six fathers were normally in permanent full-time jobs. The girls came from predominantly manual working-class homes (five) with two having a father in a manual but a mother in a non-manual job; one girl had both parents in non-manual employment.

Although the sub-culture comprised girls in the same age-group attending the same school, in many important respects it was not simply or mainly a school-based subculture, for in order to make sense of its structure and values it is necessary to look outside the school, to the situation of black minorities in Britain generally and also to the situation of women in comparison with men. The girls consciously drew on these when discussing themselves and the other girls in their group. In particular they drew on their knowledge and experience of the West Indies.

West Indian roots

Most of the black students whom I interviewed had themselves visited the West Indies in the relatively recent past; all were closely connected with others who had also returned from visits, and were in other ways kept apprised of life in the West Indies. In large part it was their awareness of their Caribbean roots and the inferences which they drew concerning themselves as females in that society which underlay and provided the basis both for the existence of the sub-culture and for an understanding of

its values and particular style. The other part is contributed by the girls'
interpretation of the fact of their female sex in British society.

From what they had themselves observed and gleaned from others'
accounts the girls had constructed a picture of a physically demanding and
financially unrewarding life for women in the West Indies, in comparison
with which their present and future lives in Britain seemed favourable.

> Women back home were really masculine. They had to be. They had to go
> and fetch water, come back and do their washing and it was really dirty
> because they don't have washing machines. And they had to get down and
> really scrub, then after that they had really old fashioned irons and had to
> burn coal to do it, plus you've got to starch it, then wet it again and iron it.
> And the men just expect them to do that. So, I mean, they can't be really
> careful what they do. (Monica)

Foner (1976) suggests that older immigrant women whom she interviewed
in London shared this perception. The girls drew a comparison between the
life-styles of women and men in the Caribbean, typifying that of men as
pleasanter and less arduous, even though male unemployment was high.
Boys, during interview, also indicated that they believed this to be the case.

One very important ramification of this picture was that the girls did not
easily envisage a future for themselves in the West Indies; on the contrary
their awareness of their West Indian roots led them to believe that they
would be better off in Britain. On the other hand a return to the homeland
(by which was meant the West Indies) featured prominently in the boys'
thoughts about the future, sentiments which were frequently given
coherence by their understanding of Rastafarianism. Within the fifth year
at Torville only boys displayed some of the externalia of Rastafarianism –
the wearing of woolly hats in orange, green and black, modified 'locks',
etc. – and had adopted its rhetoric. It may be that because the option of
returning was less (psychologically) available to the girls that they found a
Rasta identity that much more difficult to contemplate.

It should not be inferred from this that the girls dissociated themselves
from their Caribbean origins or wanted to be anything other than black.
None of the girls indicated in any way that she would prefer to be white,
and indeed they were proud to be black. For example, Janice having
explicitly defined herself as 'pure black' on several occasions in the
interview returned to the theme of blacks who 'go on as if they are a white
person', who are the opposite of 'pure black'. She also suggested that
'. . . if a black goes over to white we regard them as traitors, but if a white
person comes over to us, we accept them as a black'.

This positive acceptance of themselves as black echoes Ladner's (1971) findings in relation to Afro-American female adolescents. As was the case with many of the Asian and white girls interviewed, the black girls expressed considerable resentment towards their brothers because of what they saw as discrimination in favour of boys within their own families. The basis of their argument was that domestic tasks were unfairly allocated, so that the main burden of the shopping, child-minding, laundry and cooking not undertaken by their mothers fell on the shoulders of the girls in the family. Boys were not expected to contribute to these domestic tasks, or only intermittently, whereas commitments of this kind absorbed considerable amounts of the girls' time out of school. (The boys confirmed that they were not expected to help and only rarely undertook such 'womanish' work.)

The girls in Driver's study were also undertaking quite onerous domestic commitments. In his discussion of conflict with parents he seems to suggest that relations between girls and their parents are relatively harmonious despite these demands made on the girls. At any rate he does not mention conflicts except in the context of boys and parents. Among the girls at Torville this was the most frequently mentioned topic of arguments with parents, and it was patently a source of considerable friction between girls and their parents as well as between girls and their brothers.

In many cases this resentment extended to boys in general. And yet at the same time the discrepancy in the demands made on girls and boys seemed to provide one of the bases of the girls' greater confidence in their ability. They were inclined to interpret the boys' behaviour as evidence of inability to do even simple things, as signifying 'childishness', 'laziness', and so on. This interpretation seemed all the more plausible to them since it echoed the division of competence, as they perceived it, between their parents within the home. Thus Marcia:

> My dad helps around the house, he only helps with the good things – he never does the washing up. . . . He's not very good practically, my mum doesn't really approve of him when he's doing his decorating. My mum did the back room actually because my dad did it in this paint and my mum didn't like it so . . . she's quite independent really. She's a lot better than my dad at things – he's good at the theory, but not on practical things.

Though they might envy the boys their greater freedom from domestic chores and freedom of movement the girls nevertheless expressed no desire to be boys, other than in 'idle talk'.

The girls were aware of racial discrimination, recounting incidents involving themselves and people whom they knew, and were conscious that such discrimination would probably continue. They were also aware from a number of sources of the high levels of unemployment locally and nationally which had double implications for them as young blacks. They had, as already described, experienced what they themselves interpreted as less favourable treatment because of their sex. The conjunction of all these – their positive identity as black but knowledge of racial discrimination in Britain, their positive identity as female but belief that both in Britain and the Caribbean women were often accorded less than their due status – meant that the girls were angry at the fore-closing of options available to them as blacks and as women.

Such a conjunction might be supposed to engender apathy and despair, but quite the reverse was the case. Discussing working-class pupils, White and Brockington (1978, p. 111) also note that 'Anger and frustration, consolidated and supported, is not wasted but can motivate to action'. The girls' forms of action and the import of their stance within school need to be understood as strategies for trying to effect some control over their present and future lives. Because they considered their futures were necessarily to be in Britain, these attempts included finding some modus vivendi with whites which did not undermine their identity as blacks.

Features of the sub-culture

The sub-culture emerged from the girls' positive acceptance of the fact of being both black and female. Its particular flavour stemmed from their critical rejection of the meanings with which those categorizations are commonly endowed. Their consequent anger and frustration, unlike that of their black male peers, was not turned against themselves or translated into an automatic general dislike of whites or the opposite sex. Rather their feelings and understandings gave particular meanings to achievement through the acquisition of educational qualifications.

The girls were all strongly committed to achievement through the job market (cf. Ladner, 1971; Slaughter, 1972), being marked out from the other girls not so much by the type of jobs to which they were aspiring as by the firmness with which they held their future job ambitions, and by their certainty that they would want to be employed whatever their future domestic circumstances might be:

> I want a proper job first and some kind of skill so that if I do get married and have children I can go back to it; don't want just relying on him for money,

'cause I've got to look after myself. There must be something I can do.
(Michelle)

and Monica's view of herself is very similar in this respect:

I should go out to work because, really, if I don't start learning to get on
with it, I maybe will just have to leave home, get married and depend on the
husband and I don't want that at all . . . the picture of myself is an active
one, always doing something, I don't know what. Maybe I'll be a housewife
or something like that, but I always picture myself working.

They were also strong believers in the value of education and educational
qualifications as a necessary preparation for the 'good' jobs which they
hoped to obtain – or more accurately, perhaps, they took such a belief for
granted. They were confident of their ability to achieve the academic
qualifications which they were aiming for, both in the short term (i.e. 'O'
level and/or CSE) and in the longer term ('A' level and/or a variety of
examinations to be taken at college, polytechnic or university).

This optimism extended to their wider life-chances. Conscious of actual
incidents of racial discrimination and the possibility of discrimination
against them because of their colour and sex, and aware of the high levels
of unemployment locally and nationally which had double implications for
them as young people and blacks, the girls nevertheless believed that in
the job market there was much that they could do to forestall ending up in
low level, dead-end jobs, or finding themselves unemployed on leaving
school. They spoke of this in terms of being 'ambitious', but equally,
ensuring that whatever ambitions they had were not deflected.

As will be clear, acquisition of academic qualifications was an integral
part of this sense of control over their future. What was less immediately
obvious was the underlying relationship of academic qualifications to the
girls' sense of self-worth. In a very real sense they perceived the obtaining
of academic qualifications as a public statement of something which they
already knew about themselves but which they were also certain was given
insufficient public recognition: that they were capable, intelligent, and the
equal of boys.

I think people trust you more when you're a boy; they say you're more
reliable, you're more trustworthy. Because my dad always says that, he says
you can take a boy and you can show him a trade, but you can take a girl and
the next minute their heads are all filled up with boys, that she just doesn't
want to know. So I'm going to show him, you see! (Beverley)

That is, their sense of self-worth did not derive from the acquisition of academic qualifications nor, in the future, from obtaining a 'good' job; rather their pursuit of these ends was given meaning by their existing knowledge of their own worth and their understanding that this was often denied. During interviews most of the girls said they thought boys considered themselves superior to girls, an idea which they viewed with amused disbelief or scepticism.

> Most West Indian boys definitely aren't going to let a woman dominate them or tell them what to do, they firmly believe that they're the boss and she has to do everything. . . . They just have this thing that they are the superior ones and women are inferior. This equality business – I don't think that it would ever work in the West Indies, don't think they'd accept it, might here. And I don't think the West Indian boys growing up here, I don't think they're going to accept it either because they always talk about it as a load of rubbish anyway, because as far as they're concerned they're superior and they're not going to be equal with a woman, or anything like that. (Christa)

The written word does not readily convey the tone in which Christa spoke, but what was clear was that she, together with most of the other girls, did not take it as self-evident that males were superior or deserved to be taken more seriously than herself.

To this point in their careers the girls' confidence appeared well-founded; they had passed a greater number of 'O' level and CSE exams, and at rather higher grades than had the black boys. The black girls achieved a mean of 7.6 passes at this level compared with 5.6 for the black boys, an achievement which put them second only to Asian boys in performance in 'O' level and CSE. Similarly, while all the girls had remained in full-time education for at least one year beyond the statutory school-leaving age, only two of the black boys had done so. Where girls had left school or college to take up employment, all mentioned that they were also continuing their education by day release or block release schemes or by attending college in the evenings; only one boy mentioned that he was continuing his education in any way.

So far the picture drawn seems to be that of the girls as archetypal 'good' pupils – ones who have high aspirations and achieve well in public examinations – but this was far from the truth in most other aspects of their lives in school. Unlike other pupils who were similarly pro-education, the black girls were not pro-school. That is to say, their intolerance of the daily routines and their criticisms of much that went on inside the school were marked. They shared with some other pupils a view of school as 'boring', 'trivial' and 'childish', and yet at the same time were markedly different from these same pupils in that they had high aspirations and a high degree of academic success. Despite their critical view of school the black girls did not define it as 'irrelevant' (as did other pupils who found school boring, etc.), because of the particular importance which they attached to academic achievement. Quine (1974) discusses a similar orientation among the boys in his study of two Midland comprehensive schools.

Most high aspirers and achievers in the school were concerned to demonstrate their seriousness of purpose to teachers and other pupils by certain kinds of classroom behaviour: punctuality, a modicum of attention to lesson content, and a 'respectful' (by no means always deferential) attitude towards teachers, in addition to actually doing the work set. Whether they actively courted a good reputation in other ways or not, such pupils tended to be seen as 'good' pupils. The reverse of this behaviour was taken by both teachers and pupils to indicate a lack of interest in school and was associated with a reputation as a 'bad' pupil.

The black girls conformed to the stereotypes of the good pupil only in so far as they worked conscientiously at the schoolwork or homework set. But they gave all the appearances in class of not doing so, and in many other ways displayed an insouciance for the other aspects of the good pupil role. They neither courted a good reputation among teachers nor seemed to want to be seen as 'serious' by the staff or other pupils. Eschewing behaviour which would bring them into serious conflict with teachers (for example, truanting, direct challenges to a teacher's authority, grossly disruptive behaviour within the classroom), the girls were frequently involved in activities which exasperated the staff and which were yet not quite clearly misdemeanours requiring comment or action on their part. The following examples drawn from field notes represent incidents which occurred with some frequency: openly engaging in some 'illegitimate' activity (reading a magazine, chatting, doing homework for another subject) so that it appeared that the girls were not listening or not working, yet when questioned by the teacher they could show that they had, in fact, taken in what had been said or had actually completed the work assigned; arriving technically late for a lesson but actually seconds before the teacher, who could see their late arrival; handing in work for marking when it suited them rather than immediately it was asked for; complying with a teacher's request somewhat slowly and with a show of complete uninterest, and so on. Studying delinquent pupils (some of them black) in an American high school, Werthman (1963) describes somewhat similar behaviour. Neither meek and passive nor yet aggressive, and obviously confrontationist in their stance towards teachers, the girls were something of a puzzle to some of their peers and teachers.

Three themes emerged in their discussions of the stance they adopted within school. First, to be seen as a 'good' pupil, i.e., showing too much eagerness in class, appearing to take school too seriously, risked the discovery of their academic and job ambitions and consequently invited ridicule and possibly more from those peers with whom the girls most frequently compared themselves – black boys.

> I find that most boys do have ambitions but they're influenced by their friends, so they never get put into practice anyway . . . I think the girls are more ambitious but if they want to do something they don't feel embarrassed about it except when boys, when they hear you're doing 'O' levels, they won't come out with it and say you're a snob but they treat you a bit differently and you can feel it . . . I think West Indian girls might feel a bit funny about that. (Joan)

> I've always got my head in a book. I don't think they [boys in school] like it because they are always commenting on it and they say 'You won't get anywhere', and sometimes I think they don't want me to learn or something like that, you know; but I spoke to my mum about it, and she said I shouldn't listen and I should keep working hard. (Marcia)

In this way their classroom behaviour may be seen as a conscious smoke-screen to confuse others and enable the girls to retain the friendship of their peer group without giving up their aspirations.

Second, to be viewed by teachers as a 'good' pupil was inconsistent with the girls' own view of themselves. 'Good' pupils were boring, were unable to have 'fun', and were in other respects 'immature'; to behave in class like them would invite comparison with people from whom the girls expressly distanced themselves.

Third, the girls believed that other highly aspiring pupils placed too great an emphasis on teachers' opinions in relation to pupils' success: in so far as public examinations were marked by people who did not know the candidates personally, pupils could expect to pass exams on the quality of their work rather than on the quality of their relationship with the teachers who taught them. Very few other pupils discussed pupil-teacher relationships in this way.

The black girls' behaviour within the classroom is, I suggest, intimately connected with their positive identity as black and female. It seems reasonable to suppose that in coming to a sense of their own worth the girls had learnt to rely on their own rather than others' opinion of them. Their weighing up of the potential relevance and importance of teachers was part of a more general stance towards others. The girls were relatively sophisticated in judging who did and did not matter in their pursuit of academic qualifications, for example, so that one could say they adopted a somewhat 'strategic' political stand in relation to other people, including whites generally and white authority in school specifically.

To some extent this can also be seen in their social relationships with other pupils. The girls appeared to treat peer relationships as a resource of essentially individualistic achievement aims rather than as a source of pleasure and/or confirmation in its own right. The girls came together as a result of each of them trying to cope with the difficulties of proving their own worth. This was to be expressed through the acquisition of paper qualifications, not through the living out of a particular peer-based life-style. In a sense the confirmation of the girls' sense of identity could not come from either their peer group or from adults, but only from their own efforts. For this reason the sub-culture was not a readily discernible entity, marked out from others by a particular and visible style. Or rather their style was not the raison d'être of their coming together.

Unlike pupils in other 'academic' sub-cultures described in the literature (e.g. Hargreaves), the girls did not confine their friendship choices only to other academically inclined pupils, but showed a fluidity of friendship choices among other black but 'non-academic' girls in the school. This indicates, I suggest, that the girls had discovered or assumed that they had little in common with other pupils (white or Asian) who, like them, had high aspirations. That the black girls in the academic band at Torville made their choices of friends from among both academic and non-academic black girls, is partly due to the relatively small number of black pupils from whom to choose. (Similar ethnocentrism in friendship choices is reported by Durojaiye, 1970; Bhatnagar. 1970; Troyna, 1978.) The girls' choice of friends does also underline the central importance of both their sex and ethnicity in the girls' identity.

This can also be discerned in their assessment of certain teachers. As already indicated, the girls did not automatically define teachers as adversaries, despite the fact that they behaved in ways which might have been interpreted as giving insufficient respect to teachers, and despite the fact that the girls were critical of many aspects of their daily life in school. Alone among the pupils, a few of the black girls indicated that they greatly admired certain teachers, whom they would like to emulate. As can be seen from the following passage from an interview with Beverley, the reasons for this admiration stem from the fact that the particular teachers in question are thought to demonstrate qualities (of persistence, struggle against convention, etc.) which have a particular resonance with the girls' own current situation. In other words, the teacher is admired not because she is a teacher or because she is white, nor even despite these factors, but only because she has succeeded in the job market. In this respect the teacher's sex is the salient point.

In reply to my question 'What is it about Miss G that you admire?' Beverley replied:

> Because she's a career woman. She succeeded in life at a time in her days when women were expected to sit around . . . she rebelled against that and she's got what she wanted, got her own car, got her own flat, completely independent, goes where she likes when she likes, she's got her own money, you know, she's succeeded and got what she wants out of life, she's getting married – everything has kind of worked out for her . . . she can be very serious and hard-working but at the same time she can be good fun, you see.

What is also clear is that this particular teacher is a living demonstration that success and femininity can be reconciled, and that success and solemnity are not synonymous. No matter that the girl's perception of the 'olden days' may be inaccurate and the difficulties to be overcome exaggerated, the teacher's example is taken to heart since struggle and resourcefulness (Ladner) are important aspects of the girls' ideas about themselves. As the following incident illustrates, the girls' persistence is already well-developed:

> When I first went for the job, I was very crafty when I wrote the letter. I put that I was a student and they thought I was coming from university, and I did it in perfectly good English so they wouldn't think that it was a foreign person. And then when I went and they actually saw that I was coloured I think they were a bit shocked, so they kept stalling and said come back tomorrow. They said the person isn't in, can you come back next week, and I wouldn't give in. Everytime they said come back I'd go back and I'd go back. My dad was backing me all the way and in the end I got through. (Christa).

This kind of persistence is much admired and is a source of considerable pride:

Michelle and I are the same really, we have this thing to succeed, determined, you know. If anything gets in the way we kick it out the way and get on. (Annette)

Summary and discussion

In trying to describe and understand the sub-culture of black girls in a particular school it has been necessary to make frequent comparisons with other people in and outside Torville school itself. There are two reasons for this. First, as is common in the development of an in-group identity, the girls saw themselves as a separate group by comparing themselves with other blacks (Rosenberg and Simmons, 1972) and contrasting themselves with others. Second, very few features of the sub-culture on their own were unique to the girls, although the specific configuration of values, attitudes, behaviour and self-perceptions did mark them out as quite distinct from other pupils in their year.

Because this sub-culture of West Indian girls contrasts with the general picture of West Indian disaffection from school and low attainment, it would be helpful to know just how prevalent or typical such a sub-culture is of West Indian pupils generally. The majority of writers do not differentiate between boys and girls, and from internal evidence it would appear that much of the work has been based on males, with perhaps the implicit assumption that what is established for males is more or less an accurate representation of the whole group. Because of this lack of differentiation or failure to specify the sex-class of those being studied, it is not possible to give an accurate estimate of the typicality of the sub-culture described of black pupils in general. For very similar reasons, that in the literature on adolescence, schooling, and sub-cultures very little specific attention has been paid to girls in their own right (a lack noted by McRobbie and Garber, 1976; Ward, 1976; among others), it is not possible to gauge just how frequently such a subculture may be found among girls. However, Lambart's account of her work in a girls' grammar school is particularly instructive, since her description of the Sisterhood (a group of third-year pupils) suggests a very similar conjunction of academic attainment and non-conformity to the rules, regulations and routines of school (Lambart, 1976, pp. 157–9):

They had a sense of fun bordering often on mischief; and they were careful of the 'respect' they have to teachers . . . despite its deviance, the Sisterhood existed as a focus for girls with more than average ability.

The relationship between academic performance and behaviour within school of the black girls at Torville and Lambart's Sisterhood contrasts with that described for boys by Hargreaves and Willis (1977). I would argue that this calls into question the necessary equation of academic striving and success with conformity, an equation which the work of Werthman, Holt (1964) and Jackson (1966) in any case indicates is not universal.

Since it is frequently argued that teachers' expectations[4] serve to depress the attainment of certain groups of pupils (including females and blacks), it is particularly interesting that the black girls' achievement was not related to whether teachers saw them as good or bad pupils. Nor was there any relationship between teachers' perception of the girls as pupils and the girls' classroom activities, which contrasts with Driver's finding of a considerable overlap (particularly in relation to black boys) in the West Midland school he studied.

A radical analysis of schools and schooling points to an underlying ethnocentrism and middle-class bias in the structure, organization and curriculum of all schools. As Reynolds (1976) points out, this leads to viewing school as a battleground of opposing values in which pupils demonstrate their resistance to alien and oppressive race and class values by refusing to conform. It becomes only too easy to assume that academic striving and achievement are synonymous with subscribing (conforming) to these values, and to see school failure as necessarily indicative of rejection of those same values. Apart from the fact that neither Reynolds nor Quine could find evidence of such polarized stances in the schools they studied, conformity and deviance within the school are rarely global, but are situation-specific (Werthman, Furlong, 1976). Moreover, if further research confirms the disjunction between academic orientation and within-school behaviour, noted by Lambart and in the present study of Torville school, it may be that the pro-education pro-school connection and its polar opposite (anti-education, anti-school) emerge as somewhat specific rather than universal tendencies – specific to boys (and perhaps only a proportion of these) and/or more typical of particular types of school.

In this chapter I have described a group of black girls whose acute awareness of their double subordination as women and black was accompanied by a refusal to accept the 'facts' of subordination for themselves. As a strategy for present and future survival the girls had adopted a programme of 'going it alone' in which those aspects of schooling to do with acquiring qualifications had an important part. No more tolerant of the 'irrelevant' aspects of schooling (e.g. the daily routines) than their black male peers, the girls were in some ways a good deal more effectively independent of adult authority than any other group of pupils (male or female) in the school.

Wilkinson (1975, p. 305) argues that:

[Black] youth are unlike their white counterparts not only with respect to placement in the social structure and their definitions of the dynamics of inter-racial relations, but also with respect to the type of attitudinal orientation which emerges from their cultural experiences. They are different in the collective symbolism and self oriented definitions of who they are and what they wish to become. For they still must contend with social issues that never confront white youth.

Miles and Phizacklea (1977, p. 495) elaborate this theme, arguing that 'it is the unique experience of blacks of racial exclusion that is the essence of black ethnicity'. As I hope has been demonstrated in this chapter, when racial exclusion is overlaid and combined with sexual exclusion, it becomes necessary to begin to recognize that black ethnicity may take different forms and point to differing strategies for females and males.[5]

Notes

1. The extensive literature in this area is treated in Fuller (1976) Experiences of Adolescents from Ethnic Minorities in the British State Education System, in P. J. Bernard (ed) Les Travailleurs Etrangers en Europe Occidentale, Mouton, Paris/The Hague.
2. See Fuller, M. (1978) Dimensions of Gender in a School, Ph.D. thesis, University of Bristol.
3. The same argument would apply whether the main focus were social class or racial category. In other words, analysis of sexual differentiation is not a special case, but the use of constant comparison is desirable in most research.
4. The classic text here is Rosenthal, R. and Jacobson, L. (1968) Pygmalion in the Classroom, New York, Holt, Rhinehart and Winston.
5. The research on which this chapter is based was carried out while I was employed at the Social Science Research Council Research Unit on Ethnic Relations. This chapter does not represent the views of SSRC, nor does it necessarily reflect those of the members of the SSRC Unit. I should like to record my thanks to Annie Phizacklea for comments on an earlier draft of this chapter, and to Sarah Pegg who typed the manuscript.

References

Coard, B. 1971, *How the West Indian child is made educationally subnormal in the British school system*, New Beacon Books, London.

Bhatnagar, J. 1970, *Immigrants at School*, Cornmarket Press.

Dhondy, F. 1974, 'The black explosion in schools', *Race Today*, February.

Driver, G. 1977, 'Cultural competence, social power and school achievement: a case study of West Indian pupils attending a secondary school in the West Midlands', *New Community*, no. 5.

Durojaiye, M. 1979, 'Race relations among junior school children', *Educational Research*, no. 11.

Foner, N. 1976, 'Women, work and migration: Jamaicans in London', *New Community*, no. 5.

Furlong, V. 1976, 'Interaction sets in the classroom', in Woods, P. and Hammersley, M., *The Process of Schooling*, Open University Press and Routledge & Kegan Paul, London.

Hargreaves, D. H. 1967, *Social Relations in a Secondary School*, Routledge & Kegan Paul, London.

Horner, M. S. 1970, 'Feminity and successful achievement: a basic inconsistency', in Bardwick, J., *Feminine Personality and Conflict*, Brooks Cole, California.

Jackson, P. 1966, 'The Student's World' *The Elementary School Journal*, no. 66.

Lacey, C. 1970, *Hightown Grammer*, Manchester University Press.

Ladner, J. 1971, *Tomorrow's Tomorrow – The Black Woman*, Doubleday, New York.

Lambart, A. 1976, 'The sisterhood', in Woods, P. and Hammersley, M., op cit.

Levy, B. 1972, 'The school's role in the sex-stereotyping of girls: a feminist review of the literature', *Feminist Studies*, no. 1.

Little, A. 1978, 'Schools and race', in *Five Views of Multiracial Britain*, Commission for Racial Equality and BBC, London.

McRobbie, A. and Garber, J. 1976, 'Girls and subcultures', in Hall, S. and Jefferson, T. 1976, *Resistance through Rituals*, Hutchinson, London.

Miles, R. and Phizacklea, A. 1977, 'Class, race, ethnicity and political action', *Political Studies*, no. 27.

Quine, W. 1974, 'Polarized cultures in comprehensive schools', *Research in Education*, no. 12.

Reynolds, D. 1976, 'When teachers and pupils refuse a truce: the secondary school and the creation of delinquency', in Mungham, G. and Pearson, G. 1976, *Working Class Youth Culture*, Routledge & Kegan Paul, London.

Rosenberg, M. and Simmons, R. 1972, *Black and White self-esteem: the urban school child*, American Sociological Association, Washington.

Slaughter, D. 1972, 'Becoming an Afro-American woman', *School Review*, no. 80.

Troyna, B. 1978, 'Race and streaming', *Educational Review*, no. 30.

Ward, J. P. 1976, 'Social Reality for the Adolescent Girl', Faculty of Education, University College, Swansea.

Werthman, C. 1963, 'Delinquents in school', *Berkeley Journal of Sociology*, no. 8.

White, R. and Brockington, D. 1978, *In and out of school*, Routledge & Kegan Paul, London.

Wilkinson, D. 1975, 'Black youth', in Havighurst, R. and Dreyer, P. *Youth*, University of Chicago Press.
Willis, P. 1977, *Learning to Labour*, Saxon House, Farnborough.

CHAPTER 5.4

CLASSROOM STRESS AND SCHOOL ACHIEVEMENT: WEST INDIAN ADOLESCENTS AND THEIR TEACHERS*
GEOFFREY DRIVER

The school and classroom

The writer's own research (Driver, 1977)[1] was concerned to document the institutional processes and outcomes, and personal experiences of members of one ethnic minority in school. The material discussed below is drawn from an ethnographic case study focusing upon a number of West Indian, predominantly Jamaican, boys and girls, aged about thirteen in 1971 and rising to about fifteen in 1973. They were all pupils in the same age-cohort, or form, in the same secondary modern school serving a West Midlands neighbourhood with a large West Indian minority population. The form contained about 140 pupils in all: 45 per cent of these were West Indians, 35 per cent were English and 20 per cent were South Asians. The majority of the West Indian pupils were from Jamaican families (around 60 per cent) and there were smaller numbers whose parents originated from St Kitts and Barbados, and a few from Trinidad. At most, three out of 35 teachers in this secondary modern school were other than English: one was a Bengali, one was a Barbadian and the other an American.

It was an important aspect of the study to compare the academic records of these pupils with their school and classroom experiences. To this end, assessment data accumulated on each pupil over the entire period of their post-primary education was documented and, during the three years of the study, the assessment procedures were carefully studied. The ethnographic account of the round of school and classroom life provided an important

* *Minority Families in Britain: Support and Stress*, ed V. S. Khan, 1979, Macmillan, pp.134–44. By permission of The Social Science Research Council and Macmillan, London and Basingstoke.

backdrop to the host of detailed events which took place in classrooms, corridors, the playground and elsewhere. The paper presents some important characteristics of social relations between English teaching staff and West Indian pupils, and suggests how these contributed to the formal outcomes of schooling for individual pupils (that is, their school achievement record up to and including the final school-leaving public examination results).

There are several aspects essential to the understanding of any classroom situation. These include the individual participants' (teacher and pupils) perceptions of their roles, their respective perceptions of their social situation and the main relationships outside the classroom to which individual participants are attached. In a 'multiracial' classroom, the situation is complicated by the fact that role perceptions, definitions of social situations, relationships outside the classroom and skills to express these perceptions may differ markedly between individual participants. Under such conditions, the chances for misunderstanding are very much higher than might normally be the case.

In the following paragraphs the special requirements, strains and responses involved in the teaching role of the 'multiracial' classrooms are considered. The outcomes of social relations between teachers and their West Indian pupils are then assessed.

The complexities of classroom management

The primary function of any teacher is to impart knowledge and skills in which he/she has received recognized qualifications, to pupils for whom such learning is deemed appropriate. The classroom role of a teacher goes beyond this. To maximize the learning that takes place, a teacher must establish conducive learning conditions. Thus the teacher is in part a social manager, as well as an instructor. Schoolteaching success depends substantially on the attainment of management skills if classroom social relations are to be an asset rather than a limitation in attaining the learning objectives of a particular curriculum.

The most common example of the difficulties experienced in executing the double role of a classroom teacher is that of any student teacher out on first teaching practice. His/her lesson plans and teaching methods may be well considered and identical with those of a more experienced colleague, but he/she will almost certainly be inexperienced in managing classroom relations. The mastery of those relations consists in subtleties of observation, information and action: knowing individuals by name and personality, discerning pupils' moods and intentions in the briefest glimpses of expressions and gestures, weighing up the potential of a situation and manoeuvring to ascertain that the best is made of it for the educational benefit of all present.

To be unskilled in these subtler managerial arts has consequences well known to teachers. Pupils who do not question the teacher's superior knowledge will nevertheless question and probe the authority and confidence used to manage the social situation. The process of negotiating the limits of acceptable behaviour, beyond which punitive sanctions might be employed, is a real part of developing classroom relationships. If it becomes apparent to some pupils that the limits are imprecise or the teacher's negotiating skills are inadequate, it is highly likely that an attempt will be made to exploit these grey areas of the classroom regime.

The presence of West Indian children in the classroom implies an additional range of expressions and behaviours from the minority's cultural repertoire. While a confident teacher may be able to execute his management role in a 'normal' classroom situation, the same teacher may find he is less skilled in the presence of an ethnic minority with distinctive cultural behaviour unknown to him. The effect of the teacher's recognition of these limitations on communications and their implications for teacher attitudes and competence in classroom control and assessment of pupils are indicated in subsequent sections.

Sources of confusion in teachers' classroom dealings with West Indian pupils

Observations of classroom relations in the Form IV classes at West Midlands School indicated some crucial managerial difficulties for teachers. In situations in which about twelve of the 30 pupils in the class were West Indian (and mostly of Jamaican origin), teachers often seemed unable to establish 'a normal' environment in the classroom. Many of the teachers' difficulties arose from a range of characteristically non-English social meanings in interactions between pupil and teacher and pupil and pupil. These included distinctive physical features, gestures and other codes of communication used by the pupils.

First, in the crucial phase of getting to know a new class, many teachers persistently mistook and confused the identities of their West Indian pupils long after they had learned the names and faces of English pupils in question. It was also likely to remain in the back of the teacher's mind as an element of uncertainty of judgement about West Indian pupils with whom he (or she) must deal.

Even where identification was no longer a problem, there was another range of potential difficulties. These had to do with elementary expectations about the ways in which body movements and postures might coincide with other sorts of expressive behaviour. It was apparent, for example, when teachers often found that the eye movements of their West Indian pupils did not signal an impending message (for example, of some expected verbal initiative or response). Individuals might look away at those moments when, according to the majority's social etiquette they would not be expected to do so. In this way the expectations of individuals socialized in two cultural settings could give rise both to misunderstandings and heightened ethnic awareness.

Turning the eyes away was observed on many occasions to be made by a West Indian pupil as a sign of deference and respect to a teacher, yet it was received and interpreted by the teacher as an expression of guilt or bad manners. The example shows that such instinctive gestures, learned in early childhood, can upset the rhythm of interaction between individuals and again rise to a sense of insecurity as each tries to cope with what is for that person an unexpected gesture or posture by the other.

It can be argued that failures of perception at this subtle yet crucial level could and did give rise to a code of classroom communication to which the teacher, though the central and managerial figure in the room, was denied access. Awareness of this development generated anxieties for the teacher, who often became aware that these asymmetrical responses could (and did) give rise to sequences of behaviours that he was not culturally attuned to anticipate. The response to these phenomena might be to become increasingly dominant and strict, or to adopt an easy-going and unflappable posture. Each of these, it is clear, require considerable emotional resources of courage and self-confidence on the part of the teacher.

Thirdly, beyond the reflexive gestures and postures, there were those signs employed by a West Indian pupil to convey specific meaning. The clicking of lips, or pouting them and plucking them with a finger are examples of derogatory expressions which many teachers failed to interpret even when those gestures were directed at them. The impact of the gesture on those children who understood it ranged from disgust to amusement. It could give rise to even more jests of a similarly exclusive kind. Alternatively, innocent ethnically-exclusive signs could be interpreted as other than innocent. The lack of skills in understanding and responding subtly to these expressions often proved counter-productive to the main business of the relationship, that is, teaching and learning a particular subject or skill.

Fourthly, there was the use of *patois*, which very few teachers understood. Most teachers appeared to discourage its use, some by the use of strict penalties. It was noteworthy that among the West Indian pupils who were assessed most highly by the staff there were a number of individuals whom the writer never heard to use *patois* in any school circumstances. There could be little doubt that a number of teachers felt threatened by the persistent use of a dialect they could not understand, and that their anxiety expressed itself in their attitudes and behaviour towards those pupils who used it.

These aspects of communication outside the cultural repertoire of the majority clearly provided the basis for obstacles to confident relations between West Indian pupils and their English teachers. Not unnaturally the confusions so generated could be expected to give rise to survival strategies on the part of teachers facing these constraints on their skills of classroom management. At one extreme there were a few teachers who took the strictly authoritarian strategy of dominating absolutely all aspects of classroom social activity (although this was only really possible in shortage-subject lessons where there were few pupils motivated to persistently offensive behaviour *vis-à-vis* the teacher in question and where any offending individual could promptly be removed from the elite set of pupils given access to the shortage subject in question). At the other extreme there were many teachers who got on with their work with the minimum of confrontation over behavioural issues. In these classrooms, the exclusively West Indian forms of behaviour and expression were frequently tolerated by teachers. They were forced to accept certain limitations upon their managerial and teaching roles, and this invariably influenced their attitudes towards those individuals who seemed to be the focus of their difficulties.

Assessment of pupils

Teachers make judgements about their pupils outside as well as inside the classroom. But it would be difficult to argue that such judgements do not reflect classroom experience. Where classroom experience is uncertain and confused, questions naturally arise concerning the reliability of any assessment of individual pupils' abilities and achievements. With this in mind, it is of interest to consider the results of an assessment made of pupils in our age-cohort, then Form IV, when their teachers were asked to rate all their pupils, whatever their ethnic affiliation, on two scales. Analysis of the results of these ratings, one for academic ability and the other for behavioural co-operation, revealed that where West Indian boys and girls were concerned (and not for any other pupil category) there was a very highly significant statistical intercorrelation between the two ratings. In other words, while teachers were in most cases well able to make some discriminating judgements about the abilities and behaviours of English and South Asian pupils, their judgements were rather confused in that there was a strong tendency among them to use the same criteria to judge West Indian children on academic and behavioural terms. From such a confusion it is to be assumed that West Indian pupils were vulnerable to poor assessment of their abilities, and that the assessment given would be most likely to reflect the teachers' subjective involvement with the complex behavioural aspects of classroom relations.

The outworking of the confusion just described was most apparent on the day when pupils were allocated to the three CSE courses at the beginning of their fourth year. Each boy or girl was put into either the top stream (or full CSE course), the middle stream (or partial CSE course), or the bottom stream (the remnant considered too poor to sit the CSE examinations in any subject). Political and professional prudence on the part of the headmaster saw to it that the major ethnic categories of the pupil population were more or less proportionately represented in both the top and bottom streams. In the middle stream the number of West Indian pupils, particularly of West Indian boys, was highly disproportionate to their presence in the age grade as a whole. In that stream, 20 out of 25 pupils were West Indian, and it is possible that this ethnic composition reflects the problematic nature of teachers' confused social and academic judgements of their West Indian pupils. One West Indian boy commented upon his allocation to the middle stream : 'Sir, we're here because we're pretty'. The comment could well have been a telling one. Later that day, Form IV's West Indian boys, particularly those of the two lower streams, were responsible for a trail of havoc as they left for home: car tyres were slashed, fire-alarm bells set off, waste-bins upturned and windows broken.

Throughout their two final years at school, West Indian pupils continued to experience difficulties in meeting their own aspirations. On the one hand their frustration was expressed by a large number of drop-outs among them; on the other hand, those who remained enjoyed such low prestige with their teachers, that they were effectively waiting out their time in school with no worthwhile academic achievements within their grasp (the demoralizing process described by Clark as 'cooling out', Clark, 1962). The average level of results obtained by West Indian boys in the final examinations were dramatically lower than for any other pupil category. Their average result of two grade 5 CSE passes each was so poor as to have little more than token value. In comparison West Indian girls did three times better than this (which was about average for pupils in the age grade as a whole).

These results for West Indian pupils are particularly poignant when it is realized that the boys' abilities, as measured on scores obtained on intelligence tests, were superior to those of the girls of their own ethnic set. The diametrically opposed trends of school achievements and intelligence ratings could only be explained for West Indian boys and girls in terms of an analysis of their approach to schoolwork and their teachers' interactions with them. To complete our analysis along these lines, it is necessary to consider the pupils' own perspectives on their secondary school experience at West Midland School.

Pupil perception and support

Certain marked attitudes and developments were noted among West Indian pupils. First, West Indian girls made increasing efforts to minimize social misunderstandings and maximize co-operating with their teachers. However, the pattern of West Indian boys' attitudes appeared to run in the converse direction. Secondly, it appeared that the ethnically distinctive social and cultural behaviours and activities were, in the case of the West Midland School, predominantly Jamaican. As children of Jamaican origin formed a numerical majority there was therefore much greater chance that the West Indian pupils who formed the focus of teachers' classroom difficulties would be Jamaican rather than non-Jamaican. There was also greater opportunity for these youngsters to maintain and develop Jamaican cultural values and styles. Thirdly, in this situation one could rightly deduce that boys from Jamaican home backgrounds were particularly likely to come into collision with their teachers. These boys were the chief protagonists of a set of vigorous and stimulating social and cultural activities.

The behavioural attitudes of the West Indian girls in Form IV must be seen as one stage in their development throughout their secondary school career. In the junior classes these girls had been more the focus of teachers' classroom difficulties than the boys. Many teachers explained the high levels of excitability and even physical violence among these girls in terms of the intense peer competition into which they moved with the onset of puberty and adolescence. However these emotional strains did not appear to persist much into adolescence, possibly due to the interest taken in them by their mother and by other members of the family at home. The evidence here suggests that girls were pressured to recognize that the supportive adults at home provided much greater long-term security for them as individuals and as potential mothers. They understood that their best contribution to that supportive unit was to obtain the best economic and social standing which they could manage. In return, the supportive unit could be guaranteed to provide protection in the child-bearing years and, later on, give the matriarchal prestige of older women in many West Indian households. The West Indian girls in Form IV were thus conformists to established family and social norms, conserving and building upon the economic and social assets to which they had access. They were more concerned with longer-term personal security than shorter-term social prestige and popularity.

By contrast, the West Indian boys whose cases were considered displayed increasingly ambivalent and even hostile attitudes towards their teachers and their school experience in general. These developments coincided in many instances with difficult relations with parents. Some had even been thrown out of the household and were compelled to seek lodgings either with relatives, older peers living in flats or bed-sitters, or in a local shelter run by community workers. As they advanced into adolescence, almost all West Indian boys gave themselves energetically to peer activities and in so doing often isolated themselves even more from both parents and teachers. Their strong and more enduring ties were largely with other West Indian boys and solidarity and distinctiveness was expressed symbolically in styles of dress, musical tastes, recreational interests, physical competitiveness, joking relationships, etc. Only a few individuals opted out of this pattern and in each case they were boys who enjoyed a more positive rapport with either parents or teachers (or both). This small minority found a social niche for themselves in the comparatively rare cases of cross-ethnic friendships with English or South Asian boys, a development approved by their teachers.

The general trend of peer pressure, however, led most West Indian boys to exploit every social opportunity to gain prestige with their ethnic peers. Their concern was most clearly played out in the social and recreational activities associated with school life, but there could be no doubt that it also interfered with what might otherwise have been normal classroom relations. As has been indicated previously, many classroom situations were ripe for manipulation in this kind of way because of the apparent limitations in the cultural competences of many teachers to perceive and interpret distinctive ethnic behaviour and expressions. As a result, though many of these boys persisted in the belief that they were able to do well at school, they found themselves to be held in poor esteem by their teachers. Here were all the ingredients for mutual suspicion and disapproval. Teachers were seen to act harshly, even vindictively, in matters of social punishments and academic grades. Ethnic peer solidarity, in the face of even further isolation and apparent hostility, was for many boys the only supportive resource.

The second general development in attitudes and loyalties among West Indian pupils at the West Midlands School was due to the influence of Jamaican cultural values and styles. The majority of those boys and girls came from rural Jamaica and shared a common *patois*, and in some cases had common recollections of life 'back home'. By contrast, the children whose families had come from the smaller British Caribbean islands did not share common backgrounds, and often felt themselves to be very different from the Jamaicans. In terms of attitudes towards the English majority in general, and towards teachers in particular, there was undoubtedly some difference. Although not all teachers readily recognized the different cultural backgrounds of their West Indian pupils, there was a strong tendency for non-Jamaican pupils to enjoy more positive relations with teachers compared to Jamaican pupils. One may only speculate that the reasons for this were partly linguistic (these pupils would be less likely to employ the predominantly Jamaican *patois*) and partly social (being less inclined to identify with predominantly Jamaican behaviour and groupings).

The sensitivity of West Indian pupils to the ethnic differences between themselves influenced their social behaviour. These subtler ethnic differences were reflected in the teachers' assessments and the pupils final examination results. The development of these patterns does not imply that they could be expected to occur in other institutional circumstances where the ethnic composition of the pupil population and the personalities of the pupils is different. However, in the specific circumstances of this study, there was a strong tendency for the critical social and educational difficulties outlined to be associated with West Indian boys from Jamaican home backgrounds, and to a lesser extent with other West Indian pupils.

Conclusion

This case study suggests that West Indian pupils were exposed to considerable personal insecurities and difficulties which arose from their teachers' confusion. Pupils turned to ethnic sources of support; for the girls these were usually within the household and family, while for the boys they lay in peer relationships. For the girls, these resources contributed to levels of school achievement which their teachers tended not to anticipate. The boys' resort to stronger peer alliances seemed to serve mainly to discredit them socially and academically in the eyes of their teachers.

The strain and stress experienced by West Indian minority pupils and their English majority teachers in their classroom dealings with one another offers a valuable explanation of the levels of school achievement attained by these pupils. The strain in classroom relations appeared more readily to be explained in terms of teachers' confusions of social judgement due to their lack of competence in the cultural repertoire of West Indian pupils than in terms of any consistent conspiracy on the part of such teachers. The reasons for their deficient knowledge and skill in this area are readily apparent if the general historical and social experience of teachers over the past twenty-five years is remembered. It is one in which the emphasis has been placed upon their status as teachers and their membership of the dominant ethnic category, defining the rules and expectations of the classroom in terms of assimilation to the wider society.

Classroom teaching in these circumstances must bring teachers increasingly into conflict with their West Indian minority pupils. The alleviation of these difficulties must be largely in the hands of teachers prepared to develop their cultural skills to interact competently with West Indian minority pupils. It is the task of the policy-makers to create the conditions in institutions and appropriate training to induce teachers to develop that competence. At its core, the change in educational policy required must acknowledge the legitimacy of cultural forms generated outside the ethnic majority's cultural setting. It must be a pluralist policy. The alternative is ethnic confrontation in which educators become oppressors.

Reference

1. Driver, G. (1977) 'Ethnicity, Cultural Competence and School Achievement: A Case Study of West Indian Pupils Attending a British Secondary Modern School' unpublished Ph.D. thesis, University of Illinois.

AUTHOR INDEX

SUBJECT INDEX